The Brink of Peace

ITAMAR RABINOVICH

The Brink of Peace

The Israeli-Syrian
Negotiations

PRINCETON UNIVERSITY PRESS

Copyright © 1998 by Princeton University Press
Published by Princeton University Press, 41 William Street,
Princeton, New Jersey 08540
In the United Kingdom: Princeton University Press,
Chichester, West Sussex

Third printing, and first paperback printing, 1999
Paperback ISBN 0-691-01023-4

The Library of Congress has cataloged the cloth edition of this book as follows

Rabinovich, Itamar, 1942–
The brink of peace : the Israeli-Syrian negotiations /
Itamar Rabinovich.
p. cm.
Includes bibliographical references and index.
ISBN 0-691-05868-7 (alk. paper)
1. Israel—Foreign relations—Syria. 2. Syria—Foreign
relations—Israel. 3. Arab-Israeli conflict—1993—Peace.
4. Rabinovich, Itamar, 1942– . 1. Title.
DS119.8.S95R33   1998
327.56940569—DC21   98-14418

This book has been composed in Baskerville

The paper used in this publication meets the minimum requirements
of ANSI/NISO Z39.48-1992 (R1997) (*Permanence of Paper*)

http://pup.princeton.edu

Printed in the United States of America

3   5   7   9   10   8   6   4

*To the memory of Yitzhak Rabin,
soldier, leader, and statesman
who, in making peace, dared
to change the conventional wisdom and his own
views and to change the reality of which
he was so clearly a part.*

CONTENTS

THIS book was born in July 1992. When I was appointed by the late Yitzhak Rabin to head the Israeli delegation to the peace talks with Syria, the huge potential in these talks was clearly visible. The prime minister made a point during our first discussion on this matter of clarifying his intention to examine thoroughly the possibility of coming to terms with Syria and he expressed his willingness to make a significant concession if a serious prospect of an agreement with Syria emerged. The change in the prime minister's position from the skepticism with regard to Syria that had characterized his attitude prior to the June elections to the comparative openness in late July had transformed the familiar pattern of the two countries' relationship. For many years a peaceful settlement between Israel and Syria had not been regarded as a realistic prospect. The change in Syria's position in the late 1980s and Asad's willingness to come to the Madrid conference signified a new beginning, but the opening positions adopted by Syria and Israel in the negotiations launched in 1991 led to an impasse. Israel's new prime minister was now offering a way out of the stalemate. This meant that whether the new phase of the negotiations led to an agreement or not, it was destined to be an important chapter in the history of the Middle East and in the Arab-Israeli peace process. A breakthrough and peace between Israel and Syria would change the face of the region, whereas a failure to come to an agreement under the prevailing new circumstances would have far-reaching consequences. In any event, a scintillating story was about to unfold.

I suppose that one of the main reasons that led Yitzhak Rabin to choose me as his negotiator with Syria was my academic specialization in that country's history and politics. The prime minister thus chose a person familiar with the fundamental issues of the negotiation and in so doing sent an early positive signal toward Syria. For me this was primarily an opportunity to take part in the effort to resolve the Israeli-Syrian conflict. It was still not known whether

an agreement acceptable to both countries was feasible, and my
first task was indeed to find an answer to that question. The baggage I brought with me to the negotiations was intended above all
to help me in that task and the negotiator's other tasks. Eventually
it would provide the perspective from which the story of the negotiations would be told.

In the event, Yitzhak Rabin's opening gambit vis-à-vis Syria did
not lead to an agreement, but it gave birth to an absorbing saga
that lasted three and a half years. In addition to its intrinsic importance and interest, this bilateral negotiation had an impact on
the general course of the peace process, on the regional politics of
the Middle East, on the Israeli-American relationship, and on Israel's domestic politics. At present, more than two years since its
suspension, the negotiation of the years 1992–1996 is increasingly
becoming, with the passage of time, a closed, self-contained chapter. This chapter is constructed around two principal themes: the
story of things that happened—how Israel and Syria communicated with each other, what they agreed upon, and where they diverged—and the story of the things that did not happen, how and
why they failed to reach an agreement.

Already in the summer of 1992 I had a sense that the give-and-
take about to open between Israel and Syria could also, as a byproduct, give rise to a valuable book. This sense was translated four
years later into the present volume. It seems to me important that
the general public as well as those specializing in foreign policy
and Middle Eastern affairs be able to understand the course of the
Israeli-Syrian negotiations. It is indispensable for an understanding of the general course of events during the period that now
seems like "the golden age" of the peace process and for an evalu-
ation of the prospects and difficulties that emanate from the
present situation.

The issue of continuity between the Israeli-Syrian negotiations
of 1992–1996 and a negotiation that may begin in the near future
is not an academic question but a political, diplomatic, and legal
issue colored by the Syrian demand that the negotiations be resumed "at the point at which they had been interrupted." The Is-

raeli-Syrian controversy in this matter and a variety of political and personal interests gave rise to disagreement concerning some of the main points discussed in the negotiations, and as we draw farther from March 1996 it becomes less likely that if the negotiations resumed they would be seen and conducted as a continuation of Hafiz al-Asad's dialogue with the governments of Yitzhak Rabin and Shimon Peres. And yet it would be important to understand what was discussed and what was agreed upon during those three and a half years of negotiations would, even without a formal linkage, become part of the basis on which every Israeli-Syrian give-and-take would be conducted in the next few years.

Clarifying the course of and the essential developments in the Israeli-Syrian negotiation is also important in two broader contexts. Some rare insights into the inner workings of three systems—the American, the Israeli, and the Syrian—are afforded when the parties to an intense negotiation interact and open up to one another. The ups and downs of the negotiation and the failure to reach an agreement contain important lessons for anyone interested in conflict resolution both on the theoretical level and in the specific Middle Eastern context.

This story can be told and examined from several vantage points: as a case study in conflict resolution, as a case study in negotiation and bargaining, or as an effort at an international mediation. My natural choice was to tell it as a diplomatic historian whose task is to convey the essential events, explain their course and meaning, and to place them in the correct context and perspective. To this vantage point a personal dimension was added, in this case, with both advantages and drawbacks. Every historian carries personal baggage that interferes with the detached and unbiased presentation expected of him. In this case the baggage carried by a participant was particularly heavy—will I be apologetic? Will I be settling scores? Will I be able to admit my own errors?

Objectivity in historical research and writing is an ideal that can never be met fully. Instead of seeking an impossible impartiality I have tried to be open and fair by presenting the reader with the constraints and biases of which I am aware.

A study of a negotiation that failed to produce an agreement inevitably raises the question of whether a deal could have been made or, in other words, whether "an opportunity for peace" was missed. The term "missed opportunities" has been part of Arab-Israeli relations and of the academic and political discussion of that relationship for many years. Preoccupation with this paradigm has derived from four principal sources. First comes the natural curiosity of the reader absorbed by the story or the course of events, who wants to understand the essential facts and to know where the turning points were and why things unfolded in a particular fashion. With regard to the Arab-Israeli conflict, curiosity is often supplemented by a heavy emotional load. An Israeli reader who encounters the argument that the conflict could have been resolved in 1947 or 1949 if only a measure of generosity or creativity had been introduced is agitated by the notion that the cost of fifty years of conflict could possibly have been saved, and the term "missed opportunity" loses its simple neutral meaning and acquires additional layers. Discussion or debate of "missed opportunities" thus became an important and contentious issue in the political and academic debate on Israel's history and on Arab-Israeli relations.

A second source is inherent in the work of the historian who studies a historical question or event, tells its story, and in the course of so doing forms an opinion or passes judgment on the actions and failures of decision makers. In order to evaluate a decision made by a leader or policy maker, the historian examines it alongside the other options that were available at that time, and in the process often wonders what the consequences of a different choice would have been. He may occasionally come to the conclusion that the wrong decision was made, and that "an opportunity was missed" to avoid a war or settle a dispute.

A third source is the effort invested by philosophers, historians, and social scientists to introduce order and methodology into this line of inquiry. From their perspective the discussion of the "ifs of history" or "missed opportunities" must not remain amateurish and should be anchored in method and discipline. The specific discussion of the issue of "missed opportunities" is conducted within the larger field of "counterfactual history." This line of inquiry has provided us during the last few years with a number of volumes and essays that have tightened the speculative discussion but failed to resolve the underlying difficulty. Once a fundamental fact has been changed in the historical picture (by assuming that a different decision has been made) a picture is created different from the one we seek to decipher. A disciplined and systematic discussion can approximate the original scenario but cannot reconstruct it fully.[1]

A fourth source is tendentiousness shaped by interests or ideology. When a negotiation or a mediation effort fails and the conflict continues, the parties to the dispute tend to accuse each other of "missing the opportunity" (that may or may not have existed) to settle it. At the same time or later, journalists, historians, and other writers address the same issues and some of them—because of a vested interest or an ideological commitment—may charge either party with responsibility for "missing an opportunity." This has been a salient dimension of the historiography and discussion of Arab-Israeli relations—could the 1948 war have been avoided? could it have been concluded with a peace agreement? could peace have been made at the Lausanne Conference or through one of the international mediators? was the 1967 war inevitable? did Golda Meir miss an opportunity to come to an agreement with Anwar al-Sadat in 1971?

In recent years, the controversy between the self-styled "new history" school of Israeli historiography and their critics has endowed this discussion and the very term "missed opportunities" with an acrimonious edge. As a rule the "new historians," like earlier critics of Israeli policies, tend to argue that in the late 1940s and early 1950s the Israeli leadership made a series of decisions that served to deepen and perpetuate the conflict rather than mitigate it. Another group of historians has responded—some moderately, others fiercely—both to the general tenor of their work and to their specific arguments.[2]

The Canadian historian Neil Caplan, the author of several vol-

umes on Arab-Jewish and Arab-Israeli diplomacy, has recently argued that the nearly obsessive discussion of "missed opportunities"
runs against the grain of the historical inquiry: "Without sufficient
detachment and even-handedness, the exercise of searching for so-
called missed opportunities for peace easily becomes polemical
and tendentious. . . . The answers to any of these questions can
never be known with certainty, and the quest for such answers is ultimately a futile exercise. Instead of speculating on the 'what-ifs' of
history, we have sought . . . to offer a thorough and sober look at
the positions and strategies which the parties did adopt."[3]

The present volume addresses the issue of "the missed opportunity" on several occasions. The question arises in and of itself in
the account of a negotiation that approached the brink but failed
to cross it, and it has been raised in the debate unfolding since
1996 over the questions of whether the negotiation could have
been concluded successfully and who is to blame for the failure to
do so. From my point of view this is one of the issues addressed by
this book without attaching to it a particular significance or a baggage of values.

IT IS my pleasant duty to thank all those who have a share in this
book. First comes the group of Israelis, Americans, and Syrians
who devoted time, thought, and goodwill in the effort to resolve
the difficult conflict between Israel and Syria. I am primarily beholden to my colleagues in the delegation to the peace talks with
Syria, the Israeli embassy in Washington, in the prime minister's
and foreign offices, and the Israeli Defense Forces (IDF) for their
contribution to the negotiations and for their help and support.
The book was written at Tel Aviv University, my professional home
for many years, which offered me a warm welcome upon my return
from Washington in the fall of 1996. To the university as a whole,
to the Dayan Center for Middle Eastern Studies, and to the
Ettinger Chair for the Contemporary History of the Middle East I
am grateful for providing the intellectual environment within
which this book was written. Lydia Gareh typed the manuscript
with her exemplary skill and devotion, and Efrat Alon-Harel has

been a very effective research assistant, and I thank them both. The staff of Princeton University Press headed by Walter Lippincott has offered credit, support, and professionalism that are all much appreciated.

This book reflects the warm feeling and high regard I have felt for the late Yitzhak Rabin. Working with him in the conduct of the Israeli-Syrian negotiations and Israel's relationship with the United States was a most unusual experience. I miss him very much as a leader and a friend, and I am proud to dedicate this book to his memory.

The Brink of Peace

ONE

Trying to Recapture
Yesterday's Shadow

TO THE STUDENTS of past history and contemporary politics nothing is more beguiling than the myriad threads that run across the invisible line which separates the two. Yesterday's events become the stuff of today's controversies, and current agendas affect the lenses through which the past is viewed and written. For three and a half years, the Israeli labor governments of Yitzhak Rabin and Shimon Peres negotiated a peace settlement with Hafiz al-Asad's Syrian Ba'th regime. Much progress was made but an agreement was not concluded before the Israeli elections of May 29, 1996, that brought Benjamin Netanyahu to power.

The unfinished negotiation stands as a scintillating and significant tale that should be told in its own right. But it also presents an important, immediate problem on the current agenda of Middle Eastern diplomacy. The Israeli-Arab peace process continues, and Israel and Syria are bound to have an active relationship in its context. They can negotiate, they can fight (directly or indirectly), and they can do both simultaneously, but they cannot and will not ignore each other.

In the immediate aftermath of the May 29 elections, these issues came to be addressed in the most fundamental fashion. As leader of the opposition, Israel's new prime minister had denounced his predecessors' policies toward Syria (among other things). His election campaign had promised the Israeli voter that, unlike Shimon Peres, who was liable to bring Israel down from the Golan Heights, Netanyahu would either construct new paradigms for the negotiations or find a different way of dealing with Syria. Once elected, the new prime minister was forced to adopt a more realistic view of Israel's relationship with Syria and, more broadly, of his ability to reshape the Israeli-Arab peace process.

This evolution was matched by the accommodation Hafiz al-Asad and the rest of the Arab world had to make to the political about-turn in Israel. Soon enough both the Netanyahu government and the Asad regime, assisted by the Clinton administration, were busy dealing with the questions of when and how the Israeli-Syrian negotiations could be resumed. Although Syria argued that the negotiations should be resumed "at the point at which they had been interrupted" in March 1996, and that important binding agreements had been made in the course of the negotiation, Israel's position was that the negotiations should be resumed "without prior conditions," and that nothing of a binding nature had been agreed between the two countries. It was in this context that an extraordinary press interview granted in January 1997 by Walid Mu'allim, Syria's ambassador to Washington and the chief negotiator with Israel, should be read. This was the longest and most detailed account of the 1992–1996 negotiations offered by a Syrian official or, in many respects, by any other knowledgeable source.

Mu'allim's revelations were clearly designed to buttress the Syrian argument that the negotiations should be resumed "at the point at which they had been interrupted" and the Syrian claim that by that time Israel had agreed to withdraw from the Golan to the "lines of June 4, 1967." As Mu'allim put it, "after Rabin became prime minister in June 1992, we still insisted on discussing withdrawal only. When Rabin finally realized that the Syrians would not move a step ahead in discussing any of the other elements of a peace settlement before being convinced of Israel's intention of full withdrawal, he made the opening. That was in August 1993."[1] As an astute, experienced diplomat, the Syrian ambassador was aware of the problems inherent in his discussion of the intimate details of a negotiation he was seeking to resume, which was of concern to both his American hosts and Israeli interlocutors. He therefore explained that "it was not President Asad who first announced the agreement of full withdrawal. Our side only mentioned it because it had been made public on the Israeli side, following the publication in September of a book in Hebrew giving *an accurate account* from Israeli sources of what happened. The Egyptian president Mubarak had said in an interview with the Arabic newspaper *al-Hayat,* that Rabin had informed him of his readiness for full withdrawal to the line of June 4, 1967."[2]

Some of the threads that run through the tissue of this story are these: the actual details of Rabin's negotiation with Syria and the need to deal with them through two transitions of power in Israel within less than one year; the American and Egyptian roles; and the current debate between Syria and Israel on the factual and legal bases on which negotiations should be resumed. The Israeli peg chosen by Ambassador Mu'allim was a biography of Shimon Peres written by the journalist Orly Azulay-Katz under the title *The Man Who Could Not Win.* The book was indeed published by Israel's mass-circulation paper *Yediot Ahronot* in September 1996. Some chapters were serialized in the paper and some of the highlights were published first as a news item in the paper's front page on September 13.[3]

The accent of the story was on Rabin's relationship with Peres. As the author had it, soon after Rabin's assassination, his successor, Peres, began to prepare for his meeting with President Clinton on the day of the funeral. Out of Rabin's safe, in the Ministry of Defense, "computer printouts and top secret documents" were brought to his desk. Peres discovered that Rabin had concealed from him the most important details of the negotiations with Syria and found, to his astonishment, how far-reaching those details were. Thus, according to Azulay-Katz, Rabin had given President Clinton a promise that in return for full peace he would be willing to withdraw to the June 4 lines. The president and the prime minister, according to the same account, had agreed that this proposal be presented to the Syrians as an American initiative. In the aftermath of the conversation with Rabin, Clinton instructed his associates to write a "non-paper" summing up this matter. According to the same set of revelations, a few days before Rabin gave his promise to the Americans, he was informed by them that Asad was willing to accept all the security arrangements that Israel had asked for. Following Rabin's promise, a statement of principles was put together between Israel and Syria with American help, which comprised the details of withdrawal, arrangements concerning water, the security arrangements, and normalization of relations between the two countries.[4]

As will be seen below, what the Syrians chose to characterize as "an accurate account" did contain some of the important and relevant facts, but in many places it was far off the mark. The book itself, once published, turned out to be quite awkward for Peres, contrary to the expectations of those who had clearly helped the author in researching it.

The book did convey many of the complexities of the Rabin-Peres relationship, and the main theme of its opening chapter and of the newspaper article drawn from it was not new. In fact, a few days after Rabin's assassination and Peres's assumption of power, a story appeared in the Israeli press citing sources close to Peres who complained about discovering unknown details regarding the negotiations with Syria.[5] This original story, as well as the fact that it had no sequel at the time, pointed to some of the conflicting forces at work during the transition from Rabin to Peres. Rabin conducted the negotiations with Syria personally, and the crucial details of the negotiations were kept within a very limited circle. The prime minister and the foreign minister used to meet quite frequently alone, with no notes taken or record kept. This channel of communication was preserved even during periods of great tension in their political and personal relationship. We do not know to what extent Rabin had briefed Peres on the details of the Syrian negotiations.

My impression at the time was that it was not Peres himself but someone in the immediate circle around him who saw fit to leak the story to the media. It may have been the reflection of genuine anger and surprise, but it also occurred to me then that members of the circle around Peres thought that since negotiations with Syria were bound to continue, it would be more politic to present the concessions that would have to be made as having been made by the late Rabin. Later, wiser counsel seems to have prevailed, or maybe Peres himself interfered, and the thread was dropped. Peres understood that he was wearing Rabin's mantle and that, whatever acrimony had characterized their relationship in the past, history decreed that in the aftermath of the assassination their partnership would become the dominant element of their remembered relationship.

The September 1996 publication of Orly Azulay-Katz's book picked up the thread that had been dropped during the previous November. More significantly, it generated a wave of discussion of the unknown aspects of the Israeli-Syrian negotiations under Rabin and Peres, and provided the Syrians with an alibi for publicizing their own version of what had been a secret negotiation.

It is interesting that the Syrians had not seized an earlier, less obvious opportunity to bring these issues into the open. In mid-July, Prime Minister Netanyahu's foreign policy advisor had complained to Israel's radio that upon assuming office he had discovered details concerning the activities of the previous government "that were hitherto unknown and caused him a bitter disappointment." The radio's correspondent suggested that the concessions alluded to by the prime minister's advisor "were apparently connected to promises given to the Americans with regard to the negotiations with Syria."[6] It appeared at the time that Prime Minister Netanyahu's aides were going through a process similar to the one that the circle around Peres had gone through during the previous November. There was, of course, one major difference. Peres was Rabin's partner and genuine successor, whereas Netanyahu was free from emotional or political commitments to the man he had just defeated. He clearly was not seeking to delegitimize his rival, but he was grappling with the difficulties of the peace process, and the temptation to explain how his hands had been tied by promises given by his predecessors was evident.

When Netanyahu himself was asked a few days after the September revelations to comment on them, he actually provided an accurate description of the give-and-take in this matter: "He [Rabin] spoke of a hypothetical possibility provided that the Syrians meet a series of conditions which in fact—they had not."[7]

The first public statement by President Asad in these matters was made after the publication of Orly Azulay-Katz's book in Israel. On September 25, the Syrian president granted an interview to the American journalist Rowland Evans that was broadcast on CNN's "Evans and Novak" program. The timing was not accidental. Evans was invited to come from Washington on short notice in order to conduct the interview. In the event, the publication was completely overshadowed by the "tunnel incident" and the upheaval that followed it, but Asad's presentation was very clear.[8] In response to the first question put to him, Asad offered a lengthy exposition of the foundations of the Madrid process, and then explained that

> great efforts were exerted, and then progress was made and achieve-
> ments accomplished which turned into commitments by the parties
> and rights for them. Within the framework of those commitments,
> agreement was reached between Syria and Israel on the Israeli with-
> drawal from the Golan up to 4 June 1967 lines. After that we moved
> to complete discussion of the other elements of peace. This has
> taken place under the supervision and with the knowledge of the
> United States. It goes without saying that the present Israeli govern-
> ment has to abide by an agreement reached by the former govern-
> ment, which was a legitimate government, and so according to our
> considerations, it represented Israel. Then came the recent devel-
> opments in Israel and the change of government there. Once the re-
> sults of the Israeli elections were announced, the new Israeli prime
> minister appeared to be obliterating all those principles and elimi-
> nating all efforts, commitments and rights. Thus, he canceled the
> peace process entirely. Therefore, talks can only be resumed once
> he makes up his mind on the peace strategy and responds to its
> requirements.[9]

As far as public statements were concerned, Mu'allim was right when he explained in his own interview that Syria's revelations about negotiations came after the Hebrew-language publication but, in fact, the Syrians had been sharing their version with foreign leaders and diplomats prior to mid-September. To cite one exam-ple: on September 8 the Japanese foreign minister, Yukihiko

Ikada, visited Damascus and was told by his Syrian hosts that they had an agreement with the previous Israeli government about withdrawal to the June 4, 1967, lines.[10]

What the Syrians were doing was a clear symptom of their predicament in the aftermath of the Israeli elections. During the previous three and a half years, Asad had conducted himself as if time were no constraint. Many foreign visitors advised him to hurry up and conclude negotiations, first with Rabin and then with Peres. They reminded him that elections in Israel were scheduled for October 1996, that public opinion polls pointed to a narrow margin at best for Labor, and they recommended that he make a deal with Rabin (and then Peres) before an election which could be won by Netanyahu, who had a very different policy toward Syria. Asad was not moved by such arguments. He may very well have seen them as a pressure tactic, or he may have calculated that if Labor's margin was so narrow and its prospect of victory so uncertain, there was no point in making a deal with Labor. Rabin was insisting on a deal that would be completed over several years. Why would Asad be interested in a deal whereby he would give Israel peace and recognition in turn for a small part of the Golan, and wait for the implementation of a larger territorial concession until after an election that Labor was not certain of winning? As for Peres in late 1995 and early 1996, he was ready to make and implement an agreement within a briefer time span. Mu'allim, in the interview quoted above, complained that if Rabin was too deliberate, Peres was too bold and swift: "He was in a hurry, he wanted to enter the elections with the Israeli-Syrian agreement in his hand. He wanted to 'fly high and fast' as he used to say. I used to say to the Israeli counterpart that it is important to fly, but it is also very important to know where and when to land—you can't continue to fly high and fast, we have our public opinion and we need to sell the agreement to them to accept it."[11]

Be that as it may, after the May 29 Israeli elections, Asad must have realized that he had badly miscalculated, and he was now trying to capture yesterday's shadow. Netanyahu was critical of Israel's agreement with the Palestinians, but Oslo I and II were signed agreements, and he was formally committed to them.[12] On the Syrian track, there was one "non-paper" and a whole host of hypothetical and conditional statements. The Syrians were determined to persuade the rest of the world that at least some of these were of a binding nature. They may or may not have realized that by claiming publicly that they had a binding agreement with the previous government on a full withdrawal from the Golan, they were tying their own hands. How could Asad conclude an agreement in the future that would offer Syria less than it had, allegedly, obtained in the past?

It is ironic that while the Syrians were busy building their case, on September 18, 1996, the American secretary of state, Warren Christopher, gave Prime Minister Netanyahu a letter in which he reportedly wrote that he, as the secretary of state, did not regard the "non-paper" on "the aims and principles of the security arrangements," reached between Israel and Syria in May 1995, as legally binding. This letter was kept secret until leaked to the Israeli press in January 1997.[13] Obtaining it was quite a coup for Netanyahu who, as the opposition's leader, had criticized the only agreement made between Israel and Syria under the Labor government. But the ramifications of Christopher's letter were far-reaching. If a "non-paper" that represented a real agreement, albeit unsigned and informal, between Israel and Syria was not binding, then clearly the much looser legacy of the negotiation was even less binding.

It is interesting to speculate on the reasons that led Secretary Christopher to send this letter to the Israeli prime minister. He would not have sent it had he not thought that it represented the legal position as it was, but it is difficult to avoid the feeling that it was also a way of venting some of his frustration accumulated during three and a half years of work on the Syrian-Israeli track.

Unaware of Christopher's letter, the Syrian effort to reinforce and document their case continued. In November 1996, speaking in a joint press conference with President Mubarak, Asad explained that "we are talking about an agreement, when both parties agree about something, particularly when there is also international sponsorship and as long as they are, they are supposed to be committed to what has been agreed because these all were agreements [that] have been made under the umbrella and sponsorship of both co-sponsors. This is political activity for the sake of the peace process and it need not turn into a debate whether it is a signed or unsigned agreement as if we are defending an issue in court. . . . When it comes to peace, things are different from verbal game and casuistry."[14]

At the end of December, Asad granted an interview to the Egyptian newspaper *Al-Ahram*. The Egyptian journalist asked him how true the rumors were "that Rabin had given the Americans something written in which he confirmed his readiness to withdrawal from the whole of the Golan." Asad's reply was:

> I am not familiar with the question of whether there are written papers. We were speaking to them in the presence of the American side, and the major role was played by the Americans between us and them, and after four years the Americans informed us that Rabin had finally been persuaded of the necessity of withdrawal from the whole Golan. This was a fact, and it was reaffirmed by Peres after Rabin, and then we entered into the issue of security arrangements and we spent a year arguing about them. At the end I suggested that we agree on the foundations and not enter into the debate, namely, that security is for both sides and not for one side on the expense of the other and that this arrangement would be equal for the two parties. We agreed on these foundations and began with the details, and then came Netanyahu.[15]

Ambassador Mu'allim's interview in January 1997 represents the most thorough and the most ambitious Syrian effort to substantiate and document Syria's version and Syria's claim. Subsequently President Asad himself offered a slightly different version of the course of events. Asad spoke on August 12, 1997, to a group of Israeli Arabs who had been invited to Syria. At that point Asad had lost faith in Netanyahu's intentions and was reaching out to what he viewed as sympathetic segments of the Israeli political spectrum—the Arab population and the Labor party. As he had not done on previous occasions, he spoke in unqualified terms about his negotiations with the Labor government: "We found that the Labor party government had a new tone and we were under the impression that they wanted peace." Asad then repeated the claim that "in a certain phase of the talks we arrived at basic issues including a commitment to withdraw from the Golan." Aware of the question that had by then been raised repeatedly, Asad raised it himself: "You might ask: Now that they have responded to this Syrian demand, why was peace not achieved?" His answer: "Many issues that constituted the elements of peace were still pending. These issues include the elements of security and other elements, and all of them are basic. The security issues might make the regained land something that is not worthwhile, and also might discount dignity and rights."[16] Asad was, in fact, trying to say that he had an Israeli commitment for his half of the bargain, while he had yet to agree to Israel's demands. He should be the first to know that this was a weak argument.

Against this background, it was curious to note Syria's failure in late August 1997 to seize the opportunity provided by yet another leak in the Israeli system. On August 28, the Israeli military commentator Ze'ev Schiff published in the daily *Ha'aretz* extensive quotations from the minutes of several conversations between Rabin and Christopher and one conversation between Rabin and American negotiator Dennis Ross regarding the Syrian demand for full withdrawal and subsequent demand for withdrawal to the line of June 4. Schiff was careful to conclude that Rabin had agreed to discuss the latter Syrian demand. His revelations were naturally rich with detail and color, but they did not alter the fundamental perception of the 1992–1996 negotiations as it had crystallized by the summer of 1997.[17] And yet it would have been natural for the Syrians to take full advantage of the revelations in order to seek to buttress their case. It is possible that on the eve of Madeleine Albright's first visit to Damascus they decided to appear at their statesmanlike best.

Prime Minister Netanyahu was on a visit to the Far East at the time and, when asked about the revelations, his brief response was that "it should be understood that there is no contractual agreement between Israel and Syria that is binding from Israel's point of view. The U.S. understands it too, so that the fundamental question does not concern matters that were discussed between various parties in the past but matters that will be discussed between the governments of Israel and Syria in the future."[18]

It clearly emerges from all of these reports that August 1993 was a crucial watershed in the history of the Israeli-Syrian negotiations. Prime Minister Rabin then took an initiative, and authorized Secretary Christopher to explore in a hypothetical way Syria's readiness for a comprehensive agreement with Israel in which the possibility of withdrawal from the Golan Heights was put on the agenda. President Asad did not quite pick up the glove, and Secretary Christopher, returning from Damascus, where he had gone with Rabin's offer, carried with him what was clearly a Syrian bargaining position. Rabin's timing was not accidental. When he spoke to Christopher in August 1993, he knew that an Israeli agreement with the PLO was being completed in Oslo. He never said so explicitly, but his move toward Syria must have been an attempt to find out whether he had a real Syrian option to weigh against the Palestinian alternative. Asad's disappointing response persuaded Rabin that the Syrian option was at best problematic, and he chose the Palestinian option that was being completed in Oslo. The choice had a profound effect on the whole Arab-Israeli peace process of these years. Rabin remained skeptical of Asad's willingness to offer or agree to a settlement that would also meet with his own criteria, but he continued to offer him opportunities to prove him wrong throughout 1994 and 1995.

The August 1993 give-and-take will be described in detail below. But like all good stories, the story of the Syrian-Israeli negotiation should be told from its inception.

TWO

Israel and Syria,
Rabin and Asad

OF ALL THE CONFLICTS between Israel and her Arab neighbors, the Syrian-Israeli dispute has traditionally been regarded as the most bitter. The Palestinian-Israeli conflict is the core conflict of the Arab-Israeli dispute, and Israelis and Palestinians have for over a century now fought over land, rights, and power—over the most fundamental and the most mundane. But the very close contact and interaction of the two societies, hostile as it has been, has also served to mitigate the mutual abstract demonization that is so characteristic of such conflicts.[1]

For many years Egypt had been Israel's most formidable military and political adversary. When the power of the Egyptian state and the mass of its population were mobilized against Israel, they presented her with the most severe challenges. But the challenge of Egypt had from the beginning been softened by raison d'état, the interests of the Egyptian state that set it apart from the Arab collective. And when an Egyptian president, Anwar al-Sadat, decided in the early 1970s that these interests required Egypt's disengagement from the conflict with Israel, it took less than a decade to complete the process of disengagement by signing the first Arab-Israeli peace agreement.[2]

Syria does not possess the weight of Egypt, but it has more than made up for the paucity of resources by zeal and perseverance. Syria's commitment to the issues of Palestine and the Palestinians and its opposition to the state of Israel and its Zionist antecedents have been profound and durable. To Israelis, Syria and the Syrians came to represent Arab enmity and rejection in their most entrenched and significant form.

This Syrian attitude, its evolution over time, and its translation into actual policies have derived from several sources. The weakness of the young Syrian state, its own search for identity, the hold of pan-Arab nationalism on its political classes, and its proximity and closeness to the Palestinian Arabs combined to produce a particularly strong commitment to the Palestinian cause. The ambiguous situation along the Syrian-Israeli armistice lines, the early role played in Syrian politics by army officers and by ideological parties, and Syria's drift into the Soviet orbit and Israel's own reaction and response to these developments turned the foothills of the Golan Heights into the most active front of the unfolding Arab-Israeli conflict in the 1950s and 1960s.[3]

Syria played a major role in generating the crisis that led to the 1967 war. Having lost the Golan Heights, Syria participated in formulating an Arab consensus which rejected the notion that in order to regain the land they lost in 1967 the Arabs should make their peace with the state of Israel as it had emerged from the 1948 war. Syria joined Egypt in the October War of 1973, but Asad's agenda was different from that of Sadat. Unlike his Egyptian partner, he did not launch war in order to set a peace process in motion. While Egypt mounted the track that led to the 1979 peace treaty with Israel, the Syrian-Israeli negotiating process dissolved in the aftermath of the May 1974 disengagement agreement. As Sadat's Egypt became increasingly committed to peace, Asad's Syria led the Arab campaign against Cairo's reconciliation with Israel. Throughout these years, the intensity of Syria's continued enmity and opposition to Israel was matched by an Israeli perception of Damascus as an implacable foe, a source of hostility, and definitely not a candidate for a future settlement.

The arena of Syrian-Israeli hostility was expanded by the collapse in 1975 of the Lebanese state, Syria's military intervention, and the establishment of Syrian presence and paramount influence in Lebanon. Initially Israel and Syria found a modus vivendi in Lebanon, but in 1981 they mounted a collision course in that country that led them to a limited war in 1982 and the war by proxy during the following years. Buoyed by her success against Israel (and the United States) in Lebanon and by her alliance with revolutionary Iran, Syria championed the doctrine of "strategic parity" with Israel and became embroiled in the mid-1980s in a campaign of terrorism against Israel and America. In 1986 and early 1987 the prospect of a Syrian-Israeli negotiation, let alone accommodation, seemed very remote. And yet forces were then at work that in less than five years made the unthinkable happen and brought Israel and Syria to the negotiating table as part of a larger effort to arrive at a comprehensive settlement of the Arab-Israeli conflict. The tale of Hafiz al-Asad's and Yitzhak Shamir's journey to the Madrid peace conference in October 1991 is scintillating. But in order to appreciate it fully we need to take a closer look at the evolution of the Syrian-Israeli dispute during the previous forty-odd years.

BETWEEN TWO WARS, 1948–1967

When the Arab armies invaded the territory of the young Israeli state in May 1948, they were implementing the Arab League's resolutions seeking to support the Palestinian Arabs in their war with the Jewish community and to prevent the establishment of a Jewish state in their midst. The United Nations General Assembly may have voted on the partition of mandatory Palestine, but for the Arabs this was an illegitimate act, giving birth to an illegitimate state, violating Arab rights, and creating an alien entity in a particularly significant part of the Arab homeland.

Of the five Arab armies taking part in the invasion, the Syrian army came closest to acting in this spirit. King Abdallah of Jordan maintained a clandestine relationship with the Jewish leadership, but at the same time pushed hard for an Arab invasion that would provide him with the opportunity to take over the Arab part of Palestine. Egypt's decision to join the war was finally made precisely in order to deny Abdallah and his Hashemite cousins in Iraq any such aggrandizement. Lebanon was a reluctant participant in the Arab coalition, yielding to domestic and external pressures to conform to the Arab consensus. Syria had her own share of calculating politicians and generals, but more than in the other Arab states her enthusiastic participation in the war reflected the hold that the ideology of pan-Arab nationalism had both on the political establishment and, in a more radical fashion, on many of its younger challengers. The impact of these ideas and sentiments was magnified by the war and its outcome. To the radical Arab nationalists the defeat sustained by the established Arab regimes was further proof of the corruption of the existing order and its inability to cope with the challenge of the West.

The 1948 War ended with a series of armistice agreements brokered by the UN mediator Ralph Bunche. Egyptian, Jordanian, Lebanese, and Israeli delegations negotiated and signed three armistice agreements on the island of Rhodes in the early part of 1949. Syria avoided the Rhodes talks altogether. Syrian negotiations with Israel began later and proved to be the most protracted and the most difficult. It is ironic from the present perspective that the chief stumbling block in these negotiations was Israel's insistence that Syria withdraw to the international border (between Syria and mandatory Palestine) and Syria's refusal to evacuate the (fairly small) territory she occupied west of that line at the war's end. The negotiation was further compounded by other issues: Syria's vague claim to parts of the Galilee, her refusal to acknowledge Israel's control of land not assigned to her by the UN partition plan, and her attempt to obtain a better hold over two important keys to the region's scarce water resources—the Jordan River and Lake Tiberias. Beyond these concrete impediments lay the reluctance of all Syrian governments and political leaders to defy the Arab nationalist taboo and sign an agreement that would recognize the state of Israel.[4]

The man who broke the taboo was Syria's first military dictator, Husni Za'im. Za'im was an unconventional leader whose person and regime were full of contradictions and incongruities. A former officer in France's colonial levy in the Levant, Za'im was at loggerheads with the Arab nationalist leaders who constituted the backbone of the civilian regime overthrown by his soldiers. In retrospect, it is clear that Za'im was a transitional figure whose regime opened the door to the radical, ideologically bent military that have dominated Syrian politics since the mid-1950s. But during his brief reign (March–August 1949), he did introduce several important changes and did take several bold decisions, one of which was the conclusion of an armistice agreement with Israel. Za'im in fact went further, to the point of proposing a meeting between himself and Israel's prime minister, David Ben-Gurion, and told his American interlocutors that he was willing, in return for significant Israeli territorial concessions, to sign a peace treaty and even to settle Palestinian refugees in Syria. Ben-Gurion refused to meet with Za'im before the conclusion of an armistice agreement, and by the time he was willing to explore the prospects of dealing with him, Za'im was deposed and killed by a fresh group of military conspirators.

This curious episode has yet to be fully explained. Za'im had close links with the CIA, and his initiative may have been part of a larger U.S. effort to resolve the Arab-Israeli conflict in league with a would-be "reformist army officer." Ben-Gurion refused to take Za'im seriously, and though his caution may have been well warranted, his initial refusal to deal with Za'im's initiative was quite startling. In Syria and in subsequent Syrian historiography and polemics, this episode left no trace. It was probably seen as too embarrassing and as an inconsequential aberration from the mainstream of Syrian politics and policies.[5]

This failure fitted into a larger pattern. In 1949 and 1950 all efforts to impose a comprehensive settlement of the Arab-Israel conflict or to resolve Israel's disputes with Egypt, Jordan, Lebanon, and the Palestinians were to no avail. To the extent that an Arab party was willing to negotiate or explore the prospect of accommodation with Israel, it insisted on terms that the Israelis found unacceptable. The concept of armistice agreements proved very effective in helping the parties to end the fighting, but not in settling their conflict and in making the transition to a state of peace. Stalemate led to festering, and by the mid-1950s the Arab-Israeli conflict reached its full-blown form: total political boycott by the Arab side, political warfare, border conflicts, and, in October 1956, a second Arab-Israeli war.[6]

Israel's specific conflict with Syria was exacerbated by geography, topography, and the complexities of the armistice agreement. The key to Israel's further development was water and irrigation, and the keys to Israel's water economy were perilously close to the armistice lines with Syria: Lake Tiberias and the Jordan River and its tributaries. Syria in this instance was not merely an unfriendly neighbor. It carried an Arab nationalist burden of responsibility—to prevent Israel from constructing the overland water carrier from the northern edge of the country to the empty spaces in its southern part, thereby laying the foundation for a larger and more viable Jewish state.

The armistice agreements of 1949 were, as the term suggests, designed to end the hostilities and facilitate the transition to a state of peace. The complex arrangements designed along the Israeli-Syrian line or, for that matter, in Jerusalem, were not meant to linger for nearly twenty years. But they did, and along the Syrian-Israeli armistice lines this prolonged arrangement served to fan an embryonic conflict into active hostility. Perched on the bluff of the Golan Heights, the Syrian army was determined to enforce its own strict interpretation of the agreement and to improve and expand Syria's territorial position. This Syrian pressure and Israel's own assertiveness in claiming and exercising sovereignty accounted for much of the strife along the Syrian-Israeli armistice line in the 1950s. During these years, Syria registered two principal territorial accomplishments: it took over the al-Hammah enclosure south of Lake Tiberias, and established a de facto presence on and control of the eastern shore of Lake Tiberias.[7]

The Syrian-Israeli conflict of the 1950s underwent a qualitative leap in the early 1960s. A series of developments combined to radicalize Syria's policy toward Israel and to turn it into the principal actor in the chain of events that was set in motion in 1963 and took the region into the May 1967 crisis and the Six Days War.

At the core of these developments was a quest for legitimacy. After they broke away from their union with Egypt, Syria's secessionist rulers (September 1961–March 1963) and their Ba'thist successors were hard-put to stand up to the still formidable 'Abd al-

Nasser. In order to embarrass him and to justify Syria's separate existence as the bastion of genuine Arab nationalist opposition to Israel, they adopted a particularly radical position toward Israel and accused Nasser of selling out to the United States and to the Israelis by endorsing the Johnston Plan for Arab-Israeli water sharing. When Israel announced in 1963 that it was about to complete the overland water carrier, Syria threatened to go to war in order to abort the project. This forced Egypt to convene the first Arab summit conference in Cairo in January 1964.[8] At the conference, a decision to divert the tributaries of the Jordan was made as part of a comprehensive Arab strategy to confront Israel.

Egypt's hope that the formation of a new Arab framework and the formulation of a new Arab strategy would moderate Syria's position failed to materialize. Internecine strife, Soviet support, interaction with the new wave of Palestinian nationalism, and Israel's own miscalculations all served as catalysts of further radicalization. An uninterrupted cycle of violence was unleashed in which a clear distinction no longer existed between cause and effect. When Israeli tanks hit Syrian bulldozers implementing the Arab diversion scheme, Syria retaliated by sending a Palestinian terrorist squad through the territory of Jordan, to which Israel retaliated with an air raid, only to invite the Syrian response of laying a mine in the Israeli patrol road in the valley dominated by the Golan Heights.

Matters came to a head in the spring of 1967. On April 7, six Syrian planes were shot down by Israeli planes in the course of an air battle near Damascus. The Israeli government came to the conclusion that the radical wing of the Ba'th, in power since February 1966, was set on a course of further and escalating friction. It felt that domestic weakness coupled with a sense that the Soviet Union and Egypt were committed to its survival kept propelling the Syrian regime toward further and more dangerous confrontation. The Syrians, Egyptians, and Soviets, in turn, became persuaded that Israel was trying to bring down the Ba'th regime. It was apparently in order to preempt this notion that the Soviets told the Egyptians in May 1967 that Israel had amassed fifteen brigades on its northern borders in order to mount an offensive against Syria.

'Abd al-Nasser decided to deter Israel by breaking the 1957 arrangements and remilitarizing the Sinai. By the time he had established that there was no Israeli military buildup in the north, a process was set in motion that could not be stopped. 'Abd al-Nasser realized that his bold moves had restored his stature in Egypt and the Arab world, and he continued to press forward. He crossed the point of no return on May 23, when he closed the Straits of Tiran to Israeli shipping.[9]

This turn of events confronted Syria with unexpected problems. Once Egypt took charge, Syria was relegated into a subsidiary role. Furthermore, her leaders realized that, given their contractual obligations vis-à-vis Egypt and their partnership in the Unified Arab Command, a war between Egypt and Israel was bound to involve them as well. Brave rhetoric notwithstanding, this was not what they had in mind. They were willing to go to the brink of war in pursuit of their political ends, but they never planned to cross it. As they later claimed, they thought that Egypt should not have made the decision to close the Straits of Tiran, thereby creating a casus belli, and they certainly thought that Egypt was not entitled to make on her own a decision that had such far-reaching ramifications for her partners.

Syria's unhappiness with Egypt's conduct accounted at least in part for the very modest role it chose to play once war broke out on June 6. While war raged on the Egyptian and Jordanian fronts, Syria was willing to settle on shelling parts of northern Israel and on staging one small land attack. In the early afternoon of the same day the Israeli air force destroyed the Syrian air force and brought the fighting along the Israeli-Syrian front to a virtual end. In the event, this strategy was nearly successful in steering Syria safely through the crisis. Israel's defense minister, Moshe Dayan, was quite willing to let this happen. Having accomplished his original aims, he was reluctant to launch an offensive and capture the Golan Heights. Dayan was anxious that if Israel scaled the Golan Heights, defeated the Syrian army, and seemed to threaten Damascus, the Soviet Union might be provoked into intervening in the war. As he tells it in his autobiography, the defense minister was also worried by the prospect of Egyptian refusal to accept a cease-fire and, therefore, by the risk of a lengthy conflict on two fronts. But there was a more profound dimension to Dayan's hesitation. In his own words, "Thirdly, the long term consequences of our action: The Syrians would not accept our permanent presence on the Golan Heights and we would be in a state of war with three Arab states. Having crossed the armistice lines on two fronts was quite sufficient. Let us not add a third state to the war against us."[10]

Dayan's position drew criticism from two quarters. There were those inside the government and among the military who felt and argued that Syria was responsible for the war, and by allowing her to escape its consequences Israel would be sowing the seeds of the next crisis. Another lobby, headed by residents of the valley dominated by the Golan Heights, argued that they must no longer be left to the mercy of Syria's artillery, and exerted pressure on Prime Minister Levi Eshkol and other cabinet members not to end the war without capturing the Golan Heights.

During the night of June 8 Moshe Dayan reconsidered his position, and at dawn he called General David Elazar, General Officer Northern Command, on the telephone and instructed him to launch an offensive against the Golan Heights in the morning. It took Israel about thirty hours to capture the Golan Heights. Given the terrain, fighting was tough and costly. The Syrian army fought well, but the country's leadership took two controversial decisions during the war. The elite units of the Syrian army were not thrown into battle in order to defend the national territory but were kept back in order to protect the regime. And during the final hours of fighting Radio Damascus announced the fall of Kuneitra, the provincial capital of the Golan Heights, several hours before it was actually taken by the Israeli Defense Forces (IDF). The radio bulletin was probably designed to exert pressure on the Soviet Union to expedite the imposition of a cease-fire by the Security Council. In the event it did cause a panicky flight from Kuneitra.

The loss of the Golan and the circumstances under which it happened were to haunt the Ba'th regime in the coming years. The party that claimed to have the formula for liberating Palestine could not protect the integrity of Syria's own territory and lost a piece of it under apparently questionable circumstances. Within the regime's own ranks the warring factions tried to pin responsibility on each other's chests. Hafiz al-Asad was acting defense minister and air force commander during the war. His rivals charged that as such he was formally responsible for the war's conduct and outcome. Asad argued back that instructions were given by others through informal channels and, in any event, he settled the argument by seizing full powers in November 1970.[11]

From War to War, June 1967–June 1974

On June 10 a cease-fire was arranged between Israel and Syria. The whole of the Golan Heights was captured by Israel; the region's civilian population of about 100,000 fled north. Only the Druze population in several large villages at the foothills of Mt. Hermon stayed in place.

War was soon replaced by diplomacy. The United States maintained that the territories captured in war should be exchanged for a solid political settlement. Israel's position diverged at two significant points: it put the West Bank and Gaza in a different category, and it insisted that a political settlement be nothing short of full-fledged formal peace. From that premise the Israeli cabinet (with Menachem Begin in its ranks) decided on June 19, 1967, with regard to Syria that:

> Israel proposes that a peace treaty be signed on the basis of the international border and Israel's security needs.
> The peace treaty will require:
> (a) Demilitarization of the Syrian Heights presently held by the IDF; (b) Absolute guarantee of the uninterrupted flow of water from the sources of the Jordan to Israel.
> Until the peace treaty with Syria is signed, Israel will continue to hold the territories it is holding now.[12]

The Arab consensus and the Soviet Union totally rejected this position. To them Israel was an aggressor and the territories captured in the war should be returned to their owners without any conditions. The Arab states consensus was formalized on September 1, 1967, at the Khartoum Arab summit.

This clash of perspectives and the balance of power between their respective supporters in the international arena produced a diplomatic stalemate. It was formalized by Security Council Resolution 242 in November 1967. The resolution drafters were masters of ambiguity and equilibrium. The Arabs welcomed the preamble that spoke of "the inadmissibility of the acquisition of territory by war" and the call to "withdrawal from territories occupied in the recent conflict." The Israelis, in turn, pointed to the call for "just and lasting peace in which every state in the area can live in security" and to the assertion of the right of every state in the area "to live in peace within secure and recognized boundaries," and underlined the fact that the resolution spoke of withdrawal from "territories" and not from "the territories." According to the Israeli interpretation, this meant partial withdrawal. Alongside with the reference to secure boundaries it implied, so the Israelis argued, a territorial compromise over the territories captured in June 1967 in return for genuine peace.

The Syrian Ba'th regime, like the other Arab regimes, was effective and successful in coping with the immediate repercussions of its military defeat. There was no organized opposition to take advantage of the regime's failure and humiliation. In short order, as behooves an ideological regime, a proper explanation for the defeat was produced and a policy line was formulated.[13] For the Syrian Ba'th, dealing with the "results of 1967" was a subsidiary issue. The fundamental issue was that of 1948, and once this fundamental issue was dealt with, the territorial losses of 1967 would in any case be rectified. Syria took a dubious view of Egypt's willingness to cooperate with the efforts of the United Nations and the superpowers to implement Security Council Resolution 242. But Syria's criticism of Egypt's diplomatic efforts was implicit. If the improbable were to happen and these efforts were to produce an Israeli withdrawal, Syria did not want to legislate herself out of the receiving line.

In a similar vein, Syria was also a partial participant in the "war of attrition," the limited war launched by Egypt against Israel in 1968. Several serious clashes took place along the Israeli-Syrian cease-fire line during this period, but in comparison to the sustained fighting along the Suez Canal and to the Israeli-Palestinian clashes along the Jordanian border the Golan front was rather quiet.

Syria also encouraged Palestinian attacks against Israel as long as they were carried out through Lebanese or Jordanian territory. Her relations with the Palestine Liberation Organization (PLO) and its constituent organizations were compounded by the Syrian claim to be as legitimate a custodian of the Palestinian cause as any Palestinian organization.

Custodianship of the Palestinian cause became excessively demanding in September 1970—"Black September"—when King Hussein and his army took on the Palestinian nationalists who had challenged and sapped their power during the previous three years. Intervention on the side of the Palestinians was debated in Syria. Initially the radical faction, arguing that Syria must intervene on the side of the Palestinian nationalists, won, and a Syrian armored column invaded Jordan. Hafiz al-Asad, defense minister and commander of the air force, argued against intervention. He could not prevent the invasion, but held back the air force. By that time, Israel in league with the United States was deployed to act against the Syrian invasion if necessary. Asad was not willing to have his air force decimated by the Israelis. Without aerial support, the invading Syrian armored column was easily repelled by the Jordanians and retreated ignominiously.[14] In the ensuing altercation, Asad's Syrian rivals charged him with responsibility for Syria's defeat and humiliation. He finally settled the issue in November by staging "the corrective movement" and seizing full power in Syria.

Asad's seizure of power was, of course, first and foremost a domestic Syrian affair, but in retrospect it can also be seen as part of a broader development that took the region to the October 1973 war: the Egyptian-Israeli cease-fire that ended the war of attrition, the death of 'Abd al-Nasser, Anwar al-Sadat's rise to power, and Black September.

Syrian politics in the late 1960s were governed by the conflict between Hafiz al-Asad and his rivals. At the core it was a personal and
factional struggle for power compounded by genuine disagreements over policy. Asad represented a more pragmatic school that
viewed the radical vision of his rivals and their call for a "popular
war of liberation" as hollow posturing. Domestically, he wanted to
find a modus vivendi with the middle classes. In foreign policy he
wanted Syria to act in concert with the Arab mainstream in order
to formulate a joint strategy for dealing with Israel and the territorial losses of 1967.[15]

'Abd al-Nasser's disappearance from the scene and his replace-
ment by the less intimidating Anwar al-Sadat facilitated the formation of an Egyptian-Syrian coalition. That Asad accepted the
principle of a diplomatic settlement as an alternative to a military
solution was made clear in March 1972. In the course of his
Revolution Day speech Asad, for the first time, accepted Security
Council Resolution 242, albeit in a conditional and very specific
fashion:

> I say this in reply to several inquiries which say we in Syria are against
> the Security Council's resolution and that Egypt supports the reso-
> lution. We support the Security Council resolution when inter-
> preted as providing for the withdrawal of the enemy from the Arab
> territory occupied in 1967 and as a confirmation, assertion, and
> realization of the rights of the Palestinian people. We are against this
> resolution when it is interpreted as the realization of new gains for
> the enemy, consolidation of the aggression, and a stab at the rights
> of our Arab people in Palestine.[16]

By 1973 Sadat decided to go to war. He was not hoping for a military victory, but reasoned that if the Arabs launched a war and
held their own for a couple of days, the international system would
be mobilized into forcing on Israel a political settlement acceptable to the Arab side. Syria was a vital military partner to such a
war. A simultaneous attack on the Suez and Golan fronts was an
essential component of an Egyptian strategy seeking to neutralize
Israel's military superiority.

Sadat's invitation to Asad to join him in launching the war presented the Syrian president with a dilemma. The war was to set in motion a diplomatic process that was likely to develop in ways unacceptable to him, and over which he would have very little control. Yet Asad knew very well that he could not afford to reject the invitation. He may also have hoped to secure a territorial gain at the war's outset that would remain his achievement even if the anticipated diplomatic process were to develop in an undesirable direction.

Indeed, neither the war nor its diplomatic sequel unfolded according to plan. The initial Egyptian and Syrian offensive caught Israel by surprise and met with unexpected success. But Syrian-Egyptian coordination soon foundered. Syria's troops were pushed back from the Golan Heights, and as Israel regrouped it captured additional Syrian territory, getting ever closer to Damascus. Asad complained later that by stopping his troops in place and by failing to launch additional attacks Sadat was denying Syria support while the latter was being pressed hard by Israel. Sadat, in turn, complained of Syria's attempt to obtain an early cease-fire through the Soviet Union, without consulting Egypt. On October 22, Syria was surprised both by the cease-fire arranged at Egypt's behest and by its terms (Security Council Resolution 338). During the following weeks and months, Asad had to come to terms with the emergence of direct Egyptian-Israeli negotiations, the formation of a close Egyptian relationship with the United States, and the signing of the Israeli-Egyptian disengagement agreement.[17]

Asad's bargaining chips were quite inferior. Syria ended the war with a new loss of territory. Its patron, the Soviet Union, did not prove to be very effective in that role, and it had yet to build a relationship with the United States. It was Asad's ability to maximize his assets and to emerge from this period with a disengagement agreement comparable to the one signed earlier by Egypt that first established his international reputation as a masterful negotiator and a formidable adversary. While he negotiated with the American secretary of state, Asad conducted his "war of attrition" against Israel in the spring of 1974. Both Israel, anxious to put the debacle of the October War behind it, and the United States, worried by the danger of renewed warfare at the height of the energy crisis, were willing to offer Asad better terms than he had expected in the war's immediate aftermath. Henry Kissinger's attempt to use the negotiations to lure Asad away from the Soviet Union failed. Asad wanted to build a new relationship with the United States, but he was determined to do it on his terms.[18]

The disengagement agreement that was finally signed between Syria and Israel in May 1974 has by now governed relations between the two countries for twenty-four years. It has been observed quite scrupulously by both sides, so much so that when they fought in Lebanon in 1982, peace and quiet prevailed along the Golan front. The agreement stipulated an Israeli withdrawal from the territory captured in 1973 as well as from the town of Kuneitra and a small adjacent area. Syria thus regained the best-known site in the Golan Heights while Israel kept the bulk of the territory. This included Mt. Hermon (site of a very valuable monitoring station) and the defense line along the hills to the east. A UN force (UNDOF) was created in order to monitor the agreement, whose mandate was to be renewed every six months.

It is noteworthy that the disengagement agreement was not actually signed by Syria. When the time came to sign the agreement in Geneva in June 1974, Syria authorized an Egyptian general to sign on its behalf. The message was clear—Syria was willing to negotiate with Israel indirectly in order to deal with the outcome of the 1973 war and, marginally, with that of the 1967 war, but it was not willing to extend the recognition implied by signing the same agreement. Denying recognition and avoiding or at least minimizing direct contact were traditional tools of Arab nationalist resistance to Israel, and Hafiz al-Asad was determined to demonstrate that he remained the champion of that resistance. Indeed, although the disengagement agreement between Egypt and Israel was seen as a first step in an unfolding process, as time went by its Syrian-Israeli counterpart came to be seen more as the final chapter of the October War and less as the initial phase of a potential peace process.[19]

This was not only Syria's choice. Israeli attitudes and policies toward Syria and the Golan had changed considerably soon after June 19, 1967. The positions adopted by the Arab consensus and Syria's own contribution to that consensus persuaded Israeli opinion and the Israeli government that peace with Syria was a remote possibility. Israel dug in for a long stay in the Golan Heights. By the end of 1967 the first Israeli settlements were established. Unlike most of the early settlers in the West Bank, the settlers in the Golan Heights tended to be identified with the Labor party and came to the Golan with the government's encouragement. At the same time, a defense line and monitoring stations were built in the Golan and integrated into Israel's national security doctrine.

The disengagement agreements of 1974 were negotiated on the Israeli side by the government of Golda Meir. But she was forced to resign by an Israeli public still smarting under the impact of the October War. Responsibility for the conduct of Israel's relations with the Arab world passed to her successor, Yitzhak Rabin. Together with his friend Henry Kissinger, he chose to proceed with a phased approach, "step-by-step diplomacy" in the language of that time. Rabin saw Egypt as the key to war and peace with the Arabs. The Sinai, furthermore, afforded the possibility of going through two more interim agreements before coming to a comprehensive agreement for which neither side was yet ready. Rabin was less keen on parallel progress with Syria. If Asad's bargaining style in 1974 was an indicator, the prospect of a further round of negotiations with him was quite alarming. Also, in contradistinction to the Sinai the Golan offered very little maneuverability. It was difficult to envisage a second interim agreement with Syria that would not affect either some of Israel's settlements or her defensive capability in the Golan. The notion of a full-fledged agreement with Syria was not considered a realistic option.[20]

The actual outcome of this round of diplomacy was the Israeli-Egyptian interim agreement of September 1, 1975. Syria rejected an offer to join the process on the basis of "cosmetic concessions" by Israel, and mounted instead an all-out campaign against Egypt's "sellout." But in short order the altercations over "Sinai II" were marginalized by three major developments: the Lebanese civil war, the formulation of a new American policy in the Middle East by the Carter administration, and Menachem Begin's rise to power in Israel.

THE UNITED STATES, ISRAEL, AND LEBANON, 1976–1984

By the mid-1970s it became clear that Hafiz al-Asad had transformed Syria's role in the region. The emergence of a comparatively stable and durable regime in Syria after decades of proverbial instability had for the first time enabled a Syrian government to pursue a systematic, ambitious regional policy rather than be buffeted by other forces. The essence of that policy was the quest for hegemony over Syria's weaker Arab neighbors: Jordan, Lebanon, and the Palestinians. As the hegemonial Arab power in that part of the Middle East, Asad's Syria planned to stand up to Egypt and to deal with her Soviet patron and with the United States from a hitherto unfamiliar position of strength. From that perspective Israel was not only the traditional enemy of Arab nationalism and the usurper of the Golan Heights but a geopolitical rival in the same part of the Middle East.

The emergence of a powerful Syrian state was an important catalyst to the collapse of the Lebanese state and political system through the civil war of 1975–1976. For Syria this presented an opportunity to establish and consolidate her hegemony over both Lebanon and the PLO, and a danger—a premature collision with Israel, which had its own vital interests in Lebanon. In March 1976 Asad, after much agonizing, decided on a direct military intervention in Lebanon. Through Henry Kissinger, a tacit, indirect understanding was worked out between him and Israel's Prime Minister Yitzhak Rabin. The Red Line agreement, as it came to be known, stipulated that Syria's troops would not cross a line drawn across the southern part of Lebanon. Thereby a Syrian-Israeli conflict was avoided for the time being, and the two countries displayed a surprising ability to tread softly in Lebanon when it came to each other's respective interests.[21]

For Syria the formation of its Lebanese patrimony brought about a profound change in perspective. The lines separating between great success and major failure, between lucrative opportunities and severe risks were very fine. As long as Syria's hold over Lebanon was not consolidated, Asad and his regime were preoccupied with their Lebanese investment, often at the expense of other foreign policy issues and considerations.

In November 1976, Jimmy Carter defeated Gerald Ford in the U.S. presidential elections. The administration he formed in January 1977 had a view of the Arab-Israeli problem that was dramatically different from the policies identified with the person and era of Henry Kissinger. Several members of the new team were among the authors of the Brookings Report, a policy study sponsored by the Brookings Institution in 1976 in anticipation of the elections. In several respects the new administration seemed to have adopted the report as a blueprint for its Middle Eastern policy. This meant abandoning the phased approach, a quest for a comprehensive settlement, and a special emphasis on the Palestinian issue as the core of the conflict and the key to its resolution.[22]

The new policies led the Carter administration to attach a particular importance to Syria. A comprehensive solution required an Arab consensus, and Syria's participation was deemed essential. Its preeminence in Lebanon also gave Syria a veto power over the PLO, and Syria offered an additional challenge of particular interest to American policy makers—it was the unfriendly actor, a Soviet client, a regime that had to be won over. Asad was invited to a meeting with Carter in Geneva in May 1977. The results were mixed. Carter was profoundly impressed by Asad and left with the impression that he had persuaded him to participate in his efforts. As he wrote in one version of his memoirs:

> I came away from our first meeting convinced that he would be powerful and flexible enough to modify his political tactics to changing times and circumstances. Even in his bitterness toward Israel, he retained a certain wry humor about their conflicting views, and he seemed to derive great patience from his obvious sense of history.

He professed to speak for other Arabs, but seemed confident that
his influence would be felt in seeking any permanent resolution of
differences.[23]

But in the other version of his memoirs, the same U.S. president
vented his frustration with the same Syrian leader: "This was the
man who would soon sabotage the Geneva peace talks by refusing
to attend under any reasonable circumstances, and would, still
later, do everything possible to prevent the Camp David accords
from being fulfilled."[24]

The policies of the Carter administration in the Middle East had
one unintended consequence: they encouraged Anwar al-Sadat
and the newly elected prime minister of Israel, Menachem Begin,
to establish a direct channel and to seek a separate Egyptian-Israeli
agreement. Washington abandoned its original scheme and
moved to play a crucial role in accomplishing the Camp David
accords (September 1978) and the Egyptian-Israeli peace treaty
(March 1979). Israel agreed to withdraw in phases from the whole
of the Sinai and to remove all Israeli presence, military and civilian. In return Egypt agreed to full peace and normalization with
Israel as well as to severe limitations on her own military presence
in the Sinai, so as to turn it into an effective buffer zone between
the two states. The agreements also provided for Palestinian self-
rule in the West Bank and the Gaza Strip for an interim period of
five years, and stipulated that "the principles and provisions described below should apply to peace treaties between Israel and
each of its neighbors: Egypt, Jordan, Syria, and Lebanon."[25]

But Syria was not mollified by this implicit reference to the
Golan. Asad had rejected Sadat's invitation to join him in his journey to Jerusalem in November 1977, and he had followed the ensuing chain of events with a mixture of disbelief and rage. As he
saw it, Sadat broke ranks with him and the other Arabs, betrayed
the most sacred Arab causes, and undermined everybody else's
capacity to stand up to Israel or to negotiate with it properly if it
ever came to that. The specific terms of the Camp David accords
were seen by him as a bad deal, an outcome to be expected when

an Arab leader reverses the obvious sequence in negotiations with Israel and begins by offering the ultimate concession—recognition and acceptance. Yet as the Egyptian-Israeli peace process progressed into implementation, Asad had to confront a significant body of opinion in Syria that pointed to the fact that Sadat did succeed in regaining the whole of the Sinai while Syria seemed to opt neither for war nor for diplomacy.[26]

Together with Iraq, Syria led the Arab opposition to Sadat's policies, and once Iraq became embroiled in war with Iran Damascus remained the sole leader of the campaign to isolate and punish Egypt and to undermine the peace that had been made with Israel. Like most Arab states, Syria severed diplomatic relations with Egypt and Asad vowed that Syria's flag would not be hoisted in Cairo as long as Israel's flag flew in that city.

The challenge presented by Egypt's peace with Israel was but one of the difficulties that plunged Asad's Ba'th regime into a long and deep crisis in the late 1970s and early 1980s. Domestically the regime contended for several years with the radical Islamic opposition that it finally crushed in the blood bath of Hama in February 1982. The Israeli government of Menachem Begin sought to take advantage of this weakness in order to change the rules of the game in Lebanon. Begin was of the opinion that Rabin's "Red Line agreement" with Syria gave the latter undue advantages in Lebanon, that under its terms Syria was consolidating her control over Lebanon, and the PLO was building a virtual ministate in Beirut and south Lebanon. Various members of Begin's government formulated different strategies for dealing with the Israeli-Syrian-Lebanese-Palestinian quadrangle: some thought that Asad would be willing to give up the Golan in return for Israeli recognition of Syria's control of Lebanon. Others cultivated an ever-expanding alliance with Bashir Jumayyil's Lebanese forces as a strategic partner against both Syria and the PLO.

In 1981 the Begin government sustained three setbacks: Syria's tactical victory in the "missile crisis" in Lebanon during the spring, the unsuccessful artillery duel with the PLO that ended with a cease-fire in July, and Sadat's assassination in October. Begin struck back by extending Israeli law over the Golan on December 14, 1981 (by choosing this formula he stopped short of actual annexation). But his more fundamental response to the growing sense that the hopes he had pinned on his peace agreement with Egypt were being frustrated was the green light he gave in November 1981 to the authors of the Lebanon War.[27]

The war was finally launched in June 1982. Its chief architect, Defense Minister Ariel Sharon, set himself ambitious goals: to destroy the PLO's infrastructure in Beirut and south Lebanon, to help Israel's ally Bashir Jumayyil take over the Lebanese state, to destroy Syria's position and military presence in Lebanon and, ultimately, to create a new balance in the region and in Israeli-Arab relations. Asad assumed erroneously at the war's outset that it was directed solely at the PLO, and sought to avoid direct confrontation with the more powerful IDF. When he discovered his mistake his anti-aircraft missile batteries and more than a hundred airplanes had been destroyed. Syria fought well on the ground and its troops' performance played a significant role in slowing down and confounding Israel's original plan.

Yet even Israel's partial success presented Syria with a dangerous challenge. By early September, Bashir Jumayyil was elected Lebanon's president and the country was likely to come under American and Israeli influence. Syria's enormous investment in Lebanon was about to be lost, and the probable repercussions for Asad's regime were alarming. Against this background Asad's ability to regroup, fight back and, ultimately, win was most impressive. He was ruthless in his choice of method (from Bashir Jumayyil's assassination to close collaboration with Iran and Lebanese Shi'ite terrorists), and cunning in manipulating the Lebanese arena, maximizing his assets, and taking full advantage of American and Israeli vulnerabilities. By 1984 the Reagan administration withdrew the troops it had dispatched to Lebanon, Israel withdrew her forces to the Awali River in the south, and the Lebanese administration of Amin Jumayyil abrogated the May 17 agreement with Israel that U.S. Secretary of State George Schultz had brokered in 1983.

In September 1984 a national unity government was formed in Israel with Shimon Peres as prime minister and Yitzhak Rabin as defense minister. Peres and Rabin carried the cabinet with them against the opposition of most of the Likud ministers to decide on a withdrawal from Lebanon. Rabin tried to repeat his success of 1976 and to negotiate through the United States a tacit understanding with Asad with regard to south Lebanon. But by that time Asad felt secure in Lebanon and saw no reason to limit his position through an agreement with Israel. Given his attitude, Israel decided on a unilateral withdrawal to the line that has since defined her "security strip" in south Lebanon.[28]

Asad's impressive string of successes against the United States, Israel, and his Lebanese adversaries endowed him with a fresh sense of confidence and security. Even a serious illness and its domestic political ramifications (November 1983–May 1984) did not cause more than a temporary setback. An emboldened Asad developed a doctrine of "strategic parity" with Israel. According to the new doctrine Syria could and should build her military forces to the point of being able to face Israel on her own without Egyptian or Iraqi participation in a prospective confrontation.

Another manifestation of Asad's new boldness was his readiness to rely on terrorism as an instrument of foreign policy, and to allow Syria to become directly involved (and implicated) in operations directed at the United States and Israel in the mid-1980s. But the methods that served Syria well in Lebanon backfired later. Syria was put on the State Department's list of states supporting terrorism and was subjected to British sanctions. Without ever accepting the Western definition of terrorism, Asad modified Syria's policies in 1986. Asad apparently instructed his subordinates to avoid direct Syrian involvement in terrorist activities, but he allowed Palestinian and other groups engaged in terrorism to remain on Syrian and Syrian-controlled soil. This fine distinction has not been shared by successive U.S. administrations that kept Syria on the terrorism and (separately) drug lists even as relations improved and a dialogue was established.[29]

In any event, Asad's sense of complacency in the mid-1980s was short-lived. By 1987 the Soviet Union was in rapid decline and Asad's universe was being transformed.

THE ROAD TO MADRID

In 1987 Hafiz al-Asad and Yitzhak Shamir, Menachem Begin's successor as leader of the Likud, probably did not envisage that in four years' time they would be taking their countries into an international peace conference seeking a comprehensive solution to the Arab-Israeli conflict and predicated on a set of terms that was as yet unacceptable to both. The remarkable transformation that accounted for this evolution resulted from the combined effect of the decline of the Soviet Union, the Palestinian *intifada* (uprising), and the Gulf crisis and Gulf War.[30]

The decline and subsequent dissolution of the Soviet Union and the end of the Cold War had a profound impact on Syria and on its Middle Eastern environment. The Soviet-Syrian relationship was rich in tension and ambivalence, but the Soviet Union was a superpower patron, the principal source of weapon systems, Syria's mainstay in the international arena and, ultimately, the guarantor of the regime's security. From mid-1987 it became increasingly and painfully clear that the Soviet Union was improving its own relationship with Israel, avoiding confrontation with the United States in the Arab-Israeli arena, and ceasing to subsidize and fund the supply of armaments to Syria. The Soviets told the Syrians that the doctrine of "strategic parity" should be replaced by a more realistic doctrine of "defensive sufficiency." Other related developments—Soviet-Jewish immigration to Israel, in particular—indicated to Syria, and to other proponents of Arab steadfastness, that after all time might not be on their side.

The first clear sign that Asad had thought through the implications of these developments for his country's foreign policies came in December 1989, when he paid his first visit to Egypt since the breakdown of the late 1970s. During his visit he accompanied President Mubarak to Sharm al-Shaykh in the Sinai Peninsula and soon thereafter restored diplomatic relations with Egypt. The message and the symbolism could not have been clearer. After twelve years of leading the campaign against Sadat and his policies, Asad was laying down his arms. The Syrian flag was hoisted in Cairo alongside the Israeli flag; and Asad must have realized that by visiting Sharm al-Shaykh he was visiting a particularly significant part of the Sinai—a territory lost in 1967 and recovered through the very peace negotiation that Asad had denounced so vehemently. Beyond the symbolism lay a substantive change of policy and direction. The disappearance of Soviet patronage required that a new relationship be built with the United States. Like Sadat in the early 1970s, Asad understood that for a qualitative change to take place in his relationship with Washington he would have to enter into a peace process with Israel.

During the same years Israel was going through a rude awakening of its own. The outbreak of the Palestinian intifada in December 1987 and its subsequent unfolding altered a fundamental reality of Israeli-Palestinian relations during the previous twenty years. Israel had coped successfully with all forms of Palestinian resistance and opposition, so that the Israeli body politic did not feel an urgent need to make the painful choices that any solution regarding the West Bank required. The form of opposition developed spontaneously through the intifada, however, was exacting a price that large segments of Israeli society were not willing to pay.

The Israeli elections of 1988 produced a second national unity government. But given the slight edge it acquired, the Likud was given the prime minister's position for the full period. Yitzhak Rabin remained defense minister, and Shimon Peres became minister of finance. Tensions surfaced soon thereafter. Labor was determined to work together with the Bush administration in order to start a negotiation process with the Palestinians. Prime Minister Shamir and some of his colleagues rejected the terms put forth by Secretary of State James Baker. In March 1990 the Labor party's leader, Shimon Peres, seized on the Likud's rejection of Jim Baker's "five-point plan" to start negotiations with the Palestinians, and brought the government down. His expectation that he would be able to form a new government was ultimately frustrated, and on June 11, 1990, Yitzhak Shamir formed a Likud government in coalition with his customary partners.

These developments and their immediate repercussions were soon overshadowed by the Iraqi invasion of Kuwait and the ensuing Gulf crisis and Gulf War. Syria's particular reaction to Saddam Hussein's move and its conduct during the following months were fashioned by a complex set of considerations. Given the profound hostility between the two regimes and the two leaders, Syria was alarmed by the prospect of an Iraqi success. If Saddam's gambit were to prove successful, a stronger and bolder Iraq would present an even greater threat to Hafiz al-Asad and his regime. As the United States began to organize an Arab and international coalition against Iraq, the potential advantages of Syrian membership were obvious—obstructing Saddam Hussein, building the dialogue with Washington that Asad had always wanted and was now eager to have and, if Damascus played its cards wisely, additional advantages that could be obtained as inducements for joining. There was also a down side. Joining the United States and Saudi Arabia in a wartime coalition against a Ba'th regime in Iraq might be awkward, and would expose the regime to domestic criticism. Asad was conscious of the fact that while Saddam Hussein was trying to rekindle the ashes of revolutionary pan-Arab nationalism he, Asad, was mounting the post–Cold-War path of dialogue with the United States and with Israel.

Asad's progression along that path was not swift or linear. He did join the coalition and did dispatch a reinforced division to Saudi Arabia, but his troops did not participate in the actual fighting. This did not constitute a real problem for the senior American partner. The United States needed Syria in the coalition not as a fighting force but in order to demonstrate that it was not a Western conservative alliance against radical Arab nationalism. On the domestic front, the regime mounted an effective campaign explaining and defending its choice of allies, and in fact encountered very little overt criticism. As a foreign policy investment Syria's participation in the coalition paid off handsomely. A new relationship was formed with the United States, Saudi Arabia provided Syria with three billion dollars, and the United States and Saudi Arabia, the two principal champions of the Taif accords, were willing to look the other way when Syria tightened its grip on Lebanon.[31]

The Bush administration, true to its word, moved soon after the end of the Gulf War to set an Arab-Israeli peace process in motion. President Bush and Secretary Baker felt that the crisis and the war served both to underline the urgency and to improve the prospects of a major effort to resolve or at least ameliorate the Arab-Israeli conflict. During the next seven months they devoted considerable resources to the task of narrowing the differences between the Arab and Israeli views of substance and process. Some of them had to do with the Palestinian issue, but Secretary Baker's greatest effort had to be invested in finding a format and a set of terms that would be acceptable to both Hafiz al-Asad and Yitzhak Shamir.

Asad's original concept was that of an international conference in which the Arab parties, Israel, the United States, and the USSR as well as the United Nations and the European Community would participate. The conference would remain in session and would serve as the principal arena of negotiation, with bilateral negotiations limited to a minimum. According to Asad the scope of negotiations would be very limited, anyway, since he demanded that the conference be convened on the basis of Security Council Resolutions 242 and 338 and on the principle of "territories for peace." Israel's full withdrawal from the Golan Heights was to be a point of departure and the negotiations could focus on the implementation of that withdrawal.

Little of this was acceptable to Shamir. He saw the international conference as a festive inaugural event to be followed by direct bilateral Israeli negotiations with the different Arab delegations. He championed the Israeli interpretation of Resolution 242 (withdrawal from some of the territories) and the Likud view that Israel had already met that demand when it withdrew from the Sinai. He was adamantly opposed to the notion of "territories for peace" and objected to the participation of the United Nations and the European Community in the conference.

In nine trips to the Middle East, Secretary Baker worked out a compromise. The conference, to be held in Madrid, would be attended by representatives of the United Nations and the European Community (as well as the Gulf Cooperation Council) but would actually serve as a prelude to bilateral negotiations. The letter of invitation would rely on Resolutions 242 and 338, but the term "territories for peace" would be used in letters of assurance addressed by the United States to the Arab participants but not to Israel. Multilateral working groups would meet to discuss five regional issues, but Syria (and Lebanon) would not attend.[32] This accomplished, the Madrid conference was convened.

There are two ways of looking at the first phase of Syrian negotiations that emerged from the Madrid conference. One would emphasize, as most accounts have, the harsh and negative aspects of what seemed more like a confrontation than a negotiation. After an initial encounter in Madrid, Israeli and Syrian delegations began to meet in scheduled negotiating rounds in Washington. Three Israeli delegations met with three Arab delegations—Syrian, Lebanese, and Jordanian-Palestinian. Progress was not made on any of the four tracks, but while civility was maintained in the Jordanian and Lebanese tracks the meetings with the Syrians and Palestinians were tense.

As his negotiator with Israel Asad appointed Muwaffaq Allaf, a retired Syrian diplomat who had served as an Arab diplomat at the United Nations and as Syria's ambassador to Vienna before his retirement. Except for one army officer, General Adnan Tayyara, in charge of foreign liaison, the delegation was composed entirely of diplomats. The Israeli delegation was headed by Yossi Ben-Aharon, the director general of the prime minister's office, a member of the inner core of Yitzhak Shamir's government, and one of the chief architects of its policies. The members of his delegation, in the best tradition of the Israeli government's pluralistic approach, represented a plethora of government departments and agencies.

Neither Ben-Aharon nor Allaf came to Washington to look for the middle ground on which a deal was to be made. Both represented leaders who sent their men to Madrid and Washington with a message defined by reluctance, skepticism, and suspicion. For both delegations the conference room in the State Department building was as much an arena for debate and vindication as a site for potential peacemaking. Since both countries assumed that the negotiations were likely to fail, much of what was said in the conference room and in the media stakeouts was designed for immediate and future public consumption.

The atmosphere in the conference room was tense and unpleasant. The Syrians, in the familiar tradition of denial of recognition, refused to shake hands with their Israeli counterparts. When a coffee break was announced they darted out of the room lest they be perceived to have shared a cup of coffee with the Israelis. In the absence of a chairperson there was often acrimonious squabbling over the right to speak. Much of the speaking was actually closer to haranguing. Yet through the rhetoric the two diametrically opposed positions could be discerned. The Syrians insisted that for peace to happen Israel had first to agree to a full withdrawal from the Golan Heights as decreed by Security Council Resolution 242 and by "international legitimacy." The Israeli position was a derivative of the Shamir government's "peace for peace" policy. Security Council Resolution 242 demanded that the Arabs give Israel peace within "secure and recognized" boundaries in return for withdrawal from some of the territory captured in June 1967. By withdrawing from the bulk of the territory (the Sinai) Israel had met her obligations and was now entitled to peace with her other Arab neighbors without offering any additional territorial concessions.

The two positions were, needless to say, irreconcilable. The gap was compounded by sharp disagreements over the past and by mutual demonization. In Syria's version Israel was an expansionist aggressor who had been violating the armistice agreement between 1949 and 1967 and then had launched an aggressive war through which it added the Golan Heights to its unlawful possessions. Israel's narrative was that of an aggressive Syria that for nineteen years had been shelling and shooting at Israeli civilians from the Golan Heights and in the 1960s plunged the region into the 1967 war. Israel took the Golan Heights in self-defense and was holding

on to them lawfully. And if the Syrians condemned the Israelis as
expansionist oppressive usurpers and occupiers, the Israelis retorted by denouncing the Syrians as the oppressive occupiers of
Lebanon and merchants of regional and international terrorism.

It is easy to make light of this chapter in the history of the Israeli-
Syrian negotiations and to register their negative impact in reinforcing the negative views and stereotypes that Israelis and Syrians
had of each other. But when I was entrusted in July 1992 with the
conduct of Israel's end of the negotiations, and took a closer and
better informed look at the first five rounds of negotiations, I could
also see their valuable side. Israeli and Syrian representatives had
not met and talked for forty years. A prenegotiating phase was required before a real negotiation could begin. The contradictory
versions of the past had to be confronted and the legacy of griev-
ances unburdened before a rational negotiation and quest for settlement began. Even when we met under different and more pleasant circumstances in August 1992 a new page could not simply be
turned, but a great deal of aggravation could be and in fact was
saved.

I subsequently found out that there was more to the Shamir government's policies and to Syrian-Israeli contacts than in the formal
accounts of the first five rounds. Alongside the mainstream Likud
position that opposed any, let alone major, territorial concessions
in the Golan as part of a settlement with Syria, there had for years
been voices in the Likud that argued the merits of repeating with
Syria what Begin had done with Egypt, as long as the principal task
of preserving Israel's control of the land of Israel was accomplished. Early in 1992, a secret, parallel, channel to Syria was
opened. I later came to know the person who had carried the messages between Jerusalem and Damascus. He continued to carry
messages between some Israelis and some Syrians in later years, as
well. Official negotiators are probably never enamored of emissaries whose raison d'être is to bypass official channels, but I had
additional reasons for doubting the value of this particular go-
between. In any event, he was authorized in 1992 to convey to his
Syrian contacts that, contrary to the line projected by Yossi Ben-

Aharon in the Washington talks, the Shamir government did not rule out the possibility of some territorial concessions in the Golan as part of an Israeli-Syrian settlement. But in the spring of 1992 the Syrians lost whatever interest they may have had in the Shamir government's gambit, as the June elections in Israel drew closer.

ISRAEL AND SYRIA, RABIN AND ASAD

The Israeli-Syrian negotiations of the years 1992–1995 were shaped by numerous forces, but they were dominated by the personalities of Yitzhak Rabin and Hafiz al-Asad. In the summer of 1992 both men were at the apex of long and impressive military and political careers that had unfolded during the previous five decades in very different environments. Both leaders had interacted in the past and had developed a grudging respect for each other. Asad, of course, was the one unquestioned leader of a personalized one-party regime whereas Rabin headed a coalition government resting on a small parliamentary majority, and was also constrained by significant limitations within his own party, cabinet, and government. Yet, in their different styles both men shaped their countries' approach to negotiations and conducted them directly or through their emissaries.

When the Labor party won the Israeli elections on June 23, 1992, Yitzhak Rabin became prime minister for the second time, fifteen years after he resigned that post in March 1977. This unusual return to power reflected Rabin's perception by the Israeli public as "Mr. National Security," the authoritative figure who could lead their country through a peace process without eroding its security. Rabin's stature was the product of his career and personality. He had volunteered for the Palmach, the elite unit of the Haganah, the IDF's precursor, in May 1941, was a young and prominent brigade commander in Israel's War of Independence, and in 1964 became the IDF's chief of staff. In that capacity he prepared and led the IDF through the brilliant military victory of 1967. Rabin had to share the glory with another major figure—Moshe Dayan, who became defense minister on the eve of the war. But to Israelis and Arabs, in the Jewish world and in the international arena, he was to remain the great chief of staff of the Six Days War.[33]

In 1968, when he retired from the IDF, he chose to become Israel's ambassador to the United States. His tenure as ambassador, the relationships he built with Richard Nixon, Henry Kissinger, and the congressional leadership, and the role he played in the high international drama of the war of attrition and the Jordanian crisis of September 1970 added significant new dimensions to his persona and public image. Rabin was designated by Golda Meir and the Labor party to a leadership role upon his return to Israel in 1973. His election to the Knesset and his appointment as minister of labor in Golda Meir's last cabinet were the standard fare for a senior Israeli general entering the political fray. It was the fall of Golda Meir's government in the aftermath of the October War debacle that catapulted Rabin to the center of Israeli politics. As a venerable military commander with international stature and diplomatic experience, his reputation untarnished by the October debacle, he was chosen by the party elders as Golda Meir's successor in May 1974. The choice was challenged by Shimon Peres, and the issue was decided by a vote in the party center, which Rabin won by a 60:40 ratio. A deal was made whereby Peres was given the Ministry of Defense in Rabin's government, and the mixed pattern of the two men's rivalry and partnership was set for the next twenty-two years.

A comparison of Rabin's two terms as prime minister reveals his capacity to learn, grow, and develop. Yitzhak Rabin of the years 1974–1977 was not the mature, confident, and authoritative statesman of the 1990s. He had been at fifty-two his country's youngest and first Israeli-born prime minister. The young prime minister was not comfortable with politics and politicians. He was cerebral, direct, and blunt. His government rested on a narrow parliamentary basis and within the government he felt challenged and undermined by the defense minister. Domestically, the country and the government were buffeted by the forces that were about to end some fifty years of Labor hegemony in prestate and independent Israel. In Israel's relations with the Arab world crucial choices had to be made. Rabin preferred a careful, gradual approach. An important interim agreement was concluded with Egypt and a crisis was averted in Lebanon, but painful decisions concerning the Palestinian issue and the future of the West Bank were avoided.

In March 1977 Rabin resigned over a personal embarrassment— a bank account maintained by his wife in Washington. It was the right thing to do, and it also kept him at some distance from the Labor party's first electoral defeat in May of that year. The next seven years were an awkward, difficult period for Yitzhak Rabin, involving the continuing rivalry with Shimon Peres inside the Labor party and the need to form responses to the policies of Menachem Begin, who took Israel to the heights of peace with Egypt and to the depth of the Lebanon War. Rabin emerged from this period with his stature rebuilt as the authority on national security, a leader who was somewhat removed from partisan politics. Within the Labor party a truce was achieved whereby Shimon Peres remained the party's leader and its candidate for prime minister, and Rabin was second in command and candidate for the post of defense minister.

These roles and images were reinforced by two versions of national unity governments between 1984 and 1990. While Peres and Menachem Begin's successor, Yitzhak Shamir, alternated as prime minister, Rabin served through the period as a powerful and quite autonomous defense minister. After March 1990, when the Labor party brought down the second national unity government, Rabin launched yet another challenge to Shimon Peres's leadership. The next parliamentary elections were scheduled for June 1992, and the thrust of Rabin's campaign within the Labor party was that he alone could return the party to power, that the particular image he projected and the more centrist policy he presented would provide the victory that had eluded Shimon Peres in 1981, 1984, and 1988.

Rabin at seventy won the Labor party's primaries in February 1992, and moved on to the general elections campaign. It was a very personalized campaign ("Labor headed by Rabin") that criticized the Likud government on two interrelated principal issues: its inability to manage both the Madrid peace process and the

American-Israeli relationship. Rabin and Labor won and on July 13, 1992, he presented his new government to the Knesset.

The new prime minister was determined to effect real changes. He had a clear sense that he was not given a rare opportunity—a second term fifteen years after his first one—just in order to spend time in office. He was determined to change the national agenda set by the previous government by reigniting the Madrid peace process. This was important in itself and as a key to improving relations with the United States. That accomplished, the loan guarantees would be released and the necessary investments could be made to absorb the new wave of immigrants and to build the infrastructure for the next phase in Israel's development.

Rabin saw no problem in removing the two difficulties that had obstructed Israel's relationship with the United States and their cooperation in moving the peace process forward. He was willing to suspend the construction of new settlements and to accept the principle of peace based on territorial compromise (as distinct from the previous government's formula of "peace for peace"). As defense minister he had been willing to resort to harsh measures in order to defeat the Palestinian intifada, because in his view it was a new round in conflict between Israel and Palestinian nationalism that Israel could not afford to lose. But the lesson of the intifada was not lost on him—after twenty years of futile resistance the Palestinians had stumbled upon an effective form of resistance that made the price of continued control of Gaza and the West Bank prohibitive. Rabin's approach to the issue was pragmatic, not ideological or moral. Israel in his eyes had as good a claim to the West Bank as the Palestinians, but the bulk of the West Bank was inhabited by Palestinians and that was an unchangeable fact. That being the case, he saw no point in constructing new settlements in the midst of Palestinian areas, in expending a significant portion of Israel's resources in the West Bank, in keeping the IDF busy policing the area, or in spoiling Israel's relationship with the United States over these issues. Nor did he believe in packing and leaving. He believed—and so stated in his election campaign— that a genuine autonomy could be agreed upon between Israel and the Palestinians, and that this could be accomplished within nine months.

Rabin was less sanguine with regard to an Israeli-Syrian settlement. The former general commanding officer of the Northern Command and the former chief of staff had vivid memories of the fierce conflicts with Syria in the 1950s and 1960s. He was impressed by his ability to reach a tacit agreement with Asad over Lebanon in 1976 and by Syria's strict enforcement of the disengagement agreement since 1974, but he was doubtful that Syria's concept of peace and Israel's stake in the Golan Heights could be reconciled. This view informed his election campaign, which laid the emphasis on reaching an agreement with the Palestinians and made virtually no mention of a serious prospect of negotiations with Syria.

Rabin's own perspective changed soon after his election. Secretary of State Baker came for his last visit in that capacity to the Middle East. He traveled first to Damascus and then to Jerusalem, where he told Rabin that Asad was seriously interested in making peace with Israel and that the Bush administration was ready to make a significant investment in obtaining and securing an Israeli-Syrian agreement. Rabin was impressed but not persuaded, and he was certainly ready to explore Syria's position and its repercussions for the peace process that he was about to galvanize.

IN THE mid-1940s, when Yitzhak Rabin was an officer in the Palmach, Hafiz al-Asad, born in 1930, was a high-school student in Latakiyya, a provincial port in northwestern Syria. Asad came from the large village of Kardaha in the hills just east of the coast. This was the land of the Alawis, a heterodox Islamic sect that makes up about 12 percent of Syria's population. The Alawis were rural, tribal, and downtrodden. For centuries they had been persecuted, exploited, and despised by Muslim-Sunni central governments and by Muslim-Sunni landlords living in cities like Hama and Latakiyya. When France took control of Syria, it cultivated the Alawis, encouraged their separatism, and recruited many of them into the colonial levy. But by the mid-1940s France was on her way out, and the Alawis were being integrated into the state of Syria by the Arab nationalist government in Damascus. Young men of Asad's generation were undergoing political socialization in a very politicized high school in the provincial capital. Of the variety of ideological movements that competed for the allegiance of his generation, Asad, like so many other young Alawis, chose the Ba'th. The Ba'th offered a radical secular version of Arab nationalism that proved to be particularly attractive to members of the minority communities.

The pattern continued. Like so many other young Alawis (and members of other minority communities), Asad proceeded from high school to the military academy in Homs. A military career was a major channel of upward mobility in Syria in the 1940s and 1950s. In the military academy and later as an air force pilot, Asad continued his membership and activities in the ranks of the Ba'th. These were exciting years. Army officers and their civilian allies toppled the old order in Syria, plunged the country into a series of coups d'état, and turned it into the focal point of regional and international conflicts. The Ba'th party allied itself with Gamal 'Abd al-Nasser, the messianic leader of pan-Arab nationalism, and in February 1958 led Syria into an unsuccessful union with Egypt. The union broke up in September 1961, but successive Syrian governments were hard put to consolidate Syria's existence as an independent state.

Hafiz al-Asad, now a retired air force major, was a member of a small secretive group that masterminded the coup which on March 8, 1963, brought the Ba'th to power in Syria. Their experience during the previous five years had set them against 'Abd al-Nasser and against the founding fathers of the Ba'th party. But as a small cell operating behind the scenes and through the military and political powers of others, they had to dissimulate and to act cautiously. It was only after the intra-Ba'th coup of February 23, 1966, that they rid themselves of their partners and took full power into their hands. Asad became acting minister of defense but retained his personal power base as commander of the air force. Asad's title "Acting Minister of Defense" was an early and curious manifestation of Asad's fondness for the formalistic and legalistic side of things. The Ba'th party's rules stipulated that a member could hold either a military command or a ministerial post. Asad was determined to hold both, but also to observe the letter if not the spirit of the party's constitution.

A much more significant aspect of Syrian politics in the mid-1960s and of Asad's rise to power was the emergence of sectarian loyalties and rivalries as a governing factor and a major issue. As we saw earlier, members of the Alawi and other minority communities (primarily Druze and Ismaili) tended to join both the military and the Ba'th party. Consequently, when a group of Ba'thi army officers seized power in Syria it included a disproportionate number of minorities. In the factional and personal conflicts of the 1960s primordial group solidarity became an important factor. And once the sectarian genie was out of the bottle, there was no containing it. At some point an invisible line was crossed and an innocuous sense of familiarity and solidarity turned into deliberate coordination. And once Asad and a group of Alawi military and civilians found themselves in control of the regime (having eliminated the Druze and Ismaili factions) they felt threatened by the resentful Sunni majority. The tension between a regime dominated by a sectarian minority and a resentful majority remained acute for nearly twenty years.

It was hardly surprising that when members of the core group of the Ba'th regime had eliminated all their partners they turned upon each other. The unexpected development was Hafiz al-Asad's victory. During the Ba'th's first years in power Asad was considered a gray, slow, somewhat awkward politician, while his chief rival Salah Jadid was regarded as a political mastermind, a cunning manipulator. But when matters came to a head in 1969–1970, it transpired that behind the stodgy façade lay a brilliant tactician. Asad was deliberate, patient, and cool-headed. He had gradually built a power base in both the army and the party. And when he decided to act in November 1970, he did not stage a coup but took full power into his hands and was soon ready to present a complete governing apparatus as well as a set of integrated policies.

The intra-Ba'th conflict of the late 1960s was first and foremost a personal and factional struggle for power. But there were also genuine differences of policy and substance. Asad represented a pragmatic approach. Within Syria he was not interested in deepening the social and economic revolution but in finding a modus vivendi with the Sunni urban groups, as long as they accepted the regime and did not meddle in politics. Regionally he sought accommodation and cooperation with Egypt and the Arab mainstream. And internationally, although he continued to rely on the Soviet Union as Syria's superpower patron, he was anxious to open a dialogue with the United States.

Asad's first years in power were on the whole a remarkable success. After twenty-five years of proverbial instability he formed a comparatively stable and durable government. On the basis of that stability he conducted an effective foreign policy that turned Syria into a regional power. His conduct of the post–October War negotiations, his role in the Lebanese crisis, and the anti-Egyptian campaign he mounted in the aftermath of the second Sinai agreement all bore testimony to Syria's new status in Middle Eastern and international politics.

Asad's personality was an important component of Syria's newly acquired stature. By the early 1980s Asad had built a reputation as a cunning and effective negotiator, an excellent strategist and tactician, and a leader whose personal charm and sense of humor served to conceal the brutal power that he and his regime would use when challenged. In the international arena it was Henry Kissinger's memoirs that did more than any other publication to build Asad's complex image. In the Middle East context it was Karim Pakardouni, a Lebanese politician, the principal liaison between Syria and the Phalanges (the essentially Maronite-Christian party), who drew Asad's fullest and most flattering profile. Despite the occasional overstatement, Pakardouni's account is very useful in offering both a description of Asad's modus operandi in the 1970s and early 1980s and a sense of the image Asad himself sought to project.

> In carrying out his designs, Assad is implacable, cautious and unyielding. He has built his authority stone by stone; he is never in

haste, he never gets excited and rarely raises his tone. He prefers to get what he wants by stealth and he employs persuasive before dissuasive methods.

He chooses his moment perfectly, waiting for the right opportunity, letting his own strength build up while his opponents get weaker. He will not negotiate from a position of weakness, lest his adversary be tempted to wring something out of him; when he is in a position of strength he regards any concession as an unnecessary gift. He believes that everything has its price, but that it is up to him to decide what the price shall be. He will not let himself be constrained by limits or conditions laid down by others.

When entering negotiations he adopts an impassive face. The stage setting is always the same. . . . He usually knows his subject in depth; he has an elephantine memory and a prodigious ability to concentrate.

Sometimes, the meeting itself will be the subject of negotiation.

He is an unpredictable, wily negotiator who is as capable of treating a serious problem in cavalier fashion as he is of declining to give an exact reply to a simple question. If he promises something it is as good as done, but when he wants to refuse he will say "I shall talk this over with X or Y" or "I shall examine this question."[34]

Asad's initial achievements were marred in the latter half of the 1970s by a host of domestic and external problems: the lingering animosity of the urban Sunni population, the Muslim fundamentalist offensive, dissension and corruption within the regime's ranks, the rivalry with Saddam's Iraq and Hussein's Jordan, the challenge of Israeli-Egyptian peace, and the mounting cost of maintaining Syria's new fiefdom in Lebanon. The difficulties reached their zenith in 1982. In February of that year Asad's soldiers quashed yet another Muslim rebellion in the city of Hama with unprecedented brutality, killing some 15,000 of the city's residents. In June Israel launched its war in Lebanon and in early September seemed to have destroyed Syria's enormous investment there. But Asad fought back, and did so with great success and brought his and his country's prestige to a new height.

The same pattern—oscillation between periods of success and

achievements and points of crisis—continued in the latter half of
the 1980s. Its persistence was a reflection of Asad's personal and
political strengths, and of his unwillingness and inability to deal
with his regime's structural flaws. Thus in the late 1980s, in response to the collapse of the Soviet Union and of close allies like
Romania's Nicolae Ceausescu, Asad moved to build new relations
with the United States and Egypt, but he failed to introduce meaningful political reforms in Syria. Having faced no serious domestic
opposition in recent years, Asad may very well feel that he did the
right thing.

During the four decades of his political career Hafiz al-Asad
went through several radical changes of direction. A member of
the Ba'th party, a paragon of Arab union in the 1940s and 1950s,
he played a crucial role in the consolidation of Syria's independent
existence in the 1960s. The leader of the Syrian Ba'th party and
regime that had at one time been closely identified with notions of
revolution, radicalism, and anti-imperialism, he took his country
in 1990–1991 into the American-led war coalition against the other
Ba'th regime in Iraq. In some respects Asad's gradual acceptance
of the notion of a political settlement with Israel in the late 1980s
and early 1990s represented a similar departure from a seminal dimension of his personal and political history and makeup. And yet
it was a different development. In Asad's own mind the transition
from the role of Arab nationalism's standard bearer in the struggle against Israel to that of a peacemaker was more difficult than
the decision to join the coalition against Iraq. Nor was Asad's soul-
searching alleviated by the need to make sharp choices. It had
been difficult to join the United States and Saudi Arabia in a
wartime coalition against a radical Arab regime, but Asad's decision was eased by the obvious threat that the prospect of Saddam's
victory represented. When it came to reconciliation with Israel, an
equally dramatic threat or attraction was absent. The Bush administration's invitation to Madrid required a significant decision by
Asad. Yet Asad could tell himself that, important as his positive answer was, it fell short of a final, irreversible choice and commitment. Whatever his concept of settlement, the Shamir govern-

ment's reluctance combined with his own reservations to produce a meaningless negotiation requiring no painful choices. It was the arrival of Rabin's government that forced Asad to grapple fully with the most fundamental issues that the prospect of a genuine settlement with Israel raised for him and for Syria.

THREE

First Cracks in the Ice

THE FIRST PHASE of Yitzhak Rabin's negotiations with Hafiz al-Asad lasted from August 24 to December 17, 1992. During this period three rounds of negotiations between the Israeli and Syrian delegations to the Washington peace talks took place. The Rabin government's opening gambit and Syria's response galvanized the Israeli-Syrian track. But by October the talks stalled under the combined impact of the American presidential elections and the limitations imposed by the two parties.

Rabin began his preparations for the new round of talks by changing his chief negotiator. He invited me to his home—we lived on the same street in Tel Aviv and were on very friendly terms—on a Saturday morning. The prime minister was typically careful. As a hedge against a negative answer he asked me to recommend a suitable academic expert on Syria with public standing to become the new head of the Israeli delegation to the peace talks with Syria. Elie Rubinstein and Uri Lubrani, two senior distinguished civil servants, were to remain chief negotiators with Jordan, the Palestinians, and Lebanon. But Yossi Ben-Aharon was too political, a member of the inner core of the Shamir government, to keep his position in the Syrian talks. I was naturally reluctant to recommend myself, but we soon found our way around the problem and I was recruited to the talks and to the scintillating experience of working closely with Rabin on two cardinal issues—the peace process and the U.S.-Israeli relationship.

Rabin then proceeded to describe his conversation with Secretary of State Baker after the latter's latest visit to Damascus (July 21–22, 1992). Rabin was impressed both by Baker's conviction that Asad was ready to make peace with Israel and by his willingness to make serious American investments and commitments in order to help Israel and Syria make peace and underwrite it. Both Rabin and Baker saw the advantage of dealing first with an authoritative head of state rather than with the diffuse Palestinian polity. My original mandate would be to explore the Syrian position and to indicate our own seriousness. Rabin wanted to proceed slowly and cautiously. The prospect of an agreement with Syria was bound to have immediate public and political repercussions in Israel. No one believed seriously in the prospect of "peace for peace," and everyone understood that peace meant at least some withdrawal that was bound to affect at least part of the 12,000 or so Israelis who lived in the Golan Heights.

The sixth round of the Washington talks was scheduled to begin on August 24, 1992. Unlike its predecessor, the Rabin government did not seek a change of venue. If the talks could be shifted to the region and Israel and Syria could negotiate, say, on or near the cease-fire lines, the advantages would be considerable. But the only advantage that a venue like Rome had over Washington was proximity. This could become significant in the event of a breakthrough, when large delegations of experts and frequent consultations would be called for. At this point, however, the issue was of a symbolic nature; and whereas the Shamir government had wanted to spite the Bush-Baker administration, the Rabin government was determined to work hand-in-glove with Washington and saw the continuation of the Washington talks as natural. The Arab participants, for their own good reasons, were equally interested in developing their own dialogues with the United States.

I had about three weeks to prepare for the resumption of the talks. The original delegation to the peace talks with Syria had been composed of experts representing various ministries and government departments. Two of Yossi Ben-Aharon's closest associates left with him, and the delegation remained a leaner and more professional body. According to the original agreement between Yitzhak Shamir and David Levy, the deputy head of the delegation represented the Foreign Ministry. In this case it was David Afeq, the head of the ministry's research division, a genuine Middle East expert, a seasoned diplomat, and a delightfully straightforward, blunt person. The other permanent members of the team were Avraham Leaf, a defense analyst of long standing; Jacques Neriya, on his way from the IDF to the prime minister's office; David Korenblut, a Foreign Office international law expert; and Ronen Hoffman, my personal assistant. In time I arranged for Shlomo Marom, our former ambassador to Hungary and, like Leaf, a sharp and experienced defense and policy analyst, to join the team.

By meeting with Yossi Ben-Aharon, talking to the members of the delegation, reading the written record, and listening to tapes of the first five rounds I could form a good impression of the previous nine months. The very word "tapes" pointed to one major problem. A formal negotiation with both delegations ostentatiously planting their cassette recorders on the table could hardly be expected to provide the setting for a breakthrough. Could we expect Muwaffaq Allaf, the chief Syrian negotiator, to offer flexibility on the Palestinian issue into the microphones of both a Syrian and an Israeli recorder? One was much more likely to be treated to a forceful reiteration of the familiar position. Clearly both format and atmosphere must be changed for a breakthrough to be achieved.

But there was a greater, more substantive, difficulty. Asad was apparently serious in his decision to make peace with Israel. But he was determined to obtain from Israel a commitment to full withdrawal from the Golan Heights as a precondition to any discussion of the nature of peace. It was an open question as to whether the Labor government would be willing to make peace with Syria on the basis of full withdrawal, but it was certainly unlikely to make such a commitment as a prelude to serious negotiations.

Preparation also entailed discussions with political leaders and in the defense establishment. Shimon Peres was formally the foreign minister, but he was clearly Rabin's chief partner and only competitor in the cabinet. In the division of labor agreed upon between the two, Rabin took charge of the bilateral peace talks and the U.S. relationship while Peres became responsible for the multilateral peace talks. But he was profoundly interested in the prospects of the negotiations with Syria and preoccupied by the price tag placed by Asad ("bringing the Syrians within ten meters of Lake Tiberias," as he used to put it). His deputy minister, Yossi Beilin—dovish, creative, and proactive—was trying to promote his approach to resolving the deadlock with Syria: Israel should begin by reiterating the Eshkol government's decision of June 19, 1967. It struck me as a useful step in a potential future sequence but as an excessive concession at that early stage.

The chief of staff, General Ehud Baraq, was interested in much more than the security aspects of the negotiations. It was a common assumption that he was designated—if not destined—for national leadership, and he was clearly thinking about relations with Syria in these terms. He was also close to Rabin and one of the few persons that the prime minister consulted within the genuine sense of term. General Uri Sagi, the director of military intelligence, was the chief advocate in Israel of the notion that Hafiz al-Asad had made a strategic choice and decided to make peace with Israel. Sagi had let this be known when he served under the Shamir government, and he became more outspoken after the elections. In private conversations he drew a complex and interesting picture of Asad's view of the contemporary world and his calculus vis-à-vis Israel. Some of it had become the conventional wisdom—the loss of the Soviet patron, the need to build a new relationship with the United States—but other aspects were novel. Thus he explained that Syria's participation in the coalition during the Gulf War had a chilling effect on Asad and his generals when they realized what the arsenal of the U.S. armed forces—and by implication of the IDF—was.

Before leaving for Washington I prepared the text of my opening remarks and had it approved by Rabin. The speech sought first and foremost to emphasize the change in policy and in the character of the negotiations with Syria that the new government was determined to introduce. The key sentence stated that "Israel accepts Security Council Resolution [242] in all its parts and provisions as a basis for the current peace talks and views it as applicable also to the peace negotiations with Syria." This was an indirect way of saying that the new government did not support the notion of "peace for peace" and was ready to seek a settlement with Syria that would include an element of withdrawal. It can, of course, be asked what the point was of conveying the message in an implied fashion. Why not state it explicitly and directly? The answer is that we had to adapt ourselves to Hafiz al-Asad's negotiating style. We knew by then that Asad gave nothing without getting something in return. It would be nice to negotiate magnanimously and swiftly, but before adopting such a mode we had to know that we had a cooperative partner.

During the same period our Syrian counterparts were making their own preparations. The Syrian media acknowledged the new and softer line of the Rabin government but did not spare it harsh criticism, arguing that it was up to the new government to prove to its Arab interlocutors that it was ready to "meet its obligations." Syria also chose to conduct a launching test for its Scud missiles on the eve of the resumption of the Washington talks. Lest a measure of flexibility be interpreted as a sign of weakness, it had to be accompanied by a show of strength. The foreign ministers of the Arab participants in the Madrid peace conference met in Damascus on July 24–25, 1992. The statement they published at the end of the meeting included a long list of demands addressed to Israel but also one indication of fresh flexibility—the term "peace agreements."

A far more elaborate message of flexibility was brought to Washington by 'Aziz Shukri, a Syrian professor of international law, the former dean of the University of Damascus Faculty of Law. Shukri was one of the very few Syrian academics who were allowed by the regime to speak abroad in a comparatively free fashion, to walk ahead of the accepted policy, and to test the water before a change was actually implemented. Professor Shukri came to Washington to speak at the Washington Institute for Near East Policy, which is considered to be sympathetic to Israel. A measure of its great success has been its ability to establish one of the most prestigious Middle East policy forums in Washington, which is usually well attended by both Israelis and Arabs.

As Shukri put it to his audience, Syria saw the negotiations as a vehicle for reaching a peace agreement that would put an end to the state of war and would introduce a state of peace whose meaning was, among other things, normalization, mutual recognition, economic and social cooperation, and so on. Being committed to the Arab cause, the Syrians would not object to the Israeli-Palestinian or Israeli-Jordanian track moving ahead first, as long as the agreement was comprehensive and the peace agreements were approved simultaneously. Syria was very supportive of security arrangements as long as they were mutual. And—of course—everything must be predicated on the full return of the Golan to Syria. Not a single square inch was negotiable. As the course of the negotiations over the next few months indicated, Professor Shukri had come to Washington with a mixed bag—some of his statements turned out to have been good indications of Syria's evolving position but other parts of his message were far too optimistic.[1]

MUCH was accomplished during the first round of the new negotiations with Syria—the sixth round since Madrid—which was held in Washington from August 24 through September 2. The immediate Syrian response to our opening gambit—accepting the applicability of the territorial element in Resolution 242 to the Golan Heights—was, predictably, an attempt to extract from us a bolder or a more explicit statement. This effort continued through the rest of the first week. By August 31, the Syrians finally gave up and handed us a paper that they had obviously completed at home by way of preparation for the new phase in the negotiations. It was an interesting, significant document. The document was titled "Draft Declaration of Principles" and consisted of two parts: the draft itself, consisting of nine paragraphs typed over three pages and a separate introductory page. To date the text of the paper has not been published. Of the various versions that appeared in the media at the time, the one published, of all places, in the East Jerusalem Arabic paper *al-Manar* was the most accurate.[2]

When they presented us with the paper, our Syrian interlocutors told us, oddly, that we should ignore the introductory page, that it was not "an integral part of the paper." Our immediate sense was that the core of that page was a paragraph explaining that the appended paper did not deal with every single element relating to the wider Arab-Israeli conflict since other "no less essential elements" such as withdrawal from "the other occupied Arab territories, Palestinian national rights and the right of return of Palestinian refugees, the solution of which was essential for the achievement of a really comprehensive peace" were being discussed on other bilateral tracks.

This was ambiguity at its best, or worst. Read literally, the covering page stated that there was no finality to any agreement we would be making in that it would not constitute the "really comprehensive peace" to which Syria was at least ostensibly committed. Indeed, the first paragraph of the Syrian draft declaration defined "the objective of peace" as the establishment of a "comprehensive, just and lasting peace in the region." The second paragraph, under the title "comprehensiveness of the solution," opened with the argument that "for peace to be real and durable it must be inclusive of all parties to the Arab-Israeli conflict and comprehensive on all fronts." But the same paragraph alluded to some flexibility: "the details of issues and problems . . . may vary from one group to the other," and comprehensiveness was to be the "ultimate outcome" of the peace process.

Here in a nutshell were two of the cardinal problems of this negotiation. In substantive terms the Syrians insisted on a clear-cut commitment to a very simple proposition—full Israeli withdrawal from the Golan Heights. On the other side of the equation were vague references to the issues that interested us—peace, security or, in this instance, the relationship of our prospective agreement to the other negotiating tracks. Would the Palestinians have the right to veto the agreement with Syria or its implementation? Would the Syrians—once we reached an agreement on our bilateral issues—insist that before we implement it Israel must resolve the explosive issue of the Palestinians' right of return?

In procedural terms it was clear to us that the format of the negotiations could only exacerbate the problem. In the stiff and formal setting of a State Department conference room, two delegations pitted against each other across a table decorated with cassette recorders, we were hardly likely to hear from the Syrian negotiators with a twinkle in their eye that they were merely paying lip service to comprehensiveness, that should Syria obtain its own particular ends it would be willing to make its own deal with Israel. In fact the more we were going to ask about it the more they were likely to dig in.

The draft declaration itself was a clear formulation of Syria's, or Asad's, concept of a peace settlement with Israel as it crystallized after the Israeli elections and before the beginning of a serious negotiation between the two countries. It rested on the Syrian interpretation of Security Council Resolutions 242 and 338 and the principle of "land for peace." Once these were accepted, there was no need for elaborate negotiations. All that was required was a "machinery of implementation" that would provide for "total Israeli withdrawal from the Syrian Golan occupied in 1967" and "dismantling of all Israeli settlements" and in return for "termination of all claims or states of belligerency between the two sides." The two parties would form working groups in order to proceed with the execution of "the steps" required by Resolution 242. The "executive steps" of Resolutions 242 and 338 and the "obligations ensuing therefrom" would be incorporated in a "peace agreement" to be endorsed by the Security Council and registered with the General Secretariat of the United Nations.

The important issue of security was addressed in two different paragraphs. They stated Syria's well-known position that security was a concern of both parties, and sought to preempt any Israeli attempt to replicate the elaborate and effective security regime in the Sinai that had been a key element of Israeli-Egyptian peace making in the late 1970s. Security arrangements, according to the Syrian draft, were to be "parallel and reciprocal" and "without any prejudice to the sovereignty of any party nor to the principle of equal rights for both." Demilitarized zones and zones of reduced armaments could be part of the security arrangements but they should be established "on both sides and on equal footing."

The limitations and the shortcomings of the Syrian draft were glaringly obvious and the tactical considerations behind it were quite transparent. As its opening gambit the Syrian delegation offered us a glorified nonbelligerency in return for full withdrawal. The Syrians were also placing markers for a future negotiation over the security arrangements, and creating a deliberate ambiguity over the issue of linkage between our track and the Palestinian issue. Typically, the heading and the text of the draft did not specifically mention Syria and Israel as the two peacemaking parties, and we had to read carefully through the document in order to establish that it dealt with peacemaking between Israel and Syria.

And yet it was significant that the Syrian delegation to the Washington talks did put on the table a draft declaration of principles as a first step to negotiating a peace agreement with Israel. We now had to start a real negotiation in order to bring the Syrians down from the formal-legalistic heights reflected in their paper to a more realistic level on which our positions could possibly be brought closer together.

In order to break the mold of the negotiations, I asked the assistant secretary of state, Edward Djerejian, to see whether he could arrange for me to meet with Muwaffaq Allaf, my Syrian counterpart, alone and in an informal setting. Ed Djerejian was now in charge of the peace process on the American side. Before being appointed to his present position, he was U.S. ambassador to Damascus. He had developed an excellent relationship with Asad and was given much credit for his role in improving the American-Syrian relationship and in facilitating Asad's journey to the Madrid conference. I was hoping that Allaf would agree to meet alone in an informal setting, say breakfast or dinner at Djerejian's home in suburban Washington. But all that Allaf agreed to (probably after checking with Damascus) was a smaller meeting at lunchtime at Djerejian's State Department office. He insisted that he come with Walid Mu'allim, Syria's ambassador to Washington and a member of his delegation as a notetaker. We thus met in a forum of six— Allaf and Mu'allim, myself and Jacques Neriya as the Israeli notetaker, and the two hosts, Ed Djerejian and his principal deputy,

Daniel Kurzer. Over the next few months we met several times in this format with limited effect. The atmosphere was a little more relaxed and questions could be asked and answered more directly. But it did not evolve into the proverbial "walk in the woods" in which two representatives meeting informally with no record kept could find out on behalf of their respective governments whether a deal was feasible. On one occasion Kurzer left the room and Djerejian was conveniently called to the phone on the other side of his spacious office. Allaf reacted nervously and the episode did not amount to much. At some point Allaf complained that there was no point in his coming to these smaller meetings if he did not hear what we failed to say to him in the larger meetings (namely, to express Israel's readiness for withdrawal).

This being the case, our give-and-take with Syria would have to continue through the regular meetings in the conference room on the sixth floor of the State Department building. A swift break-through was clearly not in the cards, and the negotiations should be viewed by us as a longer-term effort seeking to accomplish several aims: to continue to identify Asad's purposes—did he really want a settlement? What were his real terms and red lines? If our perspectives could not be matched, would he be interested in an interim settlement? What about a gradual, phased approach, beginning with confidence-building steps in Lebanon? Another task would be the gradual expansion of the agenda of the talks in Washington. The tone and atmosphere having been improved, we should continue in the same vein. Let us ask questions and comment on each other's media and on statements made by political leaders and public officials on both sides. Our countries had not been speaking to each other for forty years. Here was a forum and a channel of communication through which the process of de-demonization could begin. Our Syrian interlocutors had a limited mandate and they were stiff and formal but they recorded the proceedings, and if I knew anything about Asad's Syria, I knew that Asad and his foreign minister, Faruq al-Shara͑, and several other leaders of the regime would be reading the transcript. So here was an opportunity to speak to Asad, albeit indirectly, and to explain how Israel viewed the most fundamental issues in her relationship with Syria and the Arab world.

Within a few weeks the Washington talks settled into a pattern. On the Israeli side four delegations would arrive for a round of negotiations aboard an air force Boeing 707. Elie Rubinstein remained secretary of the cabinet, head of the combined delegation to the talks with the Jordanians and the Palestinians, and coordinator of the talks for the Israeli side. Uri Lubrani remained our chief negotiator with Lebanon. Elie Rubinstein's delegation was, in fact, composed of two different groups, one meeting with the Jordanians and the other with the Palestinians.

All members of the delegations stayed on one floor of a large Washington hotel, usually the Mayflower. Every morning three delegations left for the State Department building to meet with their Arab counterparts. The meetings were scheduled for three hours from Monday through Thursday from 10 A.M. to 1 P.M. In the afternoons Elie Rubinstein's other delegation would meet with either the Palestinians or the Jordanians. Every evening the heads of the delegations accompanied by Eytan Ben-Tsur, then deputy director general of the Foreign Ministry, and Zalman Shuval, our ambassador to Washington, would meet to compare notes and discuss common issues.

Around the hours of actual negotiations revolved a busy day. Morning began with an update and consultation of our delegation; we read the summary of Israeli and Arab and international media prepared by a very efficient press operation, spoke on the telephone to the prime minister's office and the Foreign Ministry, and finalized the paper work for the day's session. At the session's end we returned to the hotel to have a brown-bag lunch and analyze among ourselves the day's proceedings. On this basis we would write the daily telegram addressed to the prime minister and the foreign minister, and we consulted on the policy line to be followed. Needless to say, the major policy decisions were made in Israel and we knew very well what our red lines were, but the latitude we had as far as tactical decisions (including written formulations) were concerned was considerable. The intellect, experience, and

Middle East expertise assembled in my delegation turned these discussions and consultations into animated, stimulating sessions that I personally enjoyed enormously. We analyzed the day's session, prepared scenarios, wrote drafts of papers to be presented to the Syrians, and dissected every Syrian statement made in Washington or Damascus.

During the afternoon I would meet with our American colleagues and do media work. As I mentioned earlier, the key figure on the U.S. side at this point was Ed Djerejian. The Madrid process was put in place by Jim Baker, whose peace process team was headed by Dennis Ross, then director of policy planning, who was assisted by Dan Kurzer and Aron Miller. Richard Haas, the senior director for the Middle East at the National Security Council, worked mostly on other issues, as did John Kelly, the assistant secretary for Near Eastern affairs. When Djerejian replaced Kelly, the Bureau of Near Eastern Affairs became more deeply involved in the peace process. Then in August 1992 Baker was asked by President Bush to leave the State Department and to return to the White House as chief of staff in order to save the president's ailing campaign for reelection. Baker moved to the White House on August 13 and took Dennis Ross along with him. They became absorbed in the campaign and were essentially removed from the peace talks.

At the State Department Lawrence Eagleburger, the deputy secretary of state, remained as acting secretary and was later given by President Bush the title of secretary. He oversaw the negotiations and occasionally met with the negotiating teams for sessions dominated by his irrepressible sense of humor and command of the subject matter. Yet the fact of the matter was that the Bush administration was fading when the Israeli-Syrian negotiations were finally galvanized.

Ross's departure to the White House meant that the conduct of the peace process became the virtually exclusive domain of Ed Djerejian. Within the U.S. team there was a natural division of labor: Djerejian by virtue of his recent experience was fascinated by the prospect of an Israeli-Syrian deal, while Kurzer and Miller focused their interest on the Palestinian track. It was a very diverse team. Djerejian, as his name indicates, is of Armenian extraction. He was born in New York to parents who had emigrated from Lebanon. A very jovial and a very professional diplomat, he had developed both a Middle Eastern and a Soviet expertise. Kurzer and Miller, both Ph.D.s and both proud American Jews, were great experts on Arab-Israeli relations and genuinely devoted to Israeli-Arab, particularly Israeli-Palestinian, reconciliation.

The presidential election dominated the American media at this time. In the absence of a breakthrough or a major event comparable to the Madrid conference, the resumption of the Washington talks remained a peripheral story in the U.S. media through the fall and winter. This was certainly not the case with the Israeli and Arab media. Large contingents of Israeli and Arab correspondents covered the Washington talks and were interested in the smallest hint of a breakthrough. Formal and informal briefings for these two groups and for the smaller group of American and European specialists consumed several hours every day. The Israeli embassy's press counsellor, Ruth Yaron, a consummate professional, was an invaluable resource in a line of work that had not been bread and butter for me at Tel Aviv University.

A particularly interesting dimension of our work with the media was provided by the press stakeouts at the entrance to the State Department building before and after every session. On a good day a group of more than twenty journalists—television crews from CNN and other interested networks, the wire services, the Israeli and Arab media—would be there to address questions to the Syrian delegation and to us. This pattern had two major effects. The pre-session stakeout was soon used by the two delegations as a mechanism for trying to affect both the atmosphere and the agenda of the day's proceedings. And although we both undertook early in the negotiations to put an end to the posturing for the galleries that had bedeviled previous negotiations, we both used the post-session stakeouts in order to advance our respective agendas and points of view. The electronic media and the wire services endowed the stakeouts with an immediate impact. When Muwaffaq Allaf sought on September 17 to create an artificial crisis in the talks and stormed out of the building, it took minutes for the Israeli media in their evening news to announce that, indeed, a crisis had broken out.

The stakeouts reinforced the feeling (on the Israeli side) that the format of the Washington talks was ill suited for effecting a breakthrough with Syria. We were scrutinized on an almost daily basis, and were under pressure to offer either a progress report or a satisfactory explanation for lack of progress. If a "walk in the woods" was a technique for helping the parties to overcome the difficulties inherent in a scrutinized negotiations, the "stakeout culture" was its antithesis.

Inside the room we normally faced a Syrian delegation composed of nine members. Muwaffaq Allaf was the high-handed head of the delegation and practically the sole speaker on the Syrian side. A small, elegant, eloquent, and irascible man in his early sixties, he was an excellent choice for the previous phase of the negotiations. Allaf was a very effective advocate and debater and, after his years at the United Nations, could recite the relevant UN resolutions and Syria's version of the history of her conflict with Israel with considerable skill.

Allaf, like most members of his delegation, was not a Ba'thi. He was, rather, an Arab nationalist who in the 1950s must have been swept up by Nasser and Nasserism and subsequently transferred his allegiance to the Ba'th regime. He had no personal relationship with Asad, and to the best of our understanding was supervised directly by the foreign minister, Faruq al-Shara'. Although Allaf was an effective advocate he was not a deal maker. It was clear to us that he came to Washington to present and promote his country's point of view and to obtain an Israeli commitment to a full withdrawal, but not to look for the common ground on which deals are made. More significantly, it was our sense that he and some of his associates conducted themselves as individuals sent by their government to perform a task. If their mission was to produce peace with Israel as defined by Asad, that would be fine, but they would actually feel more comfortable if the negotiations led nowhere.

Allaf's deputy as head of the delegation was Zakariyya Isma'il, a

retired senior Foreign Ministry official who at some point had
been Syria's vice minister of foreign affairs and, as such, Allaf's su-
perior. Allaf often referred to him as "my deputy," clearly taking
pleasure at this reversal of hierarchy. Isma'il, like two other members of the delegation, Rafiq Juweijati and Muhammad Fattal, was
in his late sixties of a generation that was still educated in the
French tradition. Together with Allaf they formed a core of older,
bourgeois-looking gentlemen incongruent with the conventional
image of a radical Arab military regime dominated by members of
the Alawi minority.

It is interesting to note that by way of removing Allaf from the
negotiations Asad appointed him in 1995 to the Syrian slot of assistant to the secretary general of the Arab League. When Allaf
passed away in 1996 he was replaced in that position by Zakariyya
Isma'il. These were two passages from the onerous task of negotiating with Israel to a virtual sinecure in the pale shadow of what
used to be the embodiment and symbol of pan-Arab nationalism.
If the peace process of the early and mid-1990s represented an effort to create new political patterns in the Middle East, the Arab
League in its shriveled contemporary form represented an effort
to hang on to a bygone past.

Although Zakariyya Isma'il was formally Allaf's deputy, the real
second in command was Walid Mu'allim, Syria's ambassador to
Washington. Mu'allim, a corpulent man with a gray head of hair,
was in his mid-fifties; a professional diplomat who had previously
served in London, as Faruq al-Shara^c's *chef de cabinet,* and as ambassador to Romania (an important assignment, given Asad's special relationship with President Nicolae Ceausescu). He was a
Ba'thi intellectual and had a good reputation in Washington.
Mu'allim was one of the few members of the delegation who spoke
during our sessions, and although he did not stray from the line
represented by Allaf he projected a pragmatism by seeking common ground and agreement.

The delegation included one senior military officer, General
Adnan Tayyara, the Syrian army's chief of foreign liaison. At the
time Tayyara was terminally ill, and indeed passed away in 1994.

Tayyara never spoke during the sessions, but rather sat glumly and smoked.

Majid Abu Saleh was nominally Syria's ambassador to Jordan, but we felt that he was chosen for the delegation as a member of the Abu Saleh clan, the dominant family in Majdal Shams, the largest Druze village in the Golan Heights.

Riad Daudi was the international law expert of the Syrian delegation. He was younger and clearly more conversant with contemporary law than his older colleagues, who were products of the traditional French system. Allaf loved to recite the Syrian interpretation of Resolution 242, but on other matters of international law he gave Daudi the floor. Daudi showed up later as a member of the Syrian delegation to the Wye Plantation, whose members were allowed to fraternize with us. We then learned that he taught law at the University of Damascus and practiced his trade in the Gulf.

Two other members of the Syrian delegation did not sit at the table but in a second row by the window. Ahmad Arnus worked in Foreign Minister Shara''s office. He was in charge of the Syrian cassette recorder, and whenever the instrument sprang open he replaced the cassette and put the old cassette in a carefully sealed envelope. Information is power, and he was clearly there to make sure that the record of the negotiations would go to the right hands and to them alone. Arnus was also in charge of the file that contained such documents as the text of Resolution 242. Allaf knew that text by heart, of course, but every so often when we got into one of our endless debates on the significance and meaning of the resolution he would feign disappointment, snap his fingers, turn around and ask Arnus for the text in order to read it to us one more time.

Next to Arnus sat Bushra Kanafani, Syria's deputy chief of mission in Washington and the delegation's spokesperson. Before Mu'allim's arrival in Washington, Ms. Kanafani ran the embassy as the chargé. She was a hard-core Ba'thi and the fashion in which she slowly warmed up to the negotiations was to me an indication that things were changing, albeit at a snail's pace.

Technically speaking the two weeks we spent in Washington

from August 24 to September 2 constituted the first half of the sixth round of the Arab-Israeli negotiations produced by the Madrid conference. The second half of the sixth round was held from September 14 to September 25. Two more rounds were held before the end of the year. The two sessions of the seventh round were held from October 21 to October 29 and from November 9 to November 19, and the eighth round's single session took place between December 7 and December 17. At that point, under the combined impact of the American transition and the crisis of the Hamas deportees, the Washington talks were suspended until the spring of 1993.[3]

The American presidential elections of November 1992 had a particularly profound impact on the Syrian-Israeli track. President Asad believes in people more than he does in institutions. From his perspective he had built a dialogue with George Bush and Jim Baker, and not with the offices of president and secretary of state. As the summer of 1992 wore on it became increasingly clear that George Bush was likely to lose the election. From Asad's point of view Bill Clinton was an enigma, and nothing certain was known about the policies he would pursue in the Middle East or about his likely choice of secretary of state.

When Muwaffaq Allaf staged a brief mini-crisis in the negotiations in mid-September, we felt that Asad was testing both us and the administration. The administration's (and Israel's) swift and firm response terminated the crisis over a weekend. But by October Bush's prospects seemed so dim that we attributed Syria's tactics in the negotiations to Asad's decision to procrastinate until the elections. Nor did Bill Clinton's victory immediately clear the picture. During the ten weeks of transition a new foreign policy and national security team were formed. Warren Christopher, Anthony Lake, and their associates were unknown to Asad and he wanted to size up the president, his administration, and his policies before making any significant commitment of his own. At that point the two delegations were firmly locked in disagreement over the most fundamental issues of the negotiations. Asad's soft pedaling and Israel's own deliberate pace reinforced the deadlock. In other words, in our November and December sessions we continued to expand the agenda, explore further issues, and seek to maintain momentum and good atmosphere, but neither side was expecting a breakthrough.

Expanding the agenda meant among other things frequent discussions of our respective media. We felt that it was an indispensable part of the dialogue between two states and societies that seek to overcome decades of hostility. Allaf was less enthusiastic and complained that this was a way for us to mark time and to avoid discussion of the real issues, namely, withdrawal. But he too was often intrigued by the complex world of the Israeli media and was swept into a discussion of a particular commentary or news item. We also noticed that over time Syria's monitoring of the Israeli media improved dramatically, so that Allaf could show up for our sessions with the latest statement by an Israeli official or with a useful detail from our daily telegram that someone in Jerusalem saw fit to leak.

Some of our discussion of each other's media was predictable, almost generic. The Syrian media is tightly controlled and monistic. It lacks even the nuance that personal and bureaucratic rivalries produce in certain authoritarian regimes. In the 1960s, during the early years of the Ba'th regime, this had indeed been the case, but since the formation of Asad's regime Syria's various media have been speaking in one voice. And yet whenever we implied that Syria's radio or television or one of its newspapers was a mouthpiece of the regime we were treated to a protest and to a lecture about the freedom of the press and the autonomy of the media that echoed our own explanations of a particular column or broadcast. The truth of the matter is that an outsider needed a great deal of expertise and empathy in order to understand and accept the fact that Israel Television, for instance, was not a government agency but a public station, under considerable governmental influence yet operated by genuine newsmen who were interested in scoops like their competitors in the commercial press. We did not mind sharing this complexity with our Syrian interlocutors as a way of introducing them to the nuances of Israel's public and political life, but they were sometimes uninterested and sometimes incredulous.

I vividly remember a particular exchange with Allaf that was prompted by a false report in a Palestinian newspaper in Cyprus announcing that a Syrian-Israeli breakthrough was imminent. Allaf wanted to know why Israel's media played up a report we knew to be untrue, specifically why the Voice of Israel publicized it as the first item in its hourly news bulletin, and why, more significantly, it was the subject of a special commentary by the "political commentator" of the IDF's radio station. "You may find it hard to believe, Ambassador Allaf," I replied, "but the Voice of Israel is not a state radio and the news editor is sovereign to play up or down whatever he receives from the different wire services. As for the IDF's radio station the political commentator is a young draftee, and in fact the chief of staff wanted to close the station down but failed." "You are right," Allaf replied, "I find it hard to believe."

THE basic mold of the negotiations had crystallized by early September. Our opening gambit and the Syrian paper established our acceptance of withdrawal as a component of the prospective settlement with Syria, while the Syrians agreed that the peace embodied in a peace agreement would be another component of such a settlement. The underlying asymmetry of our positions, so characteristic of the larger Arab-Israeli relationship, soon transpired. For one thing, withdrawal could be defined easily and briefly. The Syrians insisted on "hearing two words," namely, "full withdrawal." Once a commitment to full withdrawal was given there was little left to discuss and negotiate. Of course the precise line, the duration, and the phasing of any withdrawal would have to be negotiated, but once the extent of withdrawal had been agreed upon the other issues would assume a secondary importance.

It is hardly necessary to spell out the difficulties involved in Israeli acceptance of the notion of full withdrawal from the Golan Heights. It is true that in June 1967 a national unity government expressed readiness to withdraw in return for peace, proper security arrangements, and a solution of the water problem. It is also true that Israel had not disputed Syrian sovereignty over the Golan Heights and that having withdrawn from the Sinai in return for a satisfactory peace agreement Israel could ill afford to deny the application of the same principle to her peacemaking with Syria. And yet any Israeli political leader, Yitzhak Rabin more than many others, would grapple first and foremost with himself before he made the decision: what is the value of a written agreement as against holding on to this dominant terrain? Would Asad and would his successors respect their commitments? And what about the settlements and the settlers? There were by now more than 12,000 Israeli settlers in the Golan Heights. The trauma of dismantling the settlements after nearly thirty years of living in the Golan with a sense of mission would be, if it came to that, unbearable.

Statesmanship is a lonely affair. An agreement based on an Israeli withdrawal from the Golan Heights would have to be approved by the cabinet, the Knesset, and the voters in a national referendum. But the crucial decision would have to be made by one ultimate decision maker and would be an excruciating decision. There was no need to speculate on the extent and intensity of the opposition to such a decision or just to the prospect of a decision. Most of the Golan settlers, certainly their leadership, became a single-issue constituency, focused on thwarting an Israeli-Syrian agreement. They found numerous allies—in the foothills of the Golan Heights, among the West Bank settlers, and in the right wing of Israeli politics—so many as to build an effective lobby that the government had to consider seriously.

In theory withdrawal could be neutralized or mitigated by spreading it over a very long period of time (say twenty years) or by introducing the notions of leasing or exchange of territory. But Asad made it clear early on that such ideas were totally unacceptable to him, as was the notion of a phased or an interim settlement.

Peace, on the other hand, was rather difficult to define briefly. We needed to obtain from Syria clear answers to several questions: was Syria ready to offer us a full contractual peace? Was Syria willing to come to an agreement with us and to keep it regardless of what happened on the Palestinian track? Was Syria willing to enter into a security regime comparable to the one constructed between Israel and Egypt in the late 1970s? And was Asad willing to invest at least some of the effort and political capital invested by Anwar al-Sadat at the time in order to build political support in both Syria and Israel for a genuine peace treaty between the two countries?

The Egyptian precedent was on everybody's mind, but whereas we raised it carefully and with certain ambivalence, Allaf usually objected to any reference to the late Egyptian president. Prime Minister Rabin often spoke in private conversations and in his public addresses about Begin and Sadat. He had several reasons for doing so. For one thing, he had a great deal of respect for the two leaders, for their vision and for their ability to break with their own past, make bold decisions, and carry their nations with them. He also believed that by agreeing to withdraw from every inch of the Sinai, Menachem Begin set a precedent that his successors negotiating with other Arab leaders over other issues would be hard put to overcome. Herein lay the cause of our ambivalence. We did not want to raise the Egyptian example in a way that would suggest that we were willing to go through the same withdrawal. But Rabin also thought that evoking Begin's deal with Sadat was good politics. If an agreement were to be made with Syria, the Likud as the main opposition party would be leading the charge against it, and the prime minister would be explaining that in this regard his hands were tied by the Likud's historic leader.

When Asad visited Egypt in 1989 and resumed diplomatic relations he also abandoned, as we saw, a twelve-year crusade against Sadat's way. But that, in Asad's eyes, was quite different from accepting or endorsing in retrospect the choice made by his slain Egyptian rival. When he decided to go to Madrid, Asad knew that he was mounting a track that could lead to a Syrian-Israeli peace agreement and he was willing to stay with this track, but only on very specific terms. Peace had to be done "with dignity" and in a fashion that would preserve Syria's geopolitical standing vis-à-vis Israel. Such a peace could be reconciled with the earlier phases of Asad's life and career, when he was consumed by and devoted to the conflict with Israel. From this perspective, the current process was conceived as a continuation of the historical struggle against Israel through other means. A peace treaty with Israel could only become legitimate if it could be presented as an honorable compromise congruent with the Arab nationalist outlook, even if that outlook could not be implemented in its purity.

In Asad's view this was not the peace Sadat had made with Israel. Yes, Egypt ended up regaining the whole of the Sinai, but at what a price. Egypt and the Arabs had been humiliated and weakened. The terrible events of the 1980s could be attributed at least in part to Sadat's breaking of ranks. To Asad, Sadat was also the epitome of bad negotiating tactics. His haste, his taste for "big decisions" and magnanimous gestures, and his disdain for "minor technical details" were all anathema. Asad's negotiating style was the perfect antithesis: deliberate, patient, mindful of the smallest details, formalistic, and legalistic. Nothing was to be given for free and every asset should be maximized in order to secure the best possible outcome.

Against this background it was hardly surprising that no reference was made to Sadat in the conference room, and any effort to point to the beneficial effect of, say, his public diplomacy in the progress of the Israeli-Egyptian negotiations was frowned upon and rebuffed by our Syrian interlocutors. Later, when the stiff rules were slightly loosened and a freer conversation developed during some coffee breaks, one of our Syrian colleagues told us squarely: "You must understand that Asad cannot settle on less than Sadat did." Our response was, naturally, that he could not ask for the same withdrawal as Sadat and not offer the same package that he had offered in return. In their different styles, Israel and Syria selected from the Israeli-Egyptian precedent the half they liked—Israel underlined the generous definition of peace that Sadat ended up giving, and Syria underscored Begin's willingness to return every single inch of the Sinai.

At the negotiating table we gradually expanded our reference to the issue of withdrawal. Our response to the Syrian paper when we returned from Israel in mid-September was an Israeli counter text that included the term "territorial dimension" (and later "territory"). In late October we introduced for the first time the term "withdrawal" without any reference to its extent. The Syrian delegation was—protestations aside—pleased with this new development but resented the linkage we made between the notion of withdrawal and the establishment of "secure and recognized boundaries" envisaged in Security Council Resolution 242. To them it smacked of territorial compromise and therefore needed to be quashed. Allaf demanded to know whether "withdrawal" referred to "full withdrawal." My instructions were not to specify and not to push the Syrians into a corner. I therefore told him that his demand was "unacceptable" and that I was rejecting it "without a negative or a positive prejudice."

We, in turn, continued to press on two issues: the nature of the peace that Syria had in mind and linkage to other tracks. I asked specifically whether the Syrian concept of peace included normalization. Allaf was evasive. It was not "the obvious outcome" of the negotiations; it was not part of Resolution 242; it would be mistaken to put the cart in front of the horses. He then tried another angle: normalization should be discussed in due course at the multilateral track (which Syria was boycotting).

The reference to the multilateral talks as the right forum for the discussion of normalization was quite alarming. One of the working groups in the multilateral talks dealt with refugees. Since reference was made by the Syrians several times (including mention by Allaf in a press interview) to the "right of return," it was quite possible that Damascus was toying with the idea that it would offer us nonbelligerency, while peace as we defined it would be linked to the solution of the most fundamental (and in fact insoluble) problems of the larger Arab-Israeli conflict. This position, Allaf's assertion—in response to our repeated prodding—that diplomatic relations were not necessarily included in their vision of peace with us, and his refusal to elucidate the issues of comprehensiveness and linkage to other tracks meant that we refused to answer his further questions with regard to withdrawal.

In the original Syrian paper the issue of withdrawal appeared in

paragraph 5a. As we laid down our counter text and began to re-
draft and reformulate, we actually made considerable progress in
coming close to a mutually acceptable text of the first four paragraphs. But when we reached paragraph 5 we were soon dead-
locked. Allaf usually rejected our suggestion to skip paragraph 5
and to continue joint drafting of paragraphs 6–9. The one exception was the paragraph dealing with security arrangements. It was,
as we suspected, of particular interest to Asad, and Allaf was allowed to deal with it. This was an area in which Asad expected to
do better than Sadat, and his delegation fought hard to retain
terms like "equal footing" in the text. We were equally determined
to replace them with a terminology that would lay the basis for Israeli claims for the elaborate security arrangements we had in
mind. One such term was "particular." If the Syrians wanted to introduce the equality of the peacemaking parties, we wanted to emphasize the difference in their respective positions and needs. This
was an early phase in the negotiations and we were dealing in code
words, but I could envisage teams of military experts like the ones
that subsequently met at the Wye Plantation dealing with concrete
and specific arrangements. If I knew Asad at all, I knew that by
fighting over code words now we were setting the stage for the real
bargaining over security issues later.

On November 17 the Syrians made an attempt to break the
deadlock by using a variety of the "hypothetical question" technique. This approach had been suggested at the time by Secretary
Baker, but to no avail. As our meeting of November 17 was drawing to a close, Allaf surprised us by placing a hypothetical question
on the table: "Supposing I would satisfy you in the area that is of
interest to you [namely, the nature of peace] would you be ready
to satisfy me in the area that is of interest to me [namely, with-
drawal]?" But soon thereafter Allaf pulled back his question and
insisted that we provide our answer before he provided his.

My instant response was that this sequence was not acceptable to
us. We would have to think about it overnight and try to turn his
initiative into a useful step in the next meeting. "Thinking about
it overnight" meant, as everybody understood, a consultation with

Jerusalem. In the morning we told the Syrians that, indeed, the sequence was unacceptable and that their use of the term "peace" was too loose and vague. For us to think seriously about resorting to the "hypothetical technique" we needed to know first whether peace meant full peace including diplomatic relations, borders open to the movement of people and goods, and normalization; second, whether peace between Israel and Syria, while being part of a comprehensive settlement would be "unencumbered" by developments on other tracks; and third, whether Syria was willing to have its conduct outside the conference room be tested as an index of the transition to peace. This may have been a heavy load, or the move may not have been thought through seriously in the first place, but Allaf abandoned the new tactic, and we were back to the all-too-familiar argument over peace and withdrawal.

The give-and-take between Israel and Syria during these months was not limited to the conference room and Washington. Asad and Rabin, the two leaders who dominated the negotiations by setting their countries' policies and by closely monitoring their delegations' work, also shaped the agenda through their public pronouncements. In keeping with their very different personal styles and the different political systems they governed, Asad spoke rarely and tersely whereas Rabin communicated regularly with the Israeli public and was regularly available to the Israeli and international media.

Hafiz al-Asad first spoke in public about the new phase of the negotiations in September 1992. During a meeting with a visiting delegation of Druzes from the Golan, Asad told them that:

> In the past we always used to say that we wanted peace and we said it sincerely. Today we want a dignified comprehensive peace that will be acceptable to our peoples, that would entail no retraction of any of our national rights and would not hurt in any way the pride and dignity of our nation. We want the peace of the brave, the peace of the knights, a true durable peace that protects everybody's interests. If the others [namely, Israel] agree to that kind of peace, it could be achieved. But if we encounter games, traps and ambushes that

would hurt national values, well, surrender is not part of our lexicon.[4]

We used the platform afforded us to speak to the Syrian delegation and through it to President Asad and to his principal assistant in the conduct of the peace process, Foreign Minister Faruq al-Sharaʿ, in order to explain what a meager contribution to public diplomacy such a statement was. We began by expounding our view that in addition to substance, the prospect of a negotiation was determined by procedure and by public diplomacy. By that time the limits imposed by Asad on procedure had been clarified to us. The smaller but still formal and rigid sessions in Ed Djerejian's office were all that Asad would allow his representatives. The Israeli-Palestinian conflict was more bitter than the Israeli-Syrian one, but my colleague Elie Rubinstein had no difficulty calling his counterpart, Haidar ʿAbdel Shafi, at the latter's hotel between sessions. In Muwaffaq Allaf's case the call would not be welcome, and I would not embarrass him or humiliate myself by making it.

But could we persuade the Syrians from Asad down that without public diplomacy and without reaching out to the Israeli public no agreement with Syria would be feasible? We did not know the extent of the concessions that would be required, but they would be considerable and in any event painful. It was useless, we now knew, to invoke Sadat's example, but it was always there and its lessons were clear. Public statements and gestures that reflected a change of heart and policy toward Israel would serve a dual purpose. They would persuade the Israeli public that a change had indeed taken place on the other side, and they would persuade the Israeli government that the peace policy of its counterpart enjoyed sufficient popular support as to be displayed publicly. Asad's "peace of the brave" statement, needless to say, did not fit this bill. It was cryptic, cold, and enigmatic. Israel was not mentioned by name, and was told that it could enjoy peace with Syria on the latter's terms.

It took two months for Asad to speak again on the subject of peace. He did that in an interview that was published on November 30 in *Time* magazine.[5] The full interview was filmed by Syrian television and broadcast on November 23. The Israeli government's analysts identified some subtle positive changes as compared with earlier interviews, but these nuances were too obscure to have any impact. My sermons on public diplomacy were clearly to no avail.

Nor did Asad's speech on December 13 signal a change of attitude. Asad spoke at the inaugural session of Syria's trade union federation conference, and the bulk of his speech dealt with domestic issues. As a statement of Syria's view of the peace process, however, this speech contained two interesting elements. One was Asad's claim that the progress in the Israeli-Syrian peace talks reported by the international media was not real. He acknowledged that Israel was now "serious about peace," but "until this moment Israel has not offered anything new that opens up the road of peace. . . . What they are saying today and calling new, as you hear in the media, was heard a long time ago. They say that they now approve Resolution 242 and they consider it new in their position. It is not new." Asad then went on to argue that the notion of Israeli withdrawal on or in the Golan was not new. Israel, after all, had already gone through a partial withdrawal on the Golan in 1974 "following the war of attrition which was an extension of the October War." He proceeded with a lengthy explanation that partial withdrawal could only be "a step toward peace and will not achieve peace." In other words, Asad was saying in this speech what he and all his spokesmen had been saying all along—without an Israeli commitment to full withdrawal Syria wouldn't budge.

But more important than these specific formulations were the general tone and tenor of the speech. The style of the speech was the style of the man—formal, rigid, meticulous, argumentative, possessed of one truth and one view of reality:

> Peace is not something that can be sold or bought; it is an issue of rights and commitments—rights which should be returned completely to their owners without any concession as well as commitments by all parties to peace and security, provided that the security of one party is not at the expense of the other.

. . .If Israel is serious about peace, it should respond to the resolutions of international legitimacy and the UN Charter. Despite our definite desire for peace it will never be at the expense of the territory because the Arabs with the Syrian people in their forefront will not relinquish their territory no matter how many years, decades or generations it takes, because territory is the dearest—it is dignity, it is the homeland.[6]

When reading this text I could close my eyes and hear the voices of our interlocutors in Washington. Asad's total control of the negotiations on the Syrian side began with the formulation of the fundamental concepts and proceeded to the very vocabulary used by his diplomatic emissaries.

Rabin's public rhetoric during this period was fashioned by his concept of public diplomacy. His statements were directed at both the Israeli public and the Syrian government. The fundamental message to both was the same: a new and serious negotiation had begun. Israel understood that in order to conclude this negotiation very painful concessions on its part would be required, but Israel would not deal with the extent of withdrawal before it had a clear indication of Syria's concept of peace and its willingness to make a real political investment in obtaining it.

Rabin's public diplomacy began, ironically, with an eloquent silence. On September 6, he met with a group representing the Golan settlers and, much to their disappointment, refused to promise them that not a single settlement would be affected in the event of an agreement with Syria. Herein lay several dilemmas and difficulties that any serious negotiation, let alone agreement with Syria, was bound to raise for Rabin and his government. Most of the Golan settlers, unlike the hard core of the West Bank settlers, were not right-wing ideologues but Labor and specifically Rabin supporters. They had settled in the Golan when the notion of an Israeli-Syrian peace seemed very remote, and did so as emissaries of the state. In the charged atmosphere of Israeli politics any talk or sign of progress with Syria was bound to agitate them. Furthermore, in the election campaign of 1992 the prospect of an Israeli-

Syrian deal was not an issue. Rabin therefore had to walk along a very fine line—to soothe the Golan settlers without sending ipso facto a message to Asad that a deal with Israel was practically impossible for domestic reasons. In early September 1992, in a lengthy radio interview in Hebrew, the prime minister expounded several of his principal positions:

> We said that in return for contractual peace or, in other words, a peace treaty that guarantees the termination of the state of war, open borders between Syria and Israel, diplomatic relations and exchanges of ambassadors and normalization, Israel will be ready to implement resolutions 242 and 338. . . . This implies, of course, a certain readiness for some kind of territorial compromise. Until Syria declares that it is ready to reach such a peace, we have not and will not enter any territorial discussions or draw up any maps.

This was followed by a strong and suggestive pitch for public diplomacy: "Sadat's arrival in Jerusalem, his statements in the Knesset and the very fact that he was willing to come to Jerusalem and address the Knesset, convinced the Israeli public—not just the government—that he really meant peace. Such an element has yet to be introduced into the framework of Syrian-Israeli relations."[7] Rabin commended Asad for his "peace of the brave" speech, but explained that much more would have to be clarified and done by Syria before Israel would be ready to spell out her concept of withdrawal.

A few days earlier, in a television interview, he had added another issue that Israel wanted to clarify: "to what extent is the attainment of such peace between us and Syria connected with other segments of the Arab-Israeli conflict, whether it is Lebanon or the Palestinians?"[8] At the end of October, in a speech to the Knesset, he found a more vivid way of conveying this notion: "The second condition is: the peace treaty with Syria will stand on its own two feet and will not depend on the development of the peace negotiations with the other Arab delegations."[9] (My counterpart, Allaf, developed a particular dislike for this term and whenever we used it he would explode: "I never saw a peace standing on somebody else's feet.")

Finally, in early November Rabin reached a formula that remained the hallmark of his Syrian policy for a long time: "The depth of withdrawal will reflect the depth of peace." This was not merely a well-rounded formula. It implied that full withdrawal was within the realm of the possible. After all, if the Syrians were to offer us "full peace" what would be the matching depth of withdrawal?

At that time the Syrians were not quite ready to take advantage of this opening. Foreign Minister Shara offered a less attractive formula, "total withdrawal for total peace." This was a clever way of addressing several problems at once. "Total" as distinct from "full" was a different way of saying "comprehensive." In other words, Syria's public offer to Israel was an ill-defined comprehensive peace with the Arab world for a total withdrawal from all the territories captured in 1967. This was an offer we could easily refuse and refute.

By December 1992 the negotiations with Syria had run out of steam. Whatever calculations both parties had made prior to the American presidential elections were superseded by Clinton's victory. Syrians and Israelis alike were preoccupied by such questions as what policies the new president would choose to pursue in the Middle East, and who would be chosen to play the key roles in the fields of foreign policy and national security in the new administration at the end of the transition on January 20, 1993.

During the transition an idea was raised inside the American administration: the outgoing Bush administration, Jim Baker in particular, should capitalize on its special relationship with Asad and on the immunity it now had (as the flip side of being a "lame duck"), and seek to effect a Syrian-Israeli breakthrough. It was also suggested that the administration's own contribution to the Israeli-Syrian deal would be getting Syria off the State Department's list of states engaged in terrorism. The idea amounted to no more than a flash in the pan. Neither Jerusalem nor Damascus was likely to jeopardize or sacrifice any real assets for the sake of an agreement that was to be arranged by an outgoing administration. But to the extent that the Syrians were made aware of this plan, some damage was caused. I have always suspected that the Syrians saw the terrorism and drug lists and the annual human rights report not as legitimate tools for the conduct of foreign policy or as outlets for an authentic commitment to the moral dimension of statecraft but rather as instruments used cynically against them or manipulated by pro-Israeli lobbies. The very idea that Syria's place on the terrorism list be used as a chip in a prospective transaction must have confirmed their suspicions.

These ideas and the plodding negotiations in the four tracks of the Washington talks were overshadowed in mid-December by a deep crisis that was generated by a successful offensive launched by Hamas, the radical Islamic Palestinian organization opposed to the PLO's indirect participation in the peace process. On December 7 a Hamas team killed three Israeli soldiers in the Gaza Strip. On December 13 another Hamas group kidnapped an Israeli border policeman. Hamas announced first that Officer Toledano was taken hostage in order to obtain the release of its leader, Sheikh Yassin, from an Israeli jail, but two days later his body was found after he had been strangled to death.

Rabin decided to break the backbone of the Hamas organization in the West Bank and the Gaza Strip. Four hundred Hamas activists were arrested and eventually put on buses and sent across the border to south Lebanon. It was an unorthodox, bold action, and the Rabin government had to contend with its repercussions for several months. One immediate outcome was a decision by the Arab delegations to the Washington talks to suspend their participation. The round of negotiations thus ended abruptly without setting a date for the resumption of the talks. The Clinton administration, once it took office, would have to contend with the crisis.

FOUR

The Wing Beats
of History

MUCH HAPPENED in the peace process during the Clinton administration's first nine months. At the end of January the new foreign policy and national security teams were installed and a new "peace process team" was in place. In March, Prime Minister Rabin came to Washington for his first visit under the new administration and for his first working session with President Clinton. It soon transpired that the Clinton administration had decided to endorse and continue the Middle East policies of its predecessor, and that a period of close cooperation between the Clinton administration and the Rabin government had been launched. The Clinton administration as a whole saw the Israeli-Syrian track as the cutting edge of the peace process. It attached due significance to the Israeli-Palestinian track, but saw a breakthrough in the Israeli-Syrian track as the key to both a comprehensive Arab-Israeli settlement and to a geopolitical realignment in the Middle East.

From this perspective it is particularly interesting to review the fluctuations of Israel's policy between the Syrian and Palestinian tracks during this period. During Rabin's visit to Washington in March 1993, foundations were laid for potential progress on both tracks. In the Palestinian context, Rabin agreed that Faysal Husseini, the prominent Palestinian political leader from Jerusalem, be added to the Washington talks in order to test whether he would act as an "authentic local leader" independently from Tunis. In the Syrian context the preparatory work was begun for a major American effort to effect an Israeli-Syrian breakthrough.

During the next three months or so these efforts—Ambassador Djerejian's secret trip to Damascus in April, Secretary Christopher's meeting with Minister Shara' in June, and rounds nine and ten of the Washington talks—yielded no results. There was also no progress on the Palestinian track of the Washington talks. It turned out that contrary to Israeli expectations, Faysal Husseini, too, took his instructions from Tunis and the American effort to table a compromise paper foundered. But these very failures moved Rabin to authorize Peres and Beilin to pursue the informal clandestine channel that had begun in Oslo and to convert it into an official channel by nominating the director general of the Foreign Office as Israel's negotiator with Arafat's emissary Abu 'Alaa.

In late July several processes matured and converged. The Oslo negotiations were about to produce an agreement. Hizballah's repeated Katyusha rocket attacks on Israel proper led Israel to launch Operation Accountability in Lebanon, which brought Israel and Syria close to a collision and enabled Secretary Christopher to work out a cease-fire and a limited agreement on south Lebanon between Israel and Syria. It was against this background that he came to the Middle East in early August. On August 3, in his meeting with Christopher in Jerusalem, Rabin made his boldest gambit in the peace process yet and provided the secretary of state with the mandate for effecting a breakthrough with Syria. When Christopher returned the next day with what Rabin, at least, viewed as a disappointing answer, the prime minister gave the green light to conclude the Oslo agreement. This was not the end of the quest for an Israeli-Syrian breakthrough, but it did mean that the peace process from that point on was predicated on a Palestinian rather than a Syrian cornerstone.

The fashion in which President Clinton constructed his national security and foreign policy team ensured that the secretary of state and the State Department remained the focal point of policy making with regard to the Middle East. The previous decades provided several examples of other actors and other agencies—the national security adviser and the National Security Council or the secretary of defense—playing important roles in the Middle East in addition to or in competition with the State Department. Les Aspin, Clinton's first secretary of defense; Anthony Lake, the national security adviser; Samuel (Sandy) Berger, his deputy; and James Wolsey, then director of central intelligence, were well versed in Middle Eastern and Arab-Israeli affairs, but they all accepted Warren Christopher's and the State Department's primacy in these areas.

As the deputy secretary of state in the Carter administration, Warren Christopher had not dealt with Arab-Israeli affairs. He was not identified with either the Camp David accord or with Carter's acrimonious relationship with both Rabin and Begin. His own Middle Eastern experience revolved around his negotiations with the Iranians over the hostage issue during the Carter administration's final weeks. Yet Christopher's appointment was received with apprehension by some Jewish groups in the United States. They feared that the former deputy secretary in the Carter administration would bring with him into the Clinton administration at least part of Carter's legacy.

But these apprehensions, like the concerns expressed in 1982 that George Schultz's arrival in the State Department from the Bechtel Corporation would turn him into a pro-Arab advocate, were unfounded and short-lived. Warren Christopher proved to be a fair-minded secretary, who devoted much of his time and energy to a genuine pursuit of a peaceful resolution between Israelis and Arabs. The contours of his brief were determined, of course, by the president, and the latter as far as we knew instructed his team that peace in the Middle East was a priority, but also that he did not want a head-on collision with the prime minister of Israel. With Yitzhak Rabin and Shimon Peres at the helm in Israel, there was no tension between the two poles of the policy. Occasional friction or controversy over tactics did occur, but the United States could predicate its peace process policy on a fundamental understanding with Israel and yet feel that it was offering Israel's Arab partners more than a fair deal. In that regard there was no difficulty for the administration in taking over and continuing the Middle East policy of the Bush administration as it had been conducted during the latter's final six months.

The initial inner circle at the Christopher State Department that oversaw U.S. policy in the peace process and the U.S.-Israeli relationship consisted of Christopher himself, his chief of staff Thomas Donilon, and Ed Djerejian. Tom Donilon, a partner in Christopher's law firm, was a Democratic operative with rich experience in presidential campaigns (he played an important role in preparing Clinton for the televised debates with Bush who, ironically, was assisted by Dennis Ross). The powers that be decided, however, that he not be appointed to a position in the White House but be assigned to help Christopher with the political and media dimensions of the secretary's work. Their loss was our gain: Donilon played a crucial role in steering his chief through the troubled waters of domestic politics and palace intrigues, and in the actual implementation of policy. His full figure and jovial face provided an interesting contrast to the elegant, austere—almost ascetic—figure of Christopher, and his political acumen was for all of us an immense resource. The deputy secretary, Clifton Wharton, was not really relevant to Middle Eastern policy. In any event he never developed a good working relationship with Christopher (he was a White House appointment), and eventually left. His successor, Strobe Talbot, was very much interested in Israel but his brief focused on other parts of the world. Peter Tarnoff, the undersecretary for political affairs, provided the regular nexus to the larger State Department.

Ed Djerejian now became the coordinator ("our quarterback" in the language of one of his senior colleagues) of a larger and more diverse peace team. The trio Djerejian-Kurzer-Miller of the late Bush period was reinforced by Ambassador Samuel Lewis, the new director of policy planning, Dr. Martin Indyk who became the senior director for the Middle East at the National Security Council, and Dennis Ross, who returned to the state department for an initial six-month period as an adviser to the secretary on both Middle Eastern and post-Soviet affairs.

Sam Lewis was the formidable former ambassador to Israel (1977–1984) who remained the foremost authority on Israel in Washington a full decade after his retirement. In January 1993, sensing the potential inherent in the unfolding peace process, Lewis resigned his position as president of the United States Peace

Institute in order to return to the State Department in a dual capacity: director of policy planning and member of the peace process team. Lewis had a very important impact as the elder statesman of the peace team, but his relationship with Christopher soured over issues unrelated to the Middle East, and he left in midterm.

Martin Indyk had for several years been director of the Washington Institute for Near East Policy. The Institute under his stewardship provided one of the best fora for studying and discussing the Middle East in Washington. It also demonstrated that one did not have to be anti-Israeli in order to attract Arabs and Arabists to its events. Indyk arrived in Washington as an Australian academic expert on the Middle East, and subsequently became an American citizen. He worked on Middle Eastern issues at the Clinton campaign and was well positioned in the White House. In 1995, when Indyk was appointed U.S. ambassador to Israel, he was replaced in the White House by Mark Parris, a Foreign Service officer who had distinguished himself as deputy chief of mission in Tel Aviv and was brought by Djerejian to the Bureau of Near Eastern Affairs (NEA) in charge of "non-peace-process" issues.

The peace team had a daily meeting every morning and traveled with the secretary of state as a team when his odyssey of Middle Eastern trips began in February 1993. During the Clinton administration's first few months in office, the key roles in the peace team's work under Ed Djerejian's stewardship were played by Dan Kurzer, out of the NEA Bureau, and by Aron Miller, who was formally positioned in policy planning.

The team's original outlook on the Middle East and on the peace process was articulated clearly and coherently in a speech delivered by Martin Indyk at the Washington Institute. The speech was prepared for the deputy national security adviser, Sandy Berger, but ended up being given by Indyk under the title "The Clinton Administration's Approach to the Middle East."[1]

Indyk himself offered "a short-hand way of encapsulating the Clinton administration's strategy"—"dual containment" of Iraq and Iran in the east; and promotion of Arab-Israeli peace in the west, backed by "energetic efforts to stem the spread of weapons of mass destruction and promote a vision of a more democratic and prosperous region for all the people of the Middle East." The full version of the speech argued that the two legs of the policy, "dual containment" and promotion of the Arab-Israeli peace process, were mutually reinforcing. It acknowledged the continuity from the Bush administration to the Clinton administration's policy toward the peace process, and stated quite openly that the Clinton administration's willingness to invest much and early in it was predicated on the Rabin government's readiness "to take risks for peace."

On the Syrian track "taking risks" meant a territorial concession. The administration's message to Damascus was that "the Syrians need to be willing to commit themselves to real peace with Israel with all that [it] means for ending the conflict, normalizing relations, opening borders, exchanging embassies and establishing commercial relations. If they were ready to engage in negotiations in this way, we are ready to do our part to ensure that a breakthrough to peace is achieved."[2]

Choosing the Middle East for his first international trip was a signal by Christopher of the importance and priority he attached to the Arab-Israeli peace process. There were also good substantive reasons for making the trip: the impasse with the Palestinians had to be broken and a working relationship had to be constructed with Rabin and Asad if the Israeli-Syrian track were to be jump-started.

The groundwork was indeed being laid during Secretary Christopher's trip. The trip began in Cairo on February 18, followed by visits to Amman and Damascus. Christopher then arrived in Israel for a four-day stay. By and large, it was a familiarization trip. The new secretary needed to acquire a sense of what the area looked like and to start building personal relationships with the principal players on the Arab and Israeli sides. In Israel in addition to the customary standard meetings he was taken on a helicopter tour with the IDF's chief of staff as a special guide. I was also on the tour.

The helicopter left Jerusalem and then crossed Israel's "narrow hips" at their slimmest point—it took just a couple of minutes to fly from the Green Line east of Tel Aviv to the U.S. embassy on Tel Aviv's shoreline. In the Galilee, we stopped at a mountain top known as "Carlucci's Point" (after the former American secretary of defense, the first dignitary to have been brought there). It afforded a panoramic view of both the Golan Heights and the Lebanese border. On the way back the helicopter went down to the Jordan Valley and then climbed to watch the rising topography of the Golan Heights. The imposing bluff seemed awesome, though I had no way of knowing what impression was registered in the secretary's mind. To an Israeli involved in negotiations that could very well lead to an Israeli descent back to the valley, the view was daunting. In previous years such a tour would have culminated with a statement to the effect of "You will now understand why we cannot begin to contemplate giving any of this back." This clearly was not the case with a host government committed to a peace process that would include very significant concessions. But the Rabin government certainly wanted the new secretary, and through him, the new president, to appreciate fully the costs and risks entailed in any concession.

The next step was Rabin's visit to the United States in mid-March. It ended up being a Washington visit; the other legs were canceled because of a spate of terrorist knifings in Tel Aviv—a reminder that in this peace process diplomacy was always conducted against a very real background of violence.

At the core of the visit was the meeting between Rabin and Clinton on March 15. It was preceded and supplemented by meetings with Christopher and Lake, but in the history of these years it stands out as a unique encounter. During the whole session, but particularly during the small meeting, a bond of mutual respect—and eventually warmth—was created. Rabin was impressed by Clinton's quick grasp and political intuition, by the charisma and warmth he oozed and by his evident care for Israel. Clinton saw Rabin as an older, mature, confident, and authoritative statesman, a soldier who now wanted to make peace, a leader who was willing to upset conventions. He appreciated his openness and directness. Rabin was clearly being transformed in his old-new role, and what could on occasion be awkward bluntness was turning into captivating candor. It is difficult to envisage the developments of the following three years without the personal relationship between these two men. About two years after that meeting, in May 1995, when both leaders appeared together before an American-Israel Public Affairs Committee (AIPAC) meeting, President Clinton described the March 1993 meeting in the following terms: "When we first met, as I have said over and over again—he was looking at me and I was looking at him and he was sort of sizing me up and I already knew he was bigger than life."[3]

There was also a lot of substance to the meeting. Little was said about the Palestinian track. It had already been agreed with Christopher that Faysal Husseini be added to the Palestinian delegation. President Clinton made it amply clear that he saw peace with Syria as the key to an Israeli-Arab settlement and to a new geopolitical order in the region. As Rabin saw it, both Syria and the Palestinians held potential keys that could unlock the peace process. There was a clear advantage to dealing with Syria, where a powerful leader could make decisions. But a deal with Syria entailed painful concessions, and Asad was clearly unwilling to invest the effort without which the Israeli public would not support such concessions. Rabin presented his view of the substantive and procedural aspects of the negotiations with Syria, explained Sadat's unique contribution in 1977, and argued that thus far Asad had not done "one percent" of what Sadat had done in his day. He also told the president that without a "meeting of leaders" peace would not be concluded between Israel and Syria. The president tried several times to extract from the prime minister whether he would be willing to accept full withdrawal as part of a settlement with Syria. Rabin evaded, but told the president that if things were to come to that point a referendum would be required. This was a crucial issue; it was not presented to the Israeli public in the 1992 elections, and Rabin felt that he did not have a mandate to make a decision on his own.

Less dramatic and significant and yet unusual in its own right was another meeting that was held during the March visit. It was a working breakfast with the American peace team. Heads of government do not normally conduct brainstorming sessions with the working levels of another government. But this was the unique U.S.-Israeli relationship and this was Rabin (and in this respect Peres as well), who never stood on protocol and who had a high regard for the team and its individual members. There was a particularly poignant moment during the breakfast. Rabin went through a thorough analysis of the difficulties of negotiating on the Palestinian track. When he finished, Sam Lewis commented that the logic of that analysis led to one conclusion—Israel should talk to the PLO. Rabin did not answer, but if there was a harbinger of the Oslo accord, there it was.

In the aftermath of Rabin's visit the effort to effect an Israeli-Syrian breakthrough was resumed along two tracks: a direct American effort vis-à-vis the Syrian government and two additional rounds of the Washington talks.

In April, prior to the convening of the ninth round of negotiations, Ambassador Djerejian went for a secret visit to Damascus. He was hoping to draw on his personal relationship with Asad, but was also carrying a letter from President Clinton. The U.S. peace team felt (as did we) that without a dramatic move of this sort no progress could be expected in the negotiations, that there wasn't enough fuel in the Syrian-Israeli negotiation to push it forward, and that an injection of American input was required in order to create fresh movement.

Djerejian came to update Asad on Rabin's visit and Faysal Husseini's expected participation in the Washington talks. More specifically, in the aftermath of Clinton's meeting with Rabin he had three questions for the Syrian president: one, what was Syria's full concept of peace? Two, was Asad willing to engage in public diplomacy? And three, was Asad willing to form a discreet military or civilian channel, apart from the Washington talks, that could improve the communication with Israel in a way that was clearly not afforded by the format of the Washington talks? Despite President

Clinton's personal involvement, Asad was in no hurry to respond. The State Department in Washington and the U.S. ambassador in Damascus, Christopher Ross, recommended that the administration (and Israel) wait patiently. They reminded us all that in 1991 Asad kept Bush and Baker waiting for six weeks before he gave the answer that finally opened the way to the Madrid conference.

The ninth round opened on April 27. It had been scheduled to begin on the 20th, but Arafat had held the Palestinian delegation back in the region. Asad contributed to the resolution of this problem by inviting Arafat to Latakiyya and by spending four hours with him, during which he persuaded him that the negotiations should be resumed. Given Asad's well-known personal animosity toward Arafat, he had no difficulty in presenting the meeting as a gesture for which the United States and Israel were beholden to him. Asad made another gesture, and renewed the exit permits for members of the Jewish community. From the outset Asad had cast the problem of Syrian Jewry as a Syrian-American issue. When we tried to put the issue on the Israeli-Syrian agenda we were rebuffed by Muwaffaq Allaf, who argued that Israel had no standing in the matter. From our perspective the important point was the actual exit of the community, and as long as this was accomplished we did not stand on principle nor did we complain that Asad was making the same gesture over and over again. Yet we were sufficiently familiar with Asad's negotiating tactics to know that he would demand a price for these two gestures or, in a similar vein, would regard and present them as a positive coating to the negative response we expected to Djerejian's mission.

It was hardly surprising that the Syrian delegation's brief for the ninth round was yet another effort to obtain from us a commitment to full withdrawal or at least a statement to that effect. Its opening move was an improvement on Faruq al-Shara''s original "total peace for total withdrawal." Allaf was authorized to offer us "full peace for full withdawal." If "total withdrawal" could be possibly interpreted as referring to withdrawal from all Arab territories captured in 1967 and was rejected by us out of hand, "full withdrawal" could conceivably be limited to the Golan. Ever since

Rabin introduced the formula that "the depth of withdrawal will reflect the depth of peace," such a Syrian move could be expected.

I welcomed Syria's introduction of the term "full peace" into the vocabulary of the negotiations, but explained that there was no symmetry between "full peace" and "full withdrawal," and that the complexity of our would-be agreement could not be reduced to a five-word gimmick. Did the Syrians want to elaborate on the meaning of "full peace"? Allaf then pulled back his offer even though, he explained, the Syrian leadership might continue to use it in its public discourse. Allaf's pressure "to hear the words" continued until, toward the end of the second week, he stated flatly that for Syria this was a "precondition," and without obtaining this commitment they would not move forward in the negotiations.

We had in the meantime resumed work on the latest version of the draft of a declaration of principles. We did succeed in persuading our interlocutors to change the concept of the now famous paragraph 5 from "machinery of implementation" to "discussion of the core issues." The Syrians did agree that there were three core issues that had to be resolved between Syria and Israel: peace, territory, and security. But they vehemently objected to the presentation of our proceedings as "negotiation of the core issues." Negotiation, one member of the delegation explained quite candidly, smacked of give-and-take, and that was inconceivable when issues of principle were involved. In the same vein a sentence referring to "the interpretation of Resolution 242" was thrown out of court. To the Syrians the resolution had only one interpretation.

Our drafting efforts produced another telling episode that shed significant light on Syria's view of a peace settlement at that phase. The original Syrian paper conceived of peacemaking as the implementation of the "executive steps" that grew out of Resolution 242. It spoke of simultaneous implementation of these steps, envisaging at the time full withdrawal as against nonbelligerency. We saw the term "simultaneous" as designed to preempt any Israeli demand to repeat the pattern of the Israeli-Egyptian peace by insisting that Syria implement her part of the bargain earlier as a confidence-building measure and as an act of public diplomacy.

When discussing and redrafting the preamble to the draft paper, I told Allaf that we understood the meaning and function of the term "simultaneous" in their paper but that at this point we decided not to make an issue of it, that we would just register our reservations and move on. But two days later it was the Syrian delegation that all of a sudden asked to change the formulation and distinguish between two categories of issues, one of which would be subject to simultaneity and the other would not. The revision reflected a tardy Syrian realization that the developments that had occurred in the negotiations had turned the word "simultaneously" into a double-edged weapon. The Syrians now realized that no peace agreement would be made with Israel without a component of normalization. They may still have been hoping that the actual implementation of that normalization could be shifted to a later phase, but they knew that it would have to be part of the treaty. They could then easily envisage an Israeli insistence that the principle of simultaneity would be applied to withdrawal and normalization, so that normalization would have to be moved up or withdrawal would have to be delayed. Needless to say, we rejected the notion of two categories of simultaneity, and insisted that our prospective agreement could only have one timetable.

The positive aspect of this episode lay in the Syrian acceptance of normalization as an indispensable dimension of peace. Throughout the ninth round a far more nuanced Syrian position on normalization was presented. The formal position was still negative, but through hint and allusion our interlocutors suggested to us that there were several elements of normalization; some of them remained unacceptable to Syria while others had to wait for a later phase. Implementation of these elements, they explained, depended on the public's will, and that will had to evolve over time. We in turn sensed that there was greater flexibility to the Syrian position in that matter and that at some future point, under greater pressure or in response to an Israeli or American gesture, they would show their hand more fully.

The most significant move during the ninth round was made by Syria outside the conference room. On May 10 Patrick Seale, the

British journalist and Asad's biographer, published in the Arabic-language London newspaper *al-Wasat* an interview given to him by Asad in Damascus two weeks earlier (parts of the interview were published by Seale a few days later as an op-ed piece in the *New York Times*).[4]

The general tenor of the interview was quite positive, but its main significance lay in a new approach that the president of Syria proposed for resolving the comprehensiveness issue. There were four negotiating tracks, Asad said, and they could each develop at its own pace. Asad did not quite say that a deal could be made in one track independently of the others, and he did mention Syria's commitment to her "legacy," but his interview suggested that there was more flexibility to the Syrian position in this matter than he wanted to spell out at that point.[5]

The ninth round ended without any real progress. In the meantime, Syria's negative reply to Djerejian's mission and Clinton's letter had been given to the United States. In consultation with us, the administration decided that the president would send a second letter to Asad and would try to take advantage of the one opening given by Asad in his own letter to Clinton. When he rejected the idea of establishing a discreet channel with Israel, Asad wrote that the way to move forward was for the United States to serve as "a repository" of the two parties' positions. Well, wrote Clinton in his second letter, Israel had already deposited its position with the United States and now it was Syria's turn to do the same. This time Asad sent his negative reply in short order. This time he also incensed the president, who felt that Asad had misled him. There followed a tense period in American-Syrian relations. Secretary Christopher met with Minister Shara' in Vienna and spoke to him sternly, and in Washington during the tenth round there was open tension between the peace team and the Syrian delegation.

The tenth round lasted three weeks (from June 15), and the Syrian track was characterized by Syrian defensiveness. As the Syrians saw it, the tension in their relationship with the United States was bound to be translated into a greater Israeli sense of closeness to the United States and hence of greater self-confidence. The Syrian delegation was apparently instructed to stand up to pressure but not to push matters to the brink. There was a new edge to Allaf's reactions. On one occasion an interesting exchange developed over the nature of negotiations. We argued that a negotiation was not an arbitration over the significance and meaning of Resolution 242 but a political transaction between two parties, and Allaf responded angrily: "You will not dictate to us." In other words, when we spoke of interests and political give-and-take Allaf heard a reference to our ability to mobilize the United States to our side.

A softer Syrian approach was tried through one more Syrian attempt to extract from us an acceptance of the notion of full withdrawal. As an apparent concession, Allaf proposed that if we chose to tell them that "the contents" of paragraph 5a were acceptable to us they would be willing to consider an alternative formulation that would be easier for us. When we failed to rise to the occasion, the Syrians offered their own "softer" version—"withdrawal of Israel's armed forces and civilians to the lines of June 4, 1967." And when we rejected the idea it was soon pulled back, since it was "unauthorized."

As the round drew to a close Syrian complaints that we acted "with a sense of power" became more frequent. Their way of indicating that Syria would not be moved by pressure was to revive talk of the Palestinian "right of return." At the session's closing they hurried out of the room, failing to shake our hands as further warning that things could deteriorate to pre-August 1992 status.

The sense of a stalemate was reinforced by developments on the Palestinian track. On May 12 an American attempt to present a "bridging paper" was rejected by the Palestinians. In June a new American draft was put together that was neither rejected nor accepted by the Palestinians. More significantly, the U.S. team to varying degrees was becoming aware of an alternative Israeli-Palestinian channel and of the growing irrelevance of the Washington talks. (I was told about the Oslo talks by Peres in March and was under strict instructions not to discuss them with anyone, but I know that at least one member of the peace team was briefed by a senior Israeli official and that information reached the U.S. government from other sources, as well.)

It was against that background that Secretary Christopher introduced an important change in the peace team in mid-June, and put Dennis Ross in charge. Ross's six-month extension was about to end, and he seemed ready for departure. Dennis was about to assume Martin Indyk's previous post as director of the Washington Institute and he collected the farewell present from his colleagues—a JFK-style rocking chair. I am not fully familiar with the chain of events within the State Department, but at the end of the day Ross was offered the conduct of the peace process under the title Special Middle East Coordinator. Ed Djerejian then asked to be sent to Tel Aviv as the ambassador. He began his tenure in January 1994, but soon thereafter he chose to resign from his post and the Foreign Service in order to become the first director of the Baker Institute at Rice University in Houston. Over time a broader change transformed the team. Ross and Indyk became the inner core. Sam Lewis left the State Department altogether, and Dan Kurzer moved to the Bureau of Intelligence and Research as its deputy director. Miller remained as Ross's deputy, and Toni Verstandig, who came to the NEA as a Democratic political appointment from Capitol Hill, gradually emerged as an effective coordinator of multilateral and economic issues. Jonathan Schwartz was the team's legal expert. In the NEA Djerejian was replaced by Robert Pelletreau, the former U.S. ambassador to Tunisia and Egypt, an understated and gentlemanly professional.

In the latter half of June, the peace team under Dennis Ross's stewardship launched a new effort to revitalize the peace process. In early July the team traveled to the region more by way of showing the new flag and preparing the secretary of state's next visit then in the hope of achieving concrete results. Upon its return to Washington we met several times to prepare Christopher's next visit to the Middle East and to explore novel ways for revitalizing the peace process.

Christopher had to make a long trip to Asia and Australia, and

his Middle Eastern trip was set for late July-early August, to be followed by his (and Ross's) summer vacation in California. The next
round of the Washington talks could then be held in early September. Given Syria's refusal to establish a direct channel with Israel and Christopher's willingness to invest a significant portion of
his time in the Israeli-Arab peace process, Ross suggested that the
secretary act as a de facto "special channel" between Rabin and
Asad. There were two main questions that I was asked to clarify with
Rabin in this context: first, what messages and questions did the
prime minister want to transmit to Asad through this channel? Beyond the specific and detailed issues, my American interlocutors
wanted to know whether Rabin wanted to proceed directly to an
"end game" or whether he preferred to begin in an incremental
fashion. Second, what would his attitude be if it transpired that
progress could be made on both the Syrian and Palestinian tracks?

Our work was interrupted by a deterioration of the situation in
south Lebanon. Since June 1985 Israel's concerns and policies in
Lebanon had focused on the security zone in the south along the
Israeli-Lebanese border. Having failed to reach a new understanding with Syria, Israel's National Unity government withdrew uni-
laterally from the Awali River to the international border, but kept
a small military presence in an expanded security zone north of
the border. The main brunt of maintaining and protecting the security zone was borne by a local militia, the South Lebanese Army,
commanded by General Antoine Lahad, but without Israeli support and the latter's increasingly direct military role it would not
be able to hold its own against a host of challengers headed by
Hizballah, the pro-Iranian Shi'ite Muslim political movement-cum-
militia.

Syria's own relationship with Hizballah was quite complex.
Hizballah operates, in fact, as an arm of the Iranian government.
Syria is the paramount power in Lebanon and the access that it af-
fords Iran to Lebanon and to its Shi'ite community has been a significant component of the Syrian-Iranian partnership for nearly
two decades. There were tensions built into that partnership; Syria

accepted—indeed facilitated—Iran's patronage over Hizballah while seeking to perpetuate and consolidate its own control of Lebanese politics, including the politics of the Shi'ite community. Syria allowed, sometimes encouraged, Hizballah's attacks against the security zone and Israel's forces as well as occasional Katyusha rocket attacks on northern Israel, because it too wanted Israel out of the security zone and was willing to take the risk of military escalation. Asad knew that Tehran was critical of his participation in the peace process and of his quest for a better relationship with the United States. Both he and his Iranian allies understood that if this policy were to succeed a choice would have to be made between Tehran and Washington, that the Iranians in turn might try to sabotage a policy that would isolate them in the region's eastern flank. But as long as the new policy remained nebulous, choices did not have to be made.

This was certainly not our view. We knew that Asad was a great believer in combining diplomacy with pressure, that he regarded his endorsement of anti-Israeli activities in southern Lebanon as fully compatible with his delegation's negotiations with us. We told our Syrian interlocutors that from our perspective this was a sign of bad faith and lingering hostility, that refusing to engage in positive public diplomacy was one thing, but persistence in the posture held by Syria in Lebanon was another.

This debate afforded us at the time a very revealing glimpse into the contrasting philosophies of negotiations held by us and by our Syrian counterparts. Our view was that when two parties had made a decision to seek an end to their conflict they should start the process of confidence building during and as part of their negotiations. As mutual trust grows, so does the parties' ability to make concessions and mobilize public support for them so that a compromise, which seems beyond their grasp at the onset of the negotiations, becomes feasible as they mature. Asad and his delegation totally rejected this approach. As they saw it, no gestures must be made until the breakthrough occurs and an agreement in principle is reached. At that moment a hostile relationship can be transformed into a friendlier one. Until that moment all assets must be used in order to maximize Syria's leverage in what essentially is an exercise in power politics and a test of wills.

The tensions and contradictions inherent in these differences came to the fore several times during the first months of the negotiations. When Israel sustained casualties in south Lebanon and Radio Damascus or Allaf in person commended the attack as a legitimate act of "national liberation," we found it emotionally and politically difficult to continue to negotiate as usual or to avoid a candid comment on Syria's role and position in Lebanon. By the same token, we found Syria's hosting of the "rejectionist" organizations in Damascus and the al-Quds radio station in southern Syria, all agitating against the peace process, profoundly disturbing.

In June the challenge to Israel's very position in south Lebanon was exacerbated by a change in Hizballah's strategy. When the Israeli military returned fire to attacks launched from areas north of the security zone, Hizballah began launching Katyusha rockets into the Galilee. Israel was faced with an awkward choice. If it wanted to avoid Katyusha attacks on Israel proper it had to jeopardize the security zone and sustain ever greater casualties (seven Israeli soldiers were killed in south Lebanon in July). Or it could bring its overwhelming military advantage to bear and stage, after a long interval, a large-scale military operation that would seek to redefine the rules of the game in the Lebanese arena.

In considering the pros and cons of such an operation, Israel was not held back by the prospect of an adverse effect on the negotiations with Syria. If Syria believed that by offering passive or indirect support to Hizballah it was acquiring greater leverage over Israel, let it be reminded of the facts of the underlying military balance and of the risks inherent in Syria's Lebanese policy. The feeling in Israel that Syria was stoking the fire in south Lebanon was reinforced by the fact that Ahmad Jibril and his organization (The Popular Front for the Liberation of Palestine—General Command), Syria's distinct protégés, had joined the fray. Our estimate was that on the eve of Secretary Christopher's important visit Hafiz al-Asad was seeking to enhance his posture.

This certainly did not constrain Rabin (as prime minister and defense minister) and Chief of Staff Ehud Baraq, who decided on the large-scale operation that eventually came to be known as Operation Accountability. It opened with air raids in the Bekaa (in the course of which several Syrian soldiers were killed and wounded), but its principal component was a broad-scale expulsion of Lebanese civilians from the southern part of the country north toward Beirut. In this fashion the Israeli authors of the operation expected to generate pressure on the Lebanese government of Rafiq Hariri and ultimately on the latter's Syrian patrons. Hizballah reacted with salvos of Katyusha rockets against towns and villages in the Galilee. During the first few days international public opinion was quite restrained in its reaction and was willing to look at both sides of the coin. But as time went by the sight of thousands of Lebanese refugees became unbearable, and in the United States (and needless to say Western Europe) criticism of Israel's conduct mounted.

At the week's end Secretary Christopher increased his efforts at obtaining a cease-fire, and at the end of a long night during which he communicated on the telephone with Rabin (through Dennis Ross and myself) and with Asad (through Foreign Minister Sharaʿ), an end to the fighting and a new set of rules were agreed upon. At the core of the understanding were an undertaking by Hizballah not to launch rockets against Israel and a matching commitment by Israel not to fire into villages north of the security zone unless fired upon from within a village. There was no undertaking to spare the security zone, and increased pressure on it could be expected. The Hariri government was a party to the oral agreement, but the real guarantor of Hizballah's good behavior was Syria. This was fine, but it did underline the question marks we had about Syria's failure or unwillingness to restrain Hizballah in the past (and indeed in the future).

If the tension and fighting in south Lebanon had threatened during the week to upset the secretary's visit, the cease-fire provided an excellent threshold for his visit. His success and the effective communication he had had with both the Israeli and Syrian sides positioned him perfectly for the role of intermediary between the two.

Christopher's trip to the region was constructed so as to enable him to meet first with Rabin, listen to his positions and questions, then meet with Asad and get his reactions to them. The secretary of state departed on August 1 to Cairo and arrived in Israel on the 2nd for a morning meeting with Rabin on the 3rd. The meeting was divided, like most such meetings, into two parts: a smaller meeting in Rabin's office and a larger meeting in the adjacent conference room. Structuring meetings in this fashion, whether in Washington or in Jerusalem, was a perpetual source of tension and aggravation, but there was no escaping it. On more than one occasion there was no real difference between the smaller and larger meetings, but on August 3, 1993, the difference was stark.

In addition to Rabin and Christopher, the smaller meeting was attended by Ross and myself as note takers. Rabin wasted no time and went directly into the heart of the matter. Israel could not move forward on two tracks simultaneously, so that progress in the peace process would have to be phased. Rabin's own preference was to move first with Syria and Lebanon, and to settle on a limited simultaneous progress with the Palestinians (on the scale of the "Gaza first" plan). Rabin saw two alternatives for dealing with Syria and Lebanon. One was to deal with Lebanon "as a pilot." If the Lebanese army were to deploy along the security zone and provide six months of quiet, Rabin was willing to sign a peace treaty and withdraw to the international border. Israel's security concerns and her commitments to her allies and partners in the security zone would also have to be addressed. But Rabin was doubtful whether Syria would agree to this plan.

The second alternative was to deal with Syria and Lebanon together. In order to find out whether this alternative was feasible, Rabin asked Christopher to explore with Asad, on the assumption that his own demand would be satisfied, first whether Syria would be willing to sign a peace treaty with Israel without linkage to the pace of progress with others; second, whether Syria was ready for a real peace including normalization, diplomatic relations, and the other paraphernalia of real peace; and third, whether Syria was ready to offer elements of peace before the completion of withdrawal. Rabin explained to Christopher that he saw the whole process completed in five years, and that given the fact that Israel was asked to give tangibles in return for intangbles he wanted tangible proofs of peace before going through a significant withdrawal. What he had in mind was the Israeli-Egyptian precedent, when Sadat agreed to the establishment of embassies after the first phase of withdrawal.

In addition to the three questions to Asad, Rabin raised four other points. First, the security arrangements were as important as the other issues. In addition to the security arrangements with Syria, he expected U.S. participation in the post-settlement security regime (I added that on the basis of what we saw in the Washington talks, particularly the Syrian demand for "equal footing" in the security arrangements, stiff Syrian opposition could be expected in this matter). Second, he emphasized that he was speaking of "an assumption." Third, he insisted on the absolute confidentiality of the exercise we were about to engage in. And fourth, he explained to the secretary of state that there would have to be a referendum in Israel before he could sign an agreement with Syria.

After clarifying some of these issues, the secretary of state wanted to know whether Jericho would be part of the concomitant "limited agreement" with the Palestinians that Rabin had in mind. (This was clearly an echo of the parallel negotiation with the Palestinians, with which the secretary of state was familiar at least in general terms.) Rabin's answer was that in the event of an agreement with Syria the agreement with the Palestinians would have to be limited to Gaza, but if the first agreement were to be made with the Palestinians, both Gaza and Jericho would be included.

Before we moved on to the larger meeting, I said to Ross that the wings of history could be heard in the room. Rabin's gambit took me by surprise, but it was clear to me that by being willing to engage in the "hypothetical approach" he opened the door wide for Asad. If Asad were to respond appropriately we could soon find ourselves in the midst of a real negotiation with Syria. Before we all departed, Rabin told me again that the details of the meeting in his office must remain secret. He would update whoever needed to know about it in the Israeli government (by which he meant first and foremost Foreign Minister Peres).

Christopher and Ross saw Asad in Damascus on the 4th and returned to Israel to report to Rabin on the 5th. They then traveled back to Damascus with Rabin's response. I was briefed by Ross on the second meeting on August 8th after we had both returned to Washington. Soon thereafter both Christopher and Ross left for their planned family vacations in California.

While Christopher and Ross saw Asad's response as positive in that he accepted "the basic equation," Rabin saw it as disappointing. Asad was willing to offer formal contractual peace for full withdrawal and was, in principle, willing to view the agreement as "standing on its own two feet," but then came a long list of "ifs and buts." Most significantly, Asad did not accept Rabin's demand that the agreement be implemented in a fashion that would offer Israel at the outset a large measure of normalization for a limited withdrawal. Nor did he accept a five-year time frame and offered instead a six-month period for implementing the agreement.

Asad's response on the issue of linkage to the other tracks, while positive in principle, was not clear. Rabin knew that Syria would insist on full linkage to the Lebanese track, and understood well that Asad needed a measure of progress with the Palestinians in order to legitimize his own move, but it was not clear what that measure was. Asad agreed to a full-fledged peace, but he told Christopher that he had difficulties with the very term "normalization." He rejected Rabin's idea of establishing a direct discreet channel; the most he agreed to were meetings between both Allaf and Mu'allim and myself, attended also by an American representative. The whole issue of security arrangements was not discussed in any detail (at least as reported to us), and Rabin's insistence that without significant Syrian investment in public diplomacy he would lack a political basis for moving on fell on deaf ears.

I was back in Washington while Rabin was digesting and con-

templating Asad's response. I had been aware of his disappointment with Asad's initial reaction, but it was only later that I learned
the full extent of his disappointment. As Rabin saw it, the move he
began was shifted to a wrong footing. He was not naive and did not
expect Asad to accept his offer without any attempt at bargaining.
But he was not willing to enter into a long process of bargaining.
Such a process could never work to Israel's advantage. If Asad's demands were a constant and that constant, we already knew, had actually been endorsed by the United States, then bargaining could
only deal with Israel's demands. The issue of the time frame provided an excellent illustration. If Rabin spoke of five years and Asad
offered six months, one could safely assume that with the United
States as a go-between Asad would persistently seek to chop away
at Israel's initial position and bring it down to two or at best just
under three years. The same dynamics would apply to the other
components of the Israeli package, which would thus be whittled
down through a lengthy process of indirect bargaining. Given this
prospect, Rabin decided to give Peres the green light to bring the
Oslo negotiations to conclusion.

The decision was not easy or simple. Oslo meant an agreement
with the PLO, and one that had far-reaching ramifications. The initial steps of the agreement were relatively easy—there was no real
attachment in Israel to the Gaza Strip, and the area around Jericho
was not heavily populated by Israeli settlers. The mechanism of a
five-year transition period with final status issues finessed during
the first two years should facilitate the Israeli public's acceptance
of the agreement. The difference in this regard between a Syrian
option and a Palestinian one was stark. Asad had rejected the notion of partial or phased settlement and insisted on a full settlement, which meant that the issues of withdrawal and settlements
had to be confronted at the outset.

These considerations had to be weighed against two major difficulties. Beyond the comparatively easy early phase of the Oslo
agreement lay the hard-core issues that would have to be confronted later on. Rabin was not prone to self-delusion, and he had
a good idea of what the red lines of any Palestinian nationalist

would be when it came to final status negotiations. And there was the immediate challenge of coming to terms with the enemy that Rabin himself had bedeviled and warned against, and the uncertainty of Arafat's ability to build a coherent political and administrative structure and to deliver his part of the deal. The difficulty of the decision was further compounded by the need to take into account Washington's reaction. True, Rabin told Clinton in March that a breakthrough could occur on either track, and Christopher and his team had been briefed on the broad lines of the Oslo talks. But it was clear to us that the Clinton administration preferred a breakthrough on the Syrian track and had invested its efforts and prestige accordingly. How would the president and the secretary of state react when told that a deal had been initialed in Oslo and that for the next few months Israel preferred to complete and implement it while the Syrian track was shifted to the back burner?

In early August Rabin preferred not to deal with the full ramifications of his decision. To the very small group of Israelis familiar with the state of the Oslo talks he expressed skepticism until the last moment, and when the agreement was provisionally signed he told Peres that his own final endorsement depended on the administration's acceptance of the move and the deal. And yet it was patently clear that a momentous decision had been made by the government of Israel and by the PLO, that the present peace process and the broader relationship between Israel and the Arab world had been transformed. To me personally it was clear that from that point on the Palestinian track would become the cutting edge of the peace process and that unless Asad was to change his style and take a bold initiative or step forward, the Syrian-Israeli track was bound to be relegated to a secondary role for some time to come.

In Washington prior to Ross's departure for California (on August 10) we were still busy planning the next step on the Syrian track. Given Asad's refusal to establish a discreet channel and the need for secrecy, it seemed best to hold a new round of the Washington talks in late August and early September, and to find a way of dealing with the new, secret, dimension of the negotiations while keeping the four formal tracks going as usual.

The course of events in the region and Syria's public conduct during the next two weeks betrayed no indication of an impending breakthrough. Syria's own media continued in their harsh criticism of Israel, and then on August 12 a Lebanese newspaper printed in London, *al-Safir*, published a strange article written by the editor, Tallal Salman, who was well known for his close connections to the Syrian government. Part of the article, the first of two segments, consisted of direct quotes from an interview with Asad. Other paragraphs were rendered as Salman's impressions, which may or may not have been gathered from Asad himself. The interview and the article were designed to ward off criticism of Asad's role in arranging the cease-fire and the set of understandings that ended Operation Accountability. The apologetic tone of the interview and the need to dress up Syria's role were understandable, but not the personal attacks and ethnic jibes directed at Secretary Christopher and his team nor the virulent attack on "the Israeli enemy" and the "Zionist entity."[6]

This unsavory publication was followed by a grave incident in south Lebanon on August 19. Nine Israeli soldiers were killed by explosive charges laid by Hizballah. Technically speaking, this attack did not constitute an infringement of the recent understanding on south Lebanon between Israel, Syria, and Lebanon. But if Hizballah acted precisely in order to demonstrate that the understanding was of a limited nature and as such did not put an end to its struggle against Israel, we expected Syria in the aftermath of Rabin's gambit to exert itself in order to prevent violence and Israeli casualties in south Lebanon. We were all too familiar with the Syrian argument that Damascus did not control Hizballah and could only exercise limited "influence." We also knew that Asad was determined to demonstrate, as his interview with Salman indicated, that the recent understanding was not a matter of capitulation. And yet we were deeply puzzled by the conduct of a would-be partner to a far-reaching agreement that could conceivably

occur soon. In the event Rabin decided against a massive retalia-
tion, and the tension subsided.

In the meantime, further progress was made in Oslo. On August
20, Peres called me on the telephone to ascertain that I could find
the secretary of state in California when the need arose. This was
a clear indication of an imminent agreement. On the 25th Rabin
called to say that Peres and Norway's foreign minister, Johan Holst,
would come by special plane to California to brief the secretary of
state on the agreement that had been initialled in Oslo. A meeting
was arranged at Point Mugu, a Marine base near Oxnard, south of
Los Angeles and close to Warren Christopher's vacation home.
The base had its own airport and would offer confidentiality.
Christopher would be joined by Ross. I left for California on the
26th to wait for Peres, Holst, and their retinues, who landed at
Point Mugu on the afternoon of the 27th.

Peres was evidently excited and worried. Not only did Rabin insist on American endorsement before he gave his own, but the
memory of George Schultz's ultimate refusal to endorse the 1987
London agreement was still fresh in his memory. But the anxiety
was not warranted. The secretary of state and his team (and more
remotely, the president) may not have been happy with this surprising shift from a "Syrian option" to a "Palestinian option" or by
the rather skimpy briefing they had been given on the Oslo talks
during the previous few weeks. In private conversation some of
their unhappiness was conveyed to us later. But they wasted no
time in grasping the full significance of an agreement between the
government of Israel headed by Yitzhak Rabin and the PLO, and
of the startling effect it was bound to have on the whole peace
process. After the initial briefing by Peres and Joel Singer (the
Foreign Ministry's legal adviser), Christopher and Ross left for a
brief consultation. They returned soon thereafter and the secretary told the visitors that subject to President Clinton's approval,
the United States would endorse the agreement and facilitate its
implementation.

Much had yet to be accomplished before an agreement could be
finalized and signed. We agreed to keep the new developments and

our own deliberations secret, but we realized that the secret could not be kept very long. For one thing the delegations to the Washington talks were about to arrive. The United States felt obliged to update its Arab allies and partners as well as Syria. Asad was not likely to react kindly to the new turn of events, and the later he was told about it the angrier he was likely to be.

During the two weeks that separated the briefing at Point Mugu and the Israeli-Palestinian signing ceremony on the White House lawn (September 13, 1993) work on the peace process continued along three tracks. For one thing, the potential created in Oslo had to be translated into a set of policies. On August 27 a signing ceremony attended by President Clinton, Prime Minister Rabin, and Chairman Arafat was not a foregone conclusion. In order to obtain the Israeli-PLO mutual recognition, Foreign Minister Holst had to invest considerable effort. Arafat had to commit the PLO to a revocation of the offensive paragraphs in the Palestinian National Charter as well as to a disavowal of terror and violence. Israeli and American Jewish public opinion had to be addressed by us and by the administration, and a parallel effort had to be invested in Arab and Palestinian public opinion. Two Arab governments in particular, Syria's and Jordan's, had to be reconciled to a breakthrough that could facilitate their own negotiations with Israel, but also raised immediate concerns. The U.S. Congress needed to be briefed and persuaded to go through an accelerated procedure that would suspend the legislation that banned U.S. government contact with the PLO because of the organization's involvement in terrorist activities. This was done through the Middle East Peace Facilitation Act.

On a second track we began a new phase of Israeli-Syrian negotiations in the aftermath of Christopher's visit. This was a particularly complex exercise, given both the ambiguities of the indirect exchanges between Rabin and Asad and the shadow cast over the Israeli-Syrian track by our agreement with the Palestinians and the impending signing ceremony in Washington. Asad could see obvious advantages to Syria and himself in the Israeli-Palestinian breakthrough. The issue of linkage was practically resolved. He would no longer have to delay potential progress in his negotiations with Israel so as not to be seen as abandoning the Palestinians or as making a separate deal reminiscent of Sadat's. And if he needed to be persuaded that Rabin had the ability to make far-reaching decisions and reverse both the conventional wisdom and his own record, then the events of the last few days provided ample proof of such ability.

But these considerations were dwarfed by emotion and calculus. It was difficult for Asad to be upstaged in this fashion by Yasser Arafat, a man he despised and disliked. Arafat's ability to break ranks and upset Asad's own plans for the peace process was humiliating and irritating for the Syrian leader. He had invested great effort in establishing at least a measure of coordination and unity in the ranks of the Arab negotiators, and had worked hard to find a way of reconciling his commitment to the Palestinian cause with Syrian raison d'état, only to find out that Arafat had made his own deal. If Asad considered himself the senior leader looking with benign eyes after the interests of his weaker Arab brothers, he was rudely awakened to find out that he was trailing Arafat.

And then there was the well-warranted Syrian concern that Rabin and his government would not want or would not be able to hoist two flags simultaneously, that once a "Palestinian option" was chosen as the first breakthrough in the peace process, Rabin would feel and argue that the Israeli political system, Israeli society, or his own government could not sustain the weight and shock of another major breakthrough and the concessions it was bound to entail.

There were in the Labor government those who believed in "shock therapy" as a strategy in the peace process. In their view it was best to seek a radical comprehensive solution to the Israeli-Arab conflict, to effect it with one fell swoop, and to confront the Israeli public with the full price and the full list of benefits entailed in a comprehensive solution. This was not Rabin's preference. He preferred a gradual, incremental approach. During the final days of August and in early September he did not say so explicitly, but his decision was to soft pedal on the Syrian track for several months while the agreement with the PLO was being implemented.

On August 29 the Syrian delegation to the peace talks had arrived in Washington. Allaf and Mu'allim met with Dennis Ross and his team. Both had been briefed on Christopher's talks with Rabin and Asad. The rest of the delegation was kept in the dark. The delegation as a whole met twice with Asad, once for five hours and once for three, and was given detailed instructions. Allaf and Mu'allim had their own brief: to hear "our message" from me directly and then repeat the Syrian message. They also had a scenario for our work during the coming period: agree on the text of a declaration of principles, form a number of working groups, and have them work out the details of a settlement. As expected, their mandate with regard to format was strict and limited: they would meet me only in Ross's office.

The first meeting in Ross's office was held on the 30th. As expected, Allaf's main interest was, indeed, in hearing from me a "commitment" to an Israeli withdrawal from the Golan Heights. His effort was based on a misunderstanding or a misrepresentation of Christopher's mission earlier in August. Rabin was very careful to emphasize to the secretary that he was engaging in a hypothetical exercise. The purpose of such an exercise is to break a deadlock in a negotiation by having both parties outline to each other the scope and limits of their respective positions in an informal and nonbinding fashion. Given Asad's response to Christopher, the last thing Rabin had in mind was converting a hypothetical formula deposited with the United States to a commitment conveyed to Syria by an authorized Israeli representative. My instructions in this matter were very clear. Before Rabin would contemplate an affirmative statement, let alone a commitment, our Syrian interlocutors would have to bring Syria's position or response much closer to the model Rabin had in mind.

Once Allaf realized that he was not about to hear any commitment to withdrawal, the meeting did not go very far. I complained about Syria's conduct in Lebanon and about the format they im-

posed on our meetings. Allaf dismissed my complaints: Israel was
the offensive party in Lebanon and the site of our meetings (Ross's
office or a private home) was of no importance. Nor was there a
need for public diplomacy. Once we reached an agreement we
would make it public, and this very act would be most significant.
Or we could publicize Christopher's conversation with Asad so that
the Syrian president could justify to his people a change in his public stance.

Ross, creative as ever, made a valiant effort to break the deadlock. He saw the formation of working groups as a potential key to
a qualitative leap in the negotiations and offered us several options. Did we want to create a distinction between a "soft" public
text and a "harder" private one, or were we interested in an American proposal to form working groups that Israel and Syria would
be responding to? I did not have to ponder our own position, since
Allaf wasted no time in rejecting Ross's offer. Syria was interested
in one thing—a clear commitment to full withdrawal—and did not
believe in fine distinctions and ambiguities.

The meeting took place on a Monday. We agreed that the delegations would meet on Tuesday, Wednesday, and Thursday and
that we would meet again in Ross's office on Friday. The three plenary meetings proceeded quite smoothly. Presumably the members of the two delegations were unaware of the parallel meetings
in Ross's office and of the hypothetical exercise performed by the
secretary of state. My sense then was that the latter secret was actually kept by both sides (and this remained the case for a surprisingly long period), but that the less dramatic existence of a second
channel was known to at least several of the members in both
delegations.

At the end of the first plenary meeting on Monday it was clear
that Syria's tactic was to seek progress (namely, on Israeli commitment to withdrawal) in the private meetings and to maintain a busi-
nesslike, but not too cozy, tone in the plenary session and in the
media. We began with a review of the course of events since the
end of the previous round. The Syrians were particularly anxious
to have as many details as we would care to provide concerning our

agreement with the Palestinians. We then spent most of our time in redrafting paragraphs 1–4 of the paper we had been working on for a year. We sensed a more flexible Syrian attitude and overcame some obstacles that had been intractable in previous months. We came close to finalizing a mutually acceptable text of paragraphs 1–4, made a measure of progress on the problematic paragraph 5, and even greater progress on the security issue. Allaf still held on to "equal footing" but allowed some flexibility—equality should be manifested in the overall security formula and not necessarily in every specific measure. That notion, however, should not form part of the actual text and should rather be included in a separate note or in the agreed minutes. Compared to the historic break-through with the Palestinians, such progress seemed and was minor, but in the context of the specific negotiation with Syria it was not meaningless.

We had two additional private meetings in which nothing new was accomplished. By then most of the problems obstructing clo-sure with the Palestinians had been resolved and the signing event was taking shape. On September 9, Clinton called Asad on the tele-phone. He wanted to reassure him that the United States remained committed to effecting a Syrian-Israeli breakthrough as well, and asked him to send a representative to the signing ceremony. Asad agreed to have his ambassador in Washington participate along-side most of the other Arab ambassadors. This was a significant de-cision. Asad was incensed by the Israeli-Palestinian agreement and was bitterly critical of both substance and procedure. In his eyes, Arafat had not merely broken ranks and undermined Syria's strat-egy in the peace talks, he had done that for the sake of an unsatis-factory agreement that failed to meet Arab nationalist criteria for a proper solution to the Palestinian problem. Asad probably sus-pected the United States and Israel of playing a double game with him. Rabin was disappointed by his response in early August, but Christopher was not. How then was he to understand the sudden switch to the Palestinian track? And yet Asad understood that he could not boycott the ceremony or launch a full-blown campaign against the Oslo accords.

Indeed, there were other elements to Asad's decision, as well as to the broader policy he adopted with regard to the Israeli-Palestinian agreement. For one thing he was responding to the U.S. president, and making a gesture that he added to the balance sheet of the Syrian-American relationship that he kept and updated at all times. He probably also concluded that he had no choice. He had joined this peace process and had invested in it; he clearly miscalculated when he assumed that he alone on the Arab side possessed the key to a breakthrough, and in the absence of a better alternative he would have to make the best of the situation as it was.

Ambassador Mu'allim's participation in the events of September 13 turned out to be more significant and salient than expected. The American team was rightly determined to extract as many gestures of Arab-Israeli reconciliation from that special day as it could. It planned the signing ceremony so as to conclude it by the signatories coming off the podium and shaking hands with all those seated in the front row. The Arab ambassadors were seated in one wing of that front row, so that all of them—most notably the ambassadors of Syria and Saudi Arabia—shook hands with Rabin and Peres. From the present perspective this episode does not necessarily seem crucial, but in the context of an historical breakthrough defined by a handshake (between Arafat and Rabin) it was a significant moment. Arab-Israeli fraternizing continued during a festive luncheon hosted by the secretary of state and attended by eight former secretaries of state and an unusual array of Arab leaders and diplomats.

At the White House, President Clinton hosted Prime Minister Rabin at a private lunch. The intimate, lengthy, and relaxed meeting provided first and foremost an opportunity for the two men to develop further the personal bond that had formed during the March visit. It also provided Rabin with an opportunity to explain to the president the domestic political constraints he had to face in Israel as he went through the decisions and concessions inherent in the peace process.

Rabin was worried by an outlook reflected in an interview granted by the president to Thomas Friedman of the *New York*

Times. The president spoke explicitly about the need to address the Israeli public and prepare it for the concessions that would have to be made, particularly toward Syria. He told Friedman of his telephone conversation with President Asad, who told him that "he was ready to endorse the accord between Israel and the PLO but had cautioned Mr. Clinton . . . that it could not stand alone, but had to be followed by a breakthrough in the Syrian-Israeli track."

Glimpses into the president's perception of a peace process and his telephone conversations with Hafiz al-Asad are rare, and the following paragraphs deserve to be quoted at some length.

> "Plainly we have to be part of any ultimate resolution of the Israel, Syria, Lebanon negotiations," Mr. Clinton said. "But I think that they have to deal with it and I think that what we have to do is to create the strongest possible conditions in which they deal with it and I think right now what that means is making the Israeli people as comfortable as they can be with this—that they are more secure not less secure because this is done and that the United States is still there. I think that is the most important thing now as they absorb this."
>
> The President continued: "Each successive day that the agreement builds up in strength I think that that enables the Government in Israel to engage Syria. I personally believe that it is a lot more important than the details of this piece of land on the Golan Heights or anything else."
>
> Mr. Clinton went on at great length about his phone conversation with President Asad of Syria, which lasted 30 minutes. That conversation seemed to underscore the challenge Mr. Clinton faces in trying not to overload the political circuits in Israel—by asking the Israelis to withdraw from the Gaza Strip and the Golan Heights at once—while also keeping the Syrian leader interested in supporting moves that might not reward him immediately.
>
> Mr. Clinton said Mr. Asad had told him: "I think you are right. It is a positive thing, this agreement, for all of us. I just want to know that you are committed to the whole process."
>
> "I said, 'I am strongly,' and I said, 'I think you should be committed to the whole process.' I reminded him the issue in Israel is se-

curity, and the opposition to the agreement are people who believe that it will weaken rather than enhance their security, and if we are going to see this all the way through, which I really believe we have to, you got to solve these inter-state conflicts.

"Monday has to be a signal to the people of Israel that this is about security. I said if your Ambassador is there it will be a pretty clear signal that you are serious about it, and he said 'Yes, I think that is right.'"

"But he also said he really wanted my commitment to continue," Mr. Clinton added. "He said, 'You know, the people on our side are restless too and they don't want to feel that our part of this will be abandoned.'"

According to an Administration official, the Syrian leader added: "If there is no comprehensive peace this will not stand on its feet. If there are long periods of time with no progress these difficulties will grow greater. We should not let time go by without serious work."[7]

Rabin was, in fact, quite alarmed by Clinton's quest to reassure Israeli public opinion. If reassurance was simply meant to prepare the Israeli public for an almost simultaneous major concession to Syria, then Rabin was worried. He explained to Clinton that there was indeed only so much that the traffic could bear, that a coalition government resting on a slim majority must not overload the circuits. As he saw it, it was wrong to present the Israeli public with a series of written agreements, let alone agreements involving far-reaching concessions in the aftermath of the Oslo accords. He would rather effect a real change on the ground, let the Israeli public digest it and appreciate the accruing benefits, and then move on to the next agreement. He told the president that he was still committed to the notion of an agreement with Syria but he needed a few months, and asked the president's help in persuading Asad to wait until the end of the year. He also repeated to the president what he had told him in March: that given his own position prior to and during the 1992 elections, any major agreement with Syria would have to be approved by a referendum. Rabin felt that he had no mandate for such an agreement and could not finalize it without one.

Rabin returned elated from his lunch with the president. As he saw the meeting, the president, a very political man, understood Rabin's perspective and concerns and was very attentive to them. President Clinton then called President Asad a second time to brief him on his discussion with Rabin, to assure him of his administration's and Israel's commitment to move forward with Syria as well in a few months, and to ask him specifically to restrain the "rejectionist" Palestinian leaders residing in Damascus who vilified Arafat for "selling out" through the Oslo accords and the White House ceremony.

By mid-September 1993, the state of the Israeli-Syrian track could be summed up in the following fashion. In the year-long competition with the Palestinian track, the latter won and the Israeli-Arab peace process was to be predicated on the Israeli-Palestinian breakthrough. The three-way discussion between Israelis, Americans, and Syrians focused now on the consequences of Israel's insistence that a breakthrough on the Syrian track would have to be postponed for several months and would depend on the actual successful implementation of the Israeli-Palestinian agreement.

From Asad's perspective it was a grievance, and it was certainly presented as such. Absent in the dialogue was an explicit American statement to the Syrians that the turn taken by events was at least in part an outcome of their unsatisfactory response in August. We never took it up directly with our American colleagues, but I sensed then and believe now that they did not see eye-to-eye with us in this matter and did not fully accept Rabin's decision to go to Oslo rather than haggle with Asad over his response. Whatever the reason, the fact of the matter was that the original U.S. embarrassment vis-à-vis Damascus over Oslo was now compounded by a commitment to return full steam to the Syrian track and a sense of obligation over Asad's cooperation with the September 13 ceremony. In the language of our negotiation, the term "commitment" was now used to refer to the United States and the Israeli promise to seek in earnest a breakthrough in the Israeli-Syrian track despite and on top of the Oslo accords.

FIVE

Between Amman and
Damascus

THE TORTUOUS COURSE of the Israeli-Syrian negotiations was punctuated more by breakthroughs on other tracks than by progress based on its own inherent strength. In the immediate aftermath of the Washington signing ceremony, the prospect of an Israeli-Jordanian agreement became clearly visible. The Israeli leadership made no secret of the preference it assigned to a peace agreement with Jordan as the second accomplishment of the Madrid process. By agreeing to an open meeting between Crown Prince Hasan and Foreign Minister Peres on October 1, 1993, and in several other ways, King Hussein signaled his own interest in that option.

But Hafiz al-Asad was not impressed. A master in the art of pressure diplomacy, he responds angrily when pressure is applied against him. Asad evidently did not believe that King Hussein would cross the Rubicon he had failed to cross so many times in previous decades, and he refused to be intimidated by Israel's thinly veiled threat to bypass him a second time. Instead he dug in further, and but for a few concessions on substance and procedure he held fast to the positions that had yielded so little during the first year of his negotiations with Yitzhak Rabin. Even the signing of the Jordanian-Israeli Washington Declaration on July 25, 1994, stipulating the end of belligerency between the two countries and indicating the imminence of full-fledged peace failed to move Asad off the track he had chosen. And so this phase ended in October 1994 with the signing of the second Israeli-Arab peace treaty and with another Syrian disappointment.

If Asad suspected that Rabin was trying to change the rules of the game in that process, to break the unified Arab front, to come to agreements with Syria's Arab partners, and to deal with a weakened Asad at a later phase, he was not being entirely paranoid. Rabin remained committed to his understanding with the Clinton administration, but he was convinced that Asad was not ready to make a deal within the terms of that understanding. He had no intention of bending the whole peace process to suit Asad's taste and priorities, and was perfectly willing to move on with the other tracks of the peace process until Asad was ready to make a deal on terms acceptable to Israel.

Asad, in turn, did not view this course of events as a net loss. By sheer persistence he did chip away at the U.S. and Israeli terms, and he did mark some progress in the construction of a new relationship with the United States—President Clinton met with him in Europe in January 1994 and came to Damascus in October of that year. And the negotiations continued under the auspices of an American administration very much committed to the notion of an Israeli-Syrian peace predicated on full Israeli withdrawal from the Golan in return for a diluted version of the Syrian package envisaged by Rabin in August 1993. And so, the Israeli-Jordanian peace treaty notwithstanding, Syria's president continued to march to the sound of his own drum.

The year that separated the signing of Israeli-Jordanian peace from the September 13 ceremony can be neatly divided into three phases: first, from September 13, 1993, to late April 1994 no progress was made in the Israeli-Syrian negotiations as Hafiz al-Asad stuck to his positions while Yitzhak Rabin asked to delay any potential breakthrough with Syria as long as the Oslo and Washington agreements were not converted into an actual agreement on implementation; second, in late April, as the signing of the Gaza-Jericho agreement on the implementation of the Oslo accords was about to take place in Cairo, serious negotiations between Israel and Syria were renewed, but these negotiations were marred by profound disagreements that were resolved only on July 20; third, that resolution opened the way to the formation of the "ambassadors' channel"—my private negotiations with my Syrian counterpart that lasted through the summer and fall of 1994.

SEPTEMBER 1993–APRIL 1994

Israel's policies in the aftermath of the White House signing were clear and coherent: turn the framework agreement with the Palestinians into a new, functioning reality, draw the appropriate political and diplomatic benefits from the historic reconciliation, seek to move ahead in the peace negotiations with Jordan, and have the United States persuade Syria to wait patiently for several months rather than seek to obstruct progress on the other tracks of the peace process.

In the region itself, the Israeli-Palestinian negotiations on the formation of Palestinian self-rule in Gaza and Jericho between teams headed by the Israeli deputy chief of staff, General Amnon Shahak, and Nabil Sha'ath began on October 13. The Oslo accords set a period of three months for that negotiation, but it proved to be much more arduous than expected and was only concluded during the signing ceremony itself on May 4 in Cairo.

A parallel effort was launched jointly by the United States and Israel to raise a sizable fund from the international community in order to help with the economic development of the areas designated for Palestinian self-rule, Gaza in particular, so as to add an economic dimension to the new reality. The Donors Conference met in Washington on October 1, and 600 million dollars were pledged.

Foreign Minister Peres returned to the United States in late September to participate in the UN's General Assembly and in the Donors Conference. Peres was visibly transformed by his success and by the domestic and international recognition that came with it. The delicate balance in the complex relationship with Rabin had shifted. Rabin had made the tough decisions and had provided the political umbrella, but Peres was considered the engine of the reconciliation with the Palestinians, and had now stepped firmly into the bilateral part of the peace process. He was quite blunt in our private discussions in New York on September 26 and more subtle in a meeting with Dennis Ross two days later: Asad must patiently wait his turn while the government of Israel was reinforced by the implementation and success of its agreement with the Palestinians.

On October 1 in Washington, Peres met openly at the White House with Crown Prince Hasan of Jordan. This was a prelude to two secret meetings of the Israeli leadership with King Hussein in Jordan. On the night of October 6–7, Prime Minister Rabin went to Jordan to deal with the fallout from the Oslo accord. The king was disappointed and angry; had Israel abandoned the tacit understanding with Jordan and had she made a clear choice for a Palestinian option? Rabin persuaded him that there was a much broader spectrum to the Israeli-Jordanian relationship: bilateral issues, a joint agenda toward the United States, the need to deal with Iraq, and other strategic threats. Beyond such arguments there lay a powerful recognition: much as the king disliked the Oslo accords, he understood that he had to face the new reality, that Palestinian self-rule was to be established soon and could later evolve into statehood, and that in order to deal effectively with the ramifications for his own country he needed a new relationship with Israel.

This realization was still a far cry from real progress toward a Jordanian-Israeli breakthrough, but the potential for such a development was certainly there. Rabin and Peres were both determined to bring it about. Peace with Jordan would add a third Arab party to the Arab-Israeli peace club. It could also prove to be a comparatively painless agreement. Jordan insisted on concessions regarding territory and water, but compared to Syria's territorial demands and to the shock of reconciliation with the PLO, this was a minor issue. Rabin's initial success in assuaging King Hussein was pursued by Peres during his trip to Jordan on November 2. Progress was made and a practical agenda was set, but the king would still not commit himself. He was also incensed by the fact that news of the meeting leaked in Israel.

There was a significant American dimension to the Israeli drive to effect a breakthrough with Jordan. Without the administration's blessing and actual support, the king was not likely to make the move. He wanted to put the controversy of his relationship with

Saddam Hussein in 1990–1991 behind him, and he wanted American financial and defense aid. Would the Clinton administration lend its support to the current effort to effect an Israeli-Jordanian breakthrough when it realized that this could further delay the renewal of Israeli-Syrian negotiations? The question was indeed debated when Ross and the U.S. peace team arrived in Israel on October 20. By that date a new timetable for the peace process had been put together. The secretary of state discarded an earlier plan to travel to the Middle East in October; he preferred to postpone the visit until after Rabin's visit to the United States in mid-November. Rabin's meeting with the president was expected to produce the clarity with regard to Syria that would enable the secretary to have a fruitful trip in early December. In the uncertainty that prevailed in October it seemed wise to dispatch Ross and company to the region rather than expose the secretary of state to the risk and cost of an unsuccessful mission.

In a similar vein, a decision was made in mid-October not to hold another round of the Washington talks later that month. Rabin was interested in holding a round in October so as to demonstrate that a broader peace process continued to unfold alongside the new Israeli-Palestinian negotiation. The State Department was of two minds in this matter, but Ambassador Mu'allim came with a persuasive message from his government—Syria was not interested in holding a round during which nothing was expected to happen and the Syrian delegation would be forced to adopt a negative posture.

Ross's first meeting in Israel was held with Foreign Minister Peres. There was no acrimony, but the disagreement was open: Peres argued that Israel's next agreement should be with Jordan while Ross and his colleagues advocated the merits of the "Syria next" approach.

Ross's meeting with Rabin illustrated both the advantages and shortcomings of a diplomatic exchange held between a head of government and a senior official of another government, albeit that of a superpower. Ross was the senior administration official working on the Middle East and he did represent and carry the authority of the president and the secretary of state. And yet Rabin knew very well that after speaking to Ross in October he would be speaking to the secretary of state and to the president in Washington in mid-November. Whatever he "gave" to Ross in Jerusalem would not be final. Therefore when Ross asked him to recommit himself to the "message" of August 1993 he declined. But on another level it was easier to speak plainly and openly to Ross. Ross told Rabin in Christopher's name that the secretary's view was that agreement had actually been reached in August. Rabin disagreed—Christopher, as he saw it, returned from Damascus without an agreement that met the conditions set by Israel. Therefore, he said, he had chosen to go to Oslo. He could not now make a second agreement based on massive Israeli concessions. Did Asad want to offer an agreement that would not affect Israeli settlements on the Golan and would be, from that perspective, comparable to the Oslo accords? Since this was not the case, he preferred to move next with Jordan. Ross explained that Christopher preferred to move with Syria for a whole host of reasons, including the fact that his own credibility was at stake.

Rabin reminded Ross that after the Shass party left his government, his coalition numbered only fifty-six members of the Knesset, and that his majority depended on the votes of the Arab members who supported his government without being part of the coalition. He needed three or four months without a controversy regarding the Golan, but that time frame was not definitive and depended among other things on the pace of the implementation with the Palestinians. Rabin never said so explicitly, but there was also a subliminal message in what the prime minister had been saying for some time now: he was, of course, committed to what he had said to the secretary of state in August. His own integrity and self-view as a man of his word and the centrality he attributed to the relationship with the United States as the cornerstone of Israel's national security required that he overrule the sense that Asad had missed his opportunity and should pay a price for it. Had the administration been able to persuade Asad to come up with a package that came close to the criteria set in August 1993, Rabin would probably have gone along with it. But the administration could evidently not deliver these goods, and Rabin could justifiably insist that the original terms be kept while pursuing progress on other tracks.

On October 22 Ross met Asad for seven hours and reported to him at length on his discussion with Rabin. Asad listened carefully to Ross's description of that discussion and to his detailed analysis of the Israeli political scene. It was another sign of the times that the president of Syria, like other Arab leaders, became well versed with the politics of Shass and other Israeli parties and factions. Asad made it clear that if it turned out that Rabin had changed his mind with regard to Syria, he would turn against the current peace process and lash out against the PLO, Jordan, and other Arabs who were "soft" on Israel.

Rabin's reassuring message was finally given to President Clinton on November 12 in Washington, during the prime minister's scheduled visit to the United States. A pattern was now established whereby the prime minister came to the United States at least twice a year, for the general assembly of the Jewish Federations in November and for the American-Israel Public Affairs Committee (AIPAC) policy conference in the spring. Soon after its formation, the Clinton administration sought to upgrade and formalize the U.S.-Israeli strategic dialogue. Given the differences between the two systems a mutually acceptable format was not found, but in the event the president and the prime minister became the principal interlocutors in an informal but very effective dialogue.

The meeting on November 12 was preceded, as was usually the case, by a brief session with the secretary of state. These sessions were designed to provide the president with a clear sense of the prime minister's intentions. In the event of a disagreement, a direct conflict between the two leaders should be averted. In this case the administration's apprehensions were by and large relieved. Rabin reaffirmed to Christopher and subsequently to Clinton that he was committed to his original message, but he placed the reaffirmation in context: his priorities were to implement the Oslo accords and to move forward with Jordan. He used the occasion to describe King Hussein's full agenda. And he emphasized yet again the importance he attached to having a direct tacit channel with Syria.

Clinton in turn told Rabin about his intention to meet Asad in Europe in January 1994. Here then was the U.S. strategy at this point: Christopher would go to the region in early December and the president would meet with Asad in January. This and a message informing the Syrians of the "reaffirmation" should keep Asad quiet until the anticipated completion of the Israeli-Palestinian negotiations. The meeting with the president should then be used in order to persuade Asad to offer the concessions that would facilitate the elusive Israeli-Syrian breakthrough.

In Damascus in early December Christopher extracted two gestures from his Syrian hosts: a delegation of congressional staffers would come to Syria to seek information on the fate of Israeli MIAs, and eight hundred Syrian Jews would be allowed to leave Syria before the end of December.

The congressional staffers worked for the congressional Committee on International Relations. The committee chairman, Lee Hamilton, a distinguished Democratic congressman from Indiana, who had been one of Christopher's competitors for the secretary of state's post, was one of the very few congressional leaders who had a relationship with Syria. Hamilton's relationship with Syria was facilitated by one of his chief aides, Michael Van Dusen, who in the 1970s wrote an excellent doctoral dissertation on Syrian politics. Hamilton also had a relationship with one of the more curious figures who operate on the margins of the American-Israeli-Syrian triangle—Ibrahim (Abe) Suleiman, a Syrian of Alawi extraction who emigrated to the United States and lives in Washington, and who maintains at least some connections in Syria. I personally have never been able to authenticate his connections and standing, and therefore his value as a channel.

Chairman Hamilton believed, like us, that a humane gesture on an issue of great sensitivity in Israel would have a very salutary effect on Asad's and Syria's image in the United States and Israel. But as we found out time and again, Asad either refused or was incapable of sharing this view. He agreed to have the staffers come to Syria to the same extent that he promised the United States to seek authoritative information regarding the fate of the missing Israeli navigator Ron Arad. In both cases no serious effort was made by Syria.

Christopher failed in his effort to persuade Asad to assign a senior Syrian general to meet discreetly with an Israeli counterpart. Washington's and Jerusalem's unhappiness with Muwaffaq Allaf's rigidity seemed to endear him further to Asad. And when Christopher complained on Rabin's behalf that Allaf was not sufficiently senior in the Syrian system, Asad resorted to his special brand of humor. If Allaf wasn't sufficiently senior he could promote him to deputy secretary of state and appoint him as his adviser, thus making him both senior and close to the president.

In Damascus and in Jerusalem the secretary and his team worked out a new format for our work during the next few weeks. The talks between Israel and Syria and Israel and Lebanon would be renewed in Washington at heads-of-delegation level. Should the Clinton-Asad summit provide a new momentum, work would continue in the new format with a view to achieving a breakthrough in April of 1994. Before returning to Washington on December 11, I worked out with Rabin a potential sequence of public Israeli steps that could lead to final agreement: a reaffirmation of the government's decisions of June 19, 1967; an announcement that the Golan Law of 1981 fell short of annexing the Golan; a statement that Israel did not seek or claim sovereignty in the Golan, and so on.

The secretary of state and the peace team were eager to begin the meetings in Washington in late December or early January with a view to using them in order to prepare for and build toward the Clinton-Asad summit that was now scheduled for January 16 in Geneva. But Rabin declined. He insisted that the summit take place first and, he hoped, provide steam for the sessions in Washington.

What we saw on our television screens on January 16, 1994, was disappointing. Asad's statement and answers during a press conference were positive but vague. Asad did use the term "normal, peaceful relations," but he did not refer specifically to Israel but rather spoke of normal, peaceful relations among all in the region. This sentence, furthermore, came at the end of a statement that reiterated Asad's previous statement with regard to the peace process. It was President Clinton who had to elaborate on Asad's statement and to emphasize the positive and innovative parts, either in his own statement or in response to questions by the journalists. The sense of disappointment was exacerbated by a decision apparently made by Swiss and American officials in charge of the technical arrangements to prevent Israeli journalists from participating in the press conference.

Furthermore, for this modest contribution Asad emerged from the meeting with President Clinton with a tall set of achievements. President Clinton described Syria as "the key to the achievement of enduring and comprehensive peace." He also put the onus on Israel by expressing "hope" that Asad's "very important statement" would "provoke a positive response in Israel." The president also went along with emphasizing the importance of comprehensiveness in the Arab-Israeli peace process and practically endorsed Syria's policy in Lebanon. As a practical measure, the establishment of a mechanism for resolving bilateral problems between Syria and the United States was announced.

Ross and Indyk flew from Geneva to Jerusalem to brief Rabin on the meeting. They arrived at his residence at midnight, accompanied by Ed Djerejian, the new American ambassador to Israel. It was an awkward meeting. Ross and Indyk tried to put the best face on the public and private aspects of the summit, but their task was not easy. Asad had agreed to peace and normalization but remained adamant on security—for both sides and on equal footing. He had actually spent a significant part of the meeting lecturing to Clinton on the pre-1967 history of the conflict, so as to persuade him that Israel had been the aggressor and that Syria needed to be protected by security arrangements at least as much as Israel did.

Rabin was displeased to the point of being dismissive. As an exercise in public diplomacy the summit produced very little; Asad did not offer enough of a positive message, and his insistence on comprehensiveness was a setback. For his part, in any event, Rabin was not given anything with which to persuade the Israeli public. In these circumstances he preferred to move on with Jordan. He was also unhappy with the substance of the meeting. The previous August he had told the U.S. government what the end game could look like if his set of conditions were met. As he understood it, the United States should have kept it as a deposit while it was trying to bring about a deal. Instead, he observed, the United States was negotiating on our behalf and his original package was being eroded. He felt strongly that as long as Asad was not willing to make an early investment comparable to that of Sadat, an agreement would not be reached.

Rabin's disappointment was shared by the Israeli media but Clinton's very meeting with Asad, the positive spin put on its outcome by the administration, and the degree of progress that was in fact achieved created expectations in Israel that had to be addressed. Rabin agreed that Ross tell the media in Jerusalem that Asad was ready for full peace and demanded in return a full withdrawal. The next day he went a step further and authorized the deputy defense minister, Mordechai (Mota) Gur to state in the Knesset that if an agreement involving "significant territorial concessions" were to be reached, the government would submit it to a popular referendum. By bringing the notion of a referendum to the open Rabin sought to achieve several goals: calm down the Israeli political system, confront Asad with the need to grapple with the need for a referendum, and provide the U.S. administration with a gesture comparable to Asad's gestures. His message to the administration was that by making a public statement in this matter he was underlining the seriousness of the negotiations with Syria. Our American interlocutors, I felt, did not quite see it that way.

Before my return to Washington, Rabin invited me to brief the "security forum," an informal group consisting of the chief of staff, the three directors of the intelligence and security services, and the prime minister's military aides. Rabin was visibly comfortable with this group. As an authoritative prime minister he dominated the cabinet, but the intimacy of his relationship with the defense and security chiefs was quite striking. To that forum I outlined our strategy for the negotiations with Allaf (who would be accompanied by Mu'allim) during the coming weeks: avoid discussion of peace and withdrawal, and try to focus on the issues of security, time frame, and phases.

On January 21 Hafiz al-Asad's favorite son, Basel, was killed in a (genuine) car accident in Damascus. Asad's pain and profound sense of loss did not interfere with the daily conduct of the peace process, but the accident did have a long-term impact on the negotiations. Ever since his health crisis in 1983–1984 Asad had been under pressure to formalize or at least institutionalize the succession, but his brother Rifat's bid for power in 1984 must have persuaded him that even the closest family member could not be fully trusted as an heir apparent. He subsequently began to groom Basel at a very deliberate pace. There was no open discussion of these issues in Syria, but ever so subtly some Syrians complained of the introduction of the dynastic element into Syrian politics while others saw stability as the main issue and were willing to accept Basel if he could provide it. His sudden death reopened the succession issue. Asad began to cultivate his son Bashar, younger and less gifted or politically inclined than his brother. Opposition to Bashar burst into the open and led to an open clash with Ali Haidar, who had once been considered one of Asad's most trusted generals. Haidar was forced to retire from active service, possibly as a first step in a series of moves designed to rejuvenate the ranks of the Syrian high command so as to facilitate young Bashar's ascension. Haidar did not take kindly to his retirement and launched a tirade against Asad's policies, including his policy in the peace process. All this did not amount to a crisis or even to a serious challenge to Asad's rule, but it did force him from that point on to think more often and more seriously about the succession and about the domestic dimension of his negotiations with Israel.

The meetings with the two Syrian diplomats began on January 24, 1994. Our American hosts made an effort to effect a change of environment and atmosphere. The venue was shifted from the

State Department building, to provide us greater proximity and to shield us from the media stakeouts. Unfortunately the site that was chosen happened to be at the corner of M Street and 24th near the Grand and Ana hotels, where Arab and Israeli official visitors to Washington often chose to stay. Within a few hours the Israeli correspondents in Washington and other journalists discovered the site and any expectation of a more discreet negotiation became unrealistic. The new site did provide a better opportunity for the small Syrian team and for my personal assistant in the embassy, Dan Arbel, to rub shoulders but not to fraternize.

During the following week we met several times, both at the site and in Ross's office. I began by offering the Israeli government's condolence to President Asad. This was acknowledged with formal gratitude but a more personal tone was not introduced into the negotiation. The scenario could have been written in advance. Allaf was buoyed by what he saw and certainly presented as the success of the Geneva summit. A new relationship was being forged between Syria and the United States, and Syria was the key to comprehensiveness, he said. In Geneva, President Clinton had held a summit meeting with the whole Arab world and by the same token a peace agreement between Israel and Syria would not be a separate deal but would lead to Israeli reconciliation with the whole Arab world. Israel need not worry about comprehensiveness. Syria would keep every agreement (but without formally defining this as "standing on its own two feet"). But the main thing was not to be forgotten—Allaf wanted me to do what I had declined to do in the fall and announce an Israeli willingness to withdraw from the Golan.

We soon returned to a familiar pattern: Allaf wanted us to complete the text of a declaration of principles and resume our work on paragraph 5, so as to corner me into discussing withdrawal, while I insisted that timing, phases, and security arrangements must be agreed upon before withdrawal could be addressed. Allaf, echoing Asad, argued that timing was not a "core issue" but a matter of implementation. Phasing the agreement, he complained, was a mechanism for "prolonging the occupation." And when we reached the issue of security arrangements he insisted on the familiar notion of "equal footing."

On February 1, Secretary Christopher made an attempt to break the deadlock by inviting Allaf, Mu'allim, and myself to his office. He had, of course, been thoroughly briefed by Ross, but he let us repeat our arguments and then adjudicated. He agreed with me that we need not deal now with paragraph 5, but sided with the Syrians in saying that timing was a less critical matter. In any event he wanted us to concentrate on security and try to reach "a meeting of the minds" on that issue. Allaf and Mu'allim were further distressed when the secretary stated that Asad had not explained his concept of peace in Geneva. I could tell by the expression on their faces that the thought of reporting to Damascus their failure to sway the secretary weighed heavily with them.

We all agreed to terminate this futile round and to recommence on February 15. By way of preparation, I was invited to see Christopher on February 4. In a four-year history of a close and intimate relationship and excellent personal relations between the Rabin and Peres governments and the Clinton administration, the late winter of 1994 stood out as a quietly acrimonious period. Christopher was angry and bitter. He doubted Rabin's "seriousness" with regard to Syria. Why was he given one new date after the other? Why was nothing happening? He felt used and taken advantage of. Why should something in the spirit of the hypothetical statement of August 1993 not be put on paper? Maybe the United States should be putting something on paper? I knew full well what Rabin's response would be. He would have been incensed by the administration's proclivity to overlook the fundamental elements of dealing with a party resorting to Asad's style of bargaining. He would have complained that the United States was acting as a mediator rather than in the agreed role of a facilitator, that it was corroding the Israeli position, that by giving Asad a direct affirmative Israeli promise, let alone a written position, all leverage on him would be lost. Moreover, by forsaking the ambiguity of his original position Rabin would lose his ability to maneuver between the pitfalls of Israel's domestic politics and the requirements of the peace process.

By the same token, if a candid exchange were to take place the secretary of state would probably have told the prime minister that the world's sole superpower, its president and secretary of state could not conceivably be an ordinary facilitator or go-between acting strictly within the terms set by two small states; that once the interests and prestige of the United States and its leadership were invested in a negotiation it would make its own judgments and take liberties in order to ensure that the mediation undertaken by the United States meet with success. Rabin knew this very well from his own experience and was willing to accept it, but he thought the mediation must not come prematurely, that it would best come at the negotiation's end in order to help the parties overcome the very last hurdles. Given the difference in the negotiating and bargaining styles of the two protagonists, any compromise formula tabled at this early phase was bound to cut more deeply into Israel's original position than would a comparable formula made at a later stage.

At this point it was not the ambassador's task to respond, even if he knew the answer. I traveled to Israel for thirty-six hours to convey to the prime minister the secretary's message and to describe his mood in graphic detail. Rabin listened carefully but was not about to change his position—phasing was at the core of his concept of an Israeli-Syrian settlement and of his understanding with Christopher the previous August. On February 15 I conveyed Rabin's reply to an unhappy Christopher. Rabin was not impressed by my report on the meeting—for Israel these were existential issues and not a matter of credibility, and he would insist on his position even at the risk of derailing the whole Israeli-Syrian track. A day later Rabin invited the American ambassador to Israel in order to convey a similar complaint and a similar message through him, as well.

My meetings with Allaf and Mu'allim were renewed on February 15. We met several times at the M Street site and in Ross's office, but the difficulties that had obstructed our talks in January remained unresolved. One novelty was the brief discussion of the visit to Syria by an Arab member of the Knesset, 'Abd al-Wahhab Darawsha. It began as an American idea—to have an Israeli Arab politician lead a delegation of Israeli Arabs to Syria to pay a condolence call on President Asad during the mourning period for his son Basel. The administration was also hoping that the visit would prove to be yet another step on the long road to Syrian-Israeli public diplomacy. Darawsha was an Arab nationalist but he was also a politician playing a role in Israel's political system. I proposed to Allaf that we deal with the visit during our meetings. His incredible response was that the visit "was not related to the peace process." In the event, Darawsha and his group were finally allowed to visit Syria provided they traveled on Egyptian (and not Israeli) passports and came by plane from Cairo (rather than by land through the Golan Heights). As an exercise in confidence building the visit was a glaring failure.

In late February 1994, then, the Israeli-Arab peace process was not faring very well. Israel's negotiation with Syria was stalemated, a breakthrough with Jordan was not yet in sight, and the Israeli-Palestinian negotiation over the implementation of the Oslo accords proceeded at a snail's pace through endless difficulties. This frail and halting process was dealt a nearly fatal blow when, on February 25, a Jewish zealot, Baruch Goldstein, perpetrated a massacre at the Tomb of the Patriarchs in Hebron, killing twenty-nine Palestinian worshipers. Ever since the signing of the Oslo accords the spectre of either lunatic or coldly calculated acts by Arabs or Israelis seeking to derail the fledgling reconciliation process was in the air. The campaign by the radical Islamic organizations Hamas and Islamic Jihad was yet to come. The Hebron massacre dealt a heavy blow to the peace process and delayed its progress, but failed to stop it altogether.

Rabin's visit to Washington in mid-March, grafted onto his address to the AIPAC policy conference, provided an opportunity for restarting the peace process. On March 15 he met with Secretary Christopher. The problem of getting Arafat back to the table was discussed first, but the bulk of the meeting was devoted to the Syrian track. Rabin and Christopher, having aired their disagreements through intermediaries, were now finally speaking directly to each other. Christopher complained about Rabin's failure to renew his "commitment." Rabin responded with the list of arguments he had used previously: he knew Asad very well and if he was given what he was after he wouldn't budge further; the Syrians expected the United States "to deliver" Israel; nothing had moved with the Egyptians and the Palestinians without a secret channel, and no progress with Syria would be made in the limelight; the Egyptians, too, in the late 1970s had seen procedure as a matter of substance, but they had been very forthcoming—they allowed Israeli visits much before Camp David; with Syria we had no real contact; the previous August Rabin had presented an integrated package that had its own logic and must not be disentangled.

The next day, March 16, the meeting with President Clinton took place. Rabin's presentation was similar to the one he had made to the secretary of state, but in the Oval Office he agreed, as expected, to a procedural concession. The United States and Israel were to put together two packages. One, addressing the timetable, phasing, and security issues, would then be presented by the United States to Syria in order to draw the Syrians out and have them present a counter package. The second would be a bilateral American-Israeli security package that would focus on the defense and security aid that the United States would be offering to Israel in the event of an Israeli-Syrian agreement. The president told the prime minister that at some point some Israeli would have to discuss the issue of withdrawal directly with some Syrian. The meeting thus ended in a compromise of sorts. The formulation chosen by President Clinton implied the administration's acceptance of Rabin's refusal to switch discussion of withdrawal from the hypothetical and indirect mode to an affirmative and direct one. Rabin for his part, by agreeing that the United States take his package and juxtapose it with a Syrian package, agreed in fact to a further erosion of his starting position, as he knew full well that the Syrians would counter with a "low bid" and the United States would seek to bridge the gap.

After Rabin's departure from Washington, Ross was dispatched to the Middle East to update Asad on the administration's discussion with Rabin and to help with the resumption of the Israeli-Palestinian negotiations that had been disrupted by the Hebron massacre. Ross's trip was also designed to prepare the ground for a visit to the region by the secretary of state, who planned to take part in the signing ceremony of the Israeli-Palestinian implementation agreement and to shuttle between Jerusalem and Damascus armed with the new latitude that emerged from Rabin's visit. The secretary's entourage was also to include a representative of the Pentagon in order to discuss the bilateral U.S.-Israeli security package.

In the event, the secretary's trip was delayed until the final days of April. The Israeli-Palestinian negotiations on the Gaza-Jericho agreement lingered, and the signing was finally set for May 4 in Cairo. In the meantime, Hamas stepped up its campaign and staged two terrorist attacks against Israeli civilians in the towns of Afula (where seven persons were killed on April 6) and Hadera (where five persons were killed on April 13). As the events of the next two years were to demonstrate so clearly, the strategy chosen by Hamas, the Islamic Jihad, and their sponsors proved to be terribly effective. Nothing served better to undermine the Israeli public's support for the government's peace policy than the sense of personal insecurity generated by terrorist attacks in Israel proper.

In anticipation of the resumption of a serious negotiation with Syria, Rabin spoke in public about his willingness to dismantle settlements on the Golan as part and parcel of peacemaking. He argued that Israel of the 1990s was different from the fledgling community and state of the late 1940s, when every settlement mattered.[1] This was, in fact, a far-reaching statement that ran against the original ethos of Israeli state formation and state building. Several generations of Israelis had grown up and acted on the belief that the extent of settlement determined the real boundaries of

the state. Rabin was now challenging this credo explicitly with regard to the Golan Heights and implicitly with regard to the West
Bank.

The statement resonated in Israel but not in Syria. The Baʿth
party paper's response was so dismissive that Christopher called
Foreign Minister Faruq al-Sharaʿ to complain about the disparity
between the Israeli and Syrian attitudes to public diplomacy.

The anticipation of an accelerated negotiation with Syria also
prompted a wave of leaks from the Israeli political system and bureaucracy. One headline quoted a policy planning paper written
in the Israeli Foreign Ministry that outlined a strategy for the negotiations predicated on "a working assumption of full Israeli withdrawal." Another journalist reported that a withdrawal plan had
been prepared at the Israeli General Staff, put on a map, and presented to Rabin.[2]

In the course of my negotiations with Syria several individuals
appeared on the scene to offer their good offices. Some of them
were self-serving or unsuitable for the task, but two of them proved
over the years to be reliable and accurate transmitters of messages.
Given Asad's absolute ban on any direct contact other than on
scheduled meetings, these channels proved useful in passing messages during idle periods. In the latter part of April 1994 the message they brought was very clear: the Syrians were averse to Rabin's
insistence on a relatively lengthy time frame and on phasing, and
were very much interested in telescoping the implementation. I
could well understand the Syrian position. Asad had disliked these
aspects of Rabin's position from the outset, and his original dislike
must have been compounded by the very passage of time. If he had
made the deal in August 1993 he would have had more than three
years before the Israeli elections scheduled for October 1996. If he
could negotiate the time frame down to under three years he
would be doing better than Sadat, and would also be able to get
his share before the Israeli elections. Stretching the implementation of his part of the deal across Israel's election date was too risky
for this very careful leader.

There was a paradox built into Asad's position, of course—the longer and harder he bargained the less likely he was to obtain his goal within the remaining time frame. Asad must have been aware of this paradox, and he probably expected to resolve it by pressing even harder for a swifter implementation of our prospective agreement.

APRIL TO JULY 1994

In late April a new phase in the negotiations began that lasted into the third week of July. As April drew to a close, it became clear that the Gaza-Jericho agreement was about to be signed. This meant that Rabin's commitment to the administration that he would renew the serious negotiation with Syria at that point had to be honored. It also meant that King Hussein was forced to make his own hard decision. Since September 13 he had been able to postpone these decisions on the assumption that the Israeli-Palestinian negotiations might yet collapse. But in early May Yasser Arafat's arrival in Gaza and Jericho became a reality, and the king decided to move ahead with Israel. In April he established to his own satisfaction that debt relief and limited security aid were feasible if he made a full-fledged peace with Israel. On May 28 a secret meeting took place between the king and Rabin in London, and the ground was prepared for further progress. From that point on two very different negotiations were conducted by Israel with Jordan and Syria. Rabin never concealed the preference he assigned to the prospect of arriving first at a peace treaty with Jordan, but he kept his commitment to the Clinton administration with regard to Syria. Yet Asad's determination to make only a very particular agreement with Israel and his negotiating style were chiefly responsible for the failure to make comparable progress on the Israeli-Syrian track.

Between late April and mid-May 1994, Secretary Christopher and his team made two trips to the Middle East. As part of the first trip Christopher participated in the Israeli-Palestinian signing ceremony in Cairo on May 4, but his main purpose was to revive and move forward the Israeli-Syrian track. The trip began in Israel. On April 28, he saw Rabin twice in the Ministry of Defense, first in a comparatively large forum and later in a two-on-two meeting. Rabin's presentation in the larger meeting focused on three major components of the Israeli package: the time frame, the phasing, and the security arrangements. At this point the American visitors must have been familiar with the prime minister's arguments, but he also made two new points. For one thing, he argued that peace with Egypt was tested and implemented over a period of four and a half years (November 1977 to April 1982). This was far more than Asad had in mind, but six months less than Rabin's original five years. He also elaborated on the three phases of implementation he had in mind. The first phase, nine months after the signing, would involve a limited withdrawal; no Israeli settlement would be affected (although a Druze village could), and Syria would have to offer normalization. A second phase would take place after eighteen or twenty-four months, and a third phase would be withdrawal to a line to be agreed upon.

Since Rabin mentioned the prospect of withdrawal from a Druze village in front of a comparatively large group of Israelis, it did not take long for the story to reach the Israeli media and make the headlines under the title "Majdal Shams First" (Majdal Shams being the largest Druze village on the Golan Heights).

In the aftermath of that meeting the U.S. peace team, reinforced by General Michael Ryan, the special assistant to the chairman of the Joint Chiefs of Staff, went to a meeting with General Ehud Baraq, Israel's chief of staff. Baraq's presentation consisted of two parts. He began with his own view of peacemaking with Syria. Baraq argued that the main purpose of the security arrangements was to minimize the danger of a surprise attack. In order to minimize this danger Baraq proposed that Syria's (and, with some modification, Israel's) territory be divided into four categories of demilitarization, reduced deployment, and mutual inspection and confidence building. He explained that from a professional military perspective he had to say that a defensible border with Syria was on the Golan, but that it was up to the political level to make the final decision. He then proceeded to describe the security aid package that Israel would be hoping to obtain from the United States in the event of a settlement with Syria.

Later in the day Christopher, accompanied by Ross, came for a second meeting with Rabin. He wanted a better understanding of the first phase in Rabin's plan, and wondered why the prime minister insisted on a five-year time frame with Syria when Begin's agreement with Sadat was implemented in three years. Rabin's answer was that, given Sadat's visit to Jerusalem in November 1977, Begin had four and a half years of normalization. We were clearly in the midst of a negotiation-cum-mediation and the bargaining had begun.

On May 2 we met again. Christopher and Ross were back from their meetings in Damascus. Before giving us his account of the Syrian counter package, the secretary spoke to the prime minister privately for a few minutes. In Damascus Asad had told him that from his point of view full withdrawal from the Golan Heights had to be to the lines of June 4, 1967, and not to the international border between Syria and Palestine.

The issue had appeared occasionally on the agenda of our negotiations during the previous eighteen months. As will be recalled, the 1948 war ended with Syria in control of some territories west of the international border. These territories were demilitarized as part of the 1949 Syrian-Israeli armistice agreement. Over time Syria took actual possession of some of these territories, most notably of the al-Hamma enclave near the meeting point of the Israeli, Syrian, and Jordanian borders. Al-Hamma and its thermal springs had by now been developed as a major tourism site, but in strategic terms the most significant repercussion of the Syrian claim was the Syrian presence established before 1967 on the shore of Lake Tiberias (the international border had deliberately been set by the British at ten meters east of the shoreline).

When Allaf mentioned al-Hamma in the course of our original sessions, I told him that he should not be raising the issue for his own good reasons. After all, Syria relied heavily on Security Council Resolution 242 and particularly on the "inadmissibility of acquisition of territory by force." By making a claim to al-Hamma, a piece of mandatory Palestine taken over by the Syrian army, they were undermining that very principle. Allaf, needless to say, was not impressed and his delegation's international lawyer crossed swords with our expert over the legal status of al-Hamma. The ongoing Israeli-Syrian argument is enriched every so often by Yasser Arafat's curious tendency to claim Palestinian ownership of the enclave.

With regard to the June 4 lines, it is true that the Syrian negotiators, other Syrian spokesmen, and the Syrian media demanded regularly that Israel withdraw to them. At the same time, it would also be true to say that the accent of the Syrian demand during the nearly first two years of the negotiations was on "full withdrawal" and not on withdrawal to the "lines of June 4, 1967." Asad's insistence on Israeli withdrawal to the lines of June 4, 1967, rather than to the international boundary can be explained on two levels. For one thing, Asad needed to show that in the event of a settlement with Israel he would have achieved a better deal than Sadat. Otherwise, how could he explain a seventeen-year delay in making a deal that could have been made in 1977–1978. By being able to point to his ability to achieve more than Israel's withdrawal to the international border, Asad would not be, in his own eyes, vulnerable to such a potential charge.

Beyond this lay Asad's long-standing campaign and tirade against the illegitimacy of the political order and boundaries imposed on the region by the colonial British and French authorities in the aftermath of World War I. Very few secretaries of state or other dignitaries passed through Asad's office without hearing a lengthy thesis about the Sykes-Picot agreements. The international line between mandatory Syria and mandatory Palestine was drawn by the British and the French in 1923, and as such embodied everything that Asad had fought against since his early days in the Ba'th party. If Asad were to get a settlement with Israel, he would rather have it on a basis detached from the colonial order and era. Four years earlier, Saddam Hussein had railed against the artificial boundaries imposed by the European colonial powers when he was trying to justify his invasion and annexation of Kuwait. Asad had joined the United States and the conservative Arab states in restoring that old order. But when it came to his own adjustment to the new reality, he was still trying to show that he had not changed his line but was merely adjusting it to new circumstances.

During Christopher's discussion of Rabin's gambit with Asad on August 4, 1993, Asad asked him whether Israel had any claims in the Golan. We did not think that we had any claims to Syrian territory and we naturally saw al-Hamma and the demilitarized areas as sovereign Israeli territory. We now realized that in August 1993 rather than make an explicit demand for the June 4, 1967, lines Asad had resorted to this oblique reference. Now, nine months later, we wondered why Asad chose this particular moment, when the negotiations were about to be resumed in earnest, to turn it into a make-or-break issue. Rabin felt reinforced in his view that Asad was not interested in a genuine give-and-take. He suspected that Asad was more interested in obtaining a clear Israeli commitment to a withdrawal from the Golan than in coming to an agreement. He saw the fresh insistence on this additional "clarity" as yet another attempt to nail down the "commitment" Asad was after. His immediate response to Christopher was, accordingly, negative.

Rabin's suspicions were further reinforced as we listened to the description of Syria's counter package. The Syrian response had been prepared in writing and was read to Christopher. To begin with, the Syrians threw the notion of a Druze village as a significant component of the first phase of an Israeli withdrawal plan out of court. They argued—quite correctly—that by allowing the story to leak to the media Israel undermined the value of the prospective concession, but they seemed to have been moved by a different consideration. "Majdal Shams First" was uncomfortably reminiscent of "Gaza First"—early withdrawal from Gaza, a key element of the Oslo accords—and any resemblance to Arafat's agreement with Israel had to be avoided.

Syria's package was clearly conceived as a first step in a lengthy bargaining process. It was predicated on a demand for full Israeli withdrawal from the territories captured from Syria in June 1967.

Asad's time frame remained six months. He could accept some of
Israel's general principles for the security arrangements, but continued to insist on "equal footing" and "on both sides." He saw
Baraq's notion of dividing the whole of Syria's territory into four
categories as far-reaching. He had in mind fourteen kilometers of
demilitarization (seven on each side of the line) and an additional
area of limited deployment. He was opposed to early-warning stations in time of peace. "Normal peaceful relations" were to be implemented in stages. Upon signing the agreement, the state of war
and the secondary and tertiary boycott would be terminated.
Diplomatic relations would be announced earlier but implemented only after a comprehensive settlement (with Lebanon and
Jordan in addition to Syria) was achieved.

Rabin said to Christopher that the Syrian package failed to respond to the three fundamental principles of the Israeli package.
It was not a matter of detail, and he did not intend to start bargaining over the specifics of the Syrian response.

A sharp exchange ensued between Rabin and Christopher.
Rabin charged that Asad was in fact trying to undermine Arafat's
position in the May 4 signing ceremony in Cairo, particularly by
raising the issue of comprehensiveness. Christopher warned Rabin
against creating "a setback" in the negotiations. He clearly expected Rabin to enter the bargaining process and did not think
much of the distinction between the international border and the
lines of June 4. Rabin attached a great deal of significance to that
distinction, as well as to Syria's very insistence on it and to Asad's
refusal to tie his demand for withdrawal to the fundamentals of Israel's package. The meeting ended in disagreement. This was a
classic instance of the stark difference between the perspective of
a small state holding on to every square inch of land and any iota
of dignity and that of a vast superpower seeking compromise and
agreement and treating the petty concerns of the local parties with
a mixture of impatience and condescension.

An important insight into the Clinton administration's view of
the Israeli-Syrian track at that phase is afforded by an address that
the national security adviser, Anthony Lake, delivered at the Wash-

ington Institute in May 1994. Lake described Syria and her role in the peace process as "the key to regional stability":

> Given these difficulties, we have decided to press ahead with efforts to achieve a breakthrough to a comprehensive peace this year. A decisive Syrian-Israeli agreement would allow Jordan and Lebanon to resolve their differences with Israel in a short order. Full normalization of relations between Israel and the Arab states of the Maghreb and the Gulf would quickly follow. In short, the logjam would be broken. An Israel-Syria peace would thus shore up the agreement between Israel and the PLO and greatly advance U.S. efforts to widen the circle of peacemakers, bolster the network of Middle East moderation, and construct a bastion against backlash states.
>
> Syria plays a critical role in the wider sweep of regional peace. Historically, its alliance with Iran and support for rejectionist groups have given the forces of extremism a vital base in the Middle East. By invoking Arab nationalism, Syria has given those forces an important claim on legitimacy. Syria has used its influence both for ill, as when it rejected Sadat's peace with Israel, and for good, as when Damascus joined the Gulf War against Saddam Hussein and, most importantly, when it entered into direct bilateral negotiations with Israel.

He then continued by describing the far-reaching impact of President Clinton's meeting with Asad in Geneva:

> Thus, when President Assad took the significant step of announcing in Geneva with President Clinton that Syria had made, in his words, a "strategic choice for peace" with Israel, his nation's erstwhile extremist allies quickly grew very nervous. Palestinian rejectionist leaders, fearful that they would lose their bases in Lebanon and Syria, went off to Libya in search of new havens. Hezbollah leaders argued how best to pursue an extremist agenda in an era of Israeli-Lebanese peace. Iranian officials hurriedly visited Damascus but apparently left empty-handed, and when they got home, the Iranian clergy began criticizing the leadership for failing to prevent the emerging isolation of their nation.[3]

Christopher returned to the region on May 15. He traveled first to Damascus, and on May 16 in the evening came to see Rabin. He had obtained a Syrian acceptance of the notion of "interfacing," and clearly expected an Israeli "clarification" on the June 4 issue. Rabin declined, and another sharp exchange ensued. During the next two days, through an additional series of meetings, tempers subsided and Ross left for Damascus with a number of compromise formulae. None of them worked.

Not much happened on the Syrian track during the latter part of May and in June. Dennis Ross and Martin Indyk met separately with Ambassador Mu'allim and with me to discuss a compromise formula, but to no avail. Christopher kept postponing his planned visit to the Middle East, and away from the public eye progress was being made in Israel's negotiation with Jordan. A meeting I had with Christopher on June 29 to discuss the Syrian track provided an opportunity to update him, at Rabin's request, on the prospects of a breakthrough with Jordan. Indeed in early July, although the king was still not ready for full peace, he was willing to come quite close to it and to announce the end of belligerency with Israel. The promises of the United States in early May and the understanding reached with Rabin later that month were two important considerations. But the king was also losing patience with Syria. Asad expected him to wait for Syria and not to conclude peace before Damascus did, but the king was not willing to wait forever. The successful implementation of the Gaza-Jericho agreement and the emergence of a new reality in the West Bank provided another important incentive.

During the following three weeks or so, preparations were completed for the signing of the July 25 Washington Declaration. It is in that context that Secretary Christopher's trip to the region from July 18–21 should be seen. The meeting with Rabin on July 19 began with a discussion of the Jordanian track. The secretary reaffirmed the president's promise to King Hussein, but was really interested in what the prime minister had to say with regard to Syria. Rabin summed up his position under ten headings. The one new element in his presentation was the offer to let Syria have an early-warning station on Israeli soil in return for agreeing to let Israel keep her station on Mt. Hermon.

Christopher then returned to the June 4 issue. Could he give Asad "clarity with regard to the end of the line"? By now Rabin had clearly decided that he could actually fit the issue into the paradigm built on August 3 as long as it was a "clarification" and not a "commitment," and told Christopher that he could tell Asad that this was his "impression."

On July 21 Christopher and his team returned from Damascus. At a small meeting in Rabin's office he told us that Asad knew that he had no commitment from Rabin but that he was willing to proceed on the basis of the clarification. Asad also moved ahead in the bargaining game. He was now willing to have the deal implemented in twelve months and in two phases of six months each. At the end of the first phase he was still offering little by way of normalization. He wanted diplomatic relations to be implemented only in the aftermath of a comprehensive settlement, comprehensiveness being now limited to Syria and Lebanon; what else could he say after Jordan had clearly decided to follow the PLO's example and make her own deal with Israel? Ambassador Walid Mu'allim could start meeting with me on August 1.

Christopher proposed to come again on August 1, but Rabin took exception. He wanted time to savor the political benefits of the unfolding peacemaking with Jordan and to see what the more intimate negotiation in the "ambassadors' channel" in Washington would produce.

THE "AMBASSADORS' CHANNEL"

The "ambassadors' channel" was inaugurated on July 29, 1994, and functioned for nearly a year. During the first three months Ambassador Mu'allim and I negotiated the full gamut of the Israeli-Syrian agenda. As of early November 1994 the security issue came to dominate the talks, both in the two meetings between the chiefs

of staff of the Israeli and Syrian armed forces, and in our negotiation of the "non-paper" on "the aims and principles of the security
arrangements."

The time frame for the first phase of my meetings with Walid
Mu'allim was defined by Israel's parallel negotiation with Jordan.
When the final breakthrough had occurred and the parties were
ready to sign a peace treaty it was decided that, unlike the two previous major signing ceremonies, the signing of Israel's second
peace treaty with an Arab state would take place in the region.
After an internal debate within the Clinton administration it was
decided that the president, after taking an active part in the
Jordanian-Israeli ceremony, would also visit Damascus. In addition
to mollifying Asad, now left behind by a second former Arab partner, the visit was designed to move the Israeli-Syrian negotiation
forward. Asad's reaction to Jordan's decision to break ranks with
him and sign separately with Israel was similar to his reaction to the
PLO's decision in August 1993. Privately he was furious, but publicly he and his spokesmen and media combined acquiescence
with subtle criticism. As long as he chose to stay in the peace
process he could not launch an all-out assault on an Arab party that
had made peace with Israel.

For Asad this was also an opportunity to engage in a brand of
public diplomacy that was acceptable to him and to curry favor
with Washington. Syrian television did show the signing ceremonies with Jordan, and did convey a message to the Syrian
public that Arab-Israeli peacemaking was progressing and might
soon affect Syria. To their American interlocutors the Syrians
would argue time and again that they were helpful rather than an-
tagonistic to Israeli-Jordanian peace, and deserved credit and
remuneration.

By this time a pattern had crystallized whereby Mu'allim and I
would explore and establish the limits of our position, and an
American official (Secretary Christopher twice and Ross once)
would travel to the region and try to get the two principal decision
makers (Rabin and Asad) to make new decisions and to move
closer to the still nonexistent line of compromise.

The first meetings between Mu'allim and myself established both the merits and the limitations of the new Israeli-Syrian channel. Mu'allim was a good counterpart. He was smart, knowledgeable, creative, and interested in coming to an agreement. Of course he was a Syrian diplomat and the agreement he was after was tailored by Asad and not acceptable to us, but he clearly believed in what he was doing. For that matter I was not perturbed by the fact that he, like Asad, was primarily interested in transforming his country's relationship with Washington, and that his acceptance of the notion of peace with Israel was a necessary prelude to that transformation and not the product of a change of heart with regard to us. If a mutually acceptable compromise could be found and an agreement could be made, the change of heart would follow. This was precisely why we wanted to spread the implementation over time, so that the depth of Syria's commitment to the new relationship could be tested. Rabin's insistence on this element and Asad's determination to telescope Rabin's time frame and phases into one compact stage were, indeed, one of the chief bones of contention in our negotiation.

Mu'allim had a good working relationship with both Asad and Foreign Minister Shara' and his success in Washington clearly built up his position in Damascus. Our negotiations were confidential and unpublicized, and we could pursue them practically free from the scrutiny of the media that had bedeviled the negotiations between the two Israeli and Syrian delegations. The smaller format and the informal environment (mostly Ross's living room or terrace in suburban Washington) facilitated a freer discussion. And despite the presence of two Americans—Dennis Ross and Martin Indyk, and subsequently Ross and Mark Parris—Mu'allim and I were not playing to the galleries or seeking an American endorsement of our respective positions, but actually talking to one another. The atmosphere was comfortable but not free; every word counted and would be used at some future point. The meetings had their lighter moments, as well. Mu'allim is a heavy smoker. When we began our meetings in the summer we could sit on the Ross's porch and Mu'allim could smoke at will. When fall came and we moved into the living room it became a question of sacrificing either Ross's principles or Mu'allim's habits. Mu'allim won.

After holding several meetings Mu'allim and I realized we were both constrained by the rules of the game. A "walk in the woods" is designed to facilitate an open, informal, nonbinding exchange of ideas and positions. It ought to enable the parties to understand each other's bottom line in order to enable the ultimate decision makers at home to determine whether a deal can be made. It can also serve as an arena for a comparatively free exploration of new ideas if a deadlock is reached. But "the ambassadors' channel" was not "a walk in the woods." For one thing, all of us took notes. None of us envisaged at the time a controversy along the lines of the Syrian-Israeli debate that broke out in the summer of 1996, but the prospect of a future disagreement and juxtapositioning of versions was on our minds.

I always assumed that a Syrian emissary representing Asad—be it Allaf, Mu'allim or, later, General Hikmat Shihabi—would not stray from Asad's strict instructions and meticulous definition of Syria's position on the key issues at stake. But in a much more benevolent fashion Rabin controlled our side of the negotiation. I had a considerable degree of tactical freedom and maneuverability, but on the fundamental issues of the negotiation—withdrawal, the security arrangements, the time frame—there were very clear red lines drawn by Rabin that I never crossed. Foreign Minister Shimon Peres expressed his criticism of these discussions by stating, often in my presence, that the negotiations ought to be conducted by a cabinet member, "because ministers can make mistakes while ambassadors may not." This was a polite way of suggesting that if one wanted a breakthrough on the Syrian track comparable to the one that had occurred in Oslo, only a member of the cabinet who could defy Rabin's guidelines should be entrusted with the Syrian negotiation. I was aware of the criticism voiced in that vein by some of Peres's aides as well as by some of our American colleagues, who sometimes became exasperated with Rabin's style and were hoping that I would be willing to exceed my brief. I never had the slightest intention of doing that. My work was based on total mutual trust with Rabin, and I was determined to keep it that way.

The combined effect of the channel's format, Mu'allim's prudence, and my caution was to limit the scope of the new negotiation. No molds were broken. What we did manage to accomplish was a much better presentation and exploration of our respective packages, to understand and present our outlooks in a much clearer fashion, and to gain much deeper insights into each other's position. I began our first meeting by explaining that, as in the past, I did not intend to discuss the territorial issue. We would have to come to agreement or understanding on the other "three legs of the table" before we could deal directly with the territorial issue. Mu'allim was not surprised and did not protest, and went directly into Asad's most crucial other concern—limiting the time frame. He argued that the longer it took to implement the agreement, the more likely we were to encounter opposition or to become mired in other issues. He also offered a tradeoff—Syria would not grant Israel the three-year time frame that Egypt did, but it would offer the key to the region. In contradiction to the separate and beleaguered peace that Sadat had made with Begin, Asad could provide the key to a comprehensive settlement.

Prior to our departure for the region on August 5 to take part in Christopher's visit, we met four more times in Washington. Mu'allim continued to argue against the notion of implementing the agreement over five years and in three phases. We also reverted to the familiar argument over the security arrangements. Mu'allim made an apparent concession by dropping "equal footing," but he immediately undid it by demanding that the security arrangements be "equal . . . in size, quantity, and quality and in range." He also put forth a whole series of arguments in support of his position: Damascus is closer to the border than Tel Aviv; when peace prevails Israel will not need the security arrangements; Syria has an excellent record of keeping her commitments.

I took advantage of the new channel in order to seek a better understanding of Asad's concept of normalization. Asad had told the Americans that "normal peaceful relations" would include "passage of people and goods according to Syria's laws and regulations." This could be either an innocuous formulation or coded language for a very limited level of normalization. A peace treaty could open Syria in theory to Israeli tourists, but a strict application of the country's "laws and regulations" could turn the treaty's text into a dead letter. After fifteen years of "cold peace" with Egypt we knew full well how this could be accomplished. Allaf in 1993 and Mu'allim with greater conviction in his voice were telling me that if we did the right thing we could enjoy a "warm peace" with Syria. But now that I had the opportunity to explore this more freely, I was doubtful that our Syrian interlocutors had thought seriously and concretely about a "warm peace" with Israel.

At the end of the first week in August, Christopher and the peace team made a brief trip to Israel and Syria. Rabin received the secretary of state on August 6 and opened the meeting by expressing his satisfaction with the new channel. When asked to reciprocate for the concessions made by Asad in July, Rabin agreed to two concessions of his own—the time frame could be shorter than five years, and Baraq's notion of four categories of territory would be taken off the table. When asked by Christopher about his projected timetable for the negotiations with Syria, Rabin replied that he was hoping "to accomplish something with Syria" within six months, but in the Middle East there was no telling when it came to timetables. This was Rabin's way of telling the secretary of state that should the unfolding final negotiation with Jordan lead to full-fledged peace, it would take precedence over an intensive negotiation with Syria.

Although the secretary was quite anxious to accelerate the pace of the Israeli-Syrian negotiation, Asad provided him with no new concessions during the August 7 meeting in Damascus. Asad did agree that Mu'allim and I tinker with new ideas, and did accept the notion that at the right time we would be joined by senior military officers to discuss the security arrangements.

Mu'allim and I renewed our meetings on August 25. September was around the corner, and in September Syria's Foreign Minister

Faruq al-Shara' was scheduled to arrive in New York for the UN's General Assembly. A visit to Washington by the foreign minister of a state included in the State Department's terrorism and drug lists was not to be expected. But given the priority assigned by the administration to the Syrian-Israeli negotiation and Shara''s critical role in that negotiation, the visit became a matter of course. The "ambassadors' channel" afforded a unique opportunity to inject a significant dose of public diplomacy into Shara''s program. A meeting with his Israeli counterpart was still not feasible, but what about interviews to the Israeli media, meetings with Jewish leaders, and a meeting with at least one family of an Israeli MIA?

Yet another lengthy discussion of the security arrangements failed to move us from our respective entrenched positions. Mu'allim then argued that there was no point in having the senior military join us when the gap was so wide, while I maintained that this was precisely the reason for expediting their arrival. Our exchange reflected the very different perspectives from which we approached the idea of a meeting between senior representatives of our military. Mu'allim and his superiors saw it as essentially a concession to their American interlocutors, a confidence building measure, a procedural step of great significance that warranted a reciprocal substantive concession by Israel. We, of course, were not blind to the symbolic value of such a meeting, but I was primarily interested in the practical value of the encounter. As the experience of conflict resolution and peacemaking with Egypt taught us, the military establishments of the two parties had to make their own peace and come to an agreement on the nature of the security regime that would be constituted between our countries. Rabin and Asad happened to have been former senior officers and leaders of the defense establishments of Israel and Syria, and they could have dealt with the issues themselves, but a meeting between them was not likely to occur any time soon. Mu'allim and I could wax long about "equal footing" and "sense of security," but in order to break the ice a candid exchange between authoritative military experts had to take place.

I thought specifically about the proximity of Damascus to the

Golan Heights. It clearly weighed heavily with Asad and his men. A significant force had to be kept around Damascus both in order to protect the regime and as a hedge against a potential future conflict with us. But how large did that force have to be so as not to pose a threat to us? And how large a force could Syria maintain in the Bekaa Valley in Lebanon without posing a similar threat? And how large or small would the Israeli force stationed in the north of the country have to be in order to allay Syria's own fears and anxieties? I could envisage a senior Syrian general and an Israeli counterpart exploring these issues after they had warmed up to one another. This would not be easy, but without it I could not imagine a resolution of the crucial security dimension of this conflict.

Mu'allim and I devoted a large part of our meeting to a discussion of "the interface" or, in more mundane language, the degree of normalization that Syria would offer Israel as withdrawal was being implemented in phases. Asad had accepted the principle, but the application was evidently difficult for him. Rabin's original position, it will be recalled, was that at the end of the first phase, after the implementation of a limited withdrawal, full normalization, symbolized by full diplomatic relations, would be given. Asad, according to Mu'allim, was adamant in his opposition to any form of diplomatic representation before Israel's withdrawal was completed. And as for the rationale of Rabin's position—that Israel needed to "test" the new relationship before implementing a significant withdrawal—Syria found the very terminology patronizing and offensive: "you are not teachers and we are not pupils."

I raised two specific questions with regard to the first phase of implementation. What would Syria's position be with regard to other Arab states establishing diplomatic relations with Israel and, more specifically, how would it view the establishment of full diplomatic relations between Israel and Lebanon? It so happened that Rabin had spoken of implementing the first phase with Syria within nine months and, in a different context, of completing a peace process with Lebanon over a period of nine months (six months for the Lebanese army to take charge in south Lebanon and pacify it, and three months for negotiating a peace treaty).

Mu'allim could not answer these questions on his own authority, and told me that he would have to consult with Damascus. Before too long he had an answer. If Arab states were to ask Syria about diplomatic relations with Israel at the end of the first phase of an Israeli-Syrian settlement, they would be given a positive answer. With regard to Lebanon, as long as the agreements with Syria and Lebanon were simultaneous and on the assumption that the time frame for Israel and Syria was one year, Damascus would have no problem with the establishment of diplomatic relations between Israel and Lebanon after nine months.

As a vehicle for obtaining specific answers to very specific questions our channel was clearly functioning well. It proved less effective for exploring some of the more complex issues that were on Rabin's mind. What kind of a relationship could Israel expect to have with Syria once peace was in place? What about Syria's strategic relationship with Iran? What could Israel expect Syria to do about her relationship with Hizballah in Lebanon and the ten rejectionist organizations headquartered in Damascus? And what policies would Syria pursue toward the Israeli-Palestinian final status talks once they began in 1996? Raising these issues entailed an interesting dilemma. We could not expect too much from the discussion of such delicate matters at this phase. From all I knew about Asad, he, speaking through his emissary, would be elliptical, vague, and indirect. He would seek to embarrass us by putting us in the awkward position of a blunt stranger gracelessly moving a heavy foot in an environment that cherishes subtlety and allusion. And yet we felt entitled to clear and explicit answers to legitimate questions when we were the ones required to take risks.

I decided not to raise the Palestinian issue at that point. It had been difficult to remove the formal linkage, and it made no sense to revive the issue. Now the informal linkages would have to be explored later. But I did ask about Iran and Hizballah, and the response was not surprising. The Iranians spoke to the Syrians about the negotiations and about their relationship with the United States. They were critical of the policy but were also certain that it was bound to fail. They told the Syrians that they would not obstruct the policy, on the assumption that it would fail anyway. This clearly was not a satisfactory answer. The reality of Syrian-Iranian relations was more complex, and if our negotiations were to proceed successfully a Syrian-Iranian crisis could be anticipated. Israel would not move on without a genuine crackdown on Hizballah in south Lebanon. Washington (Congress more than the administration) would not normalize relations with Damascus before the Syrian-Iranian nexus was seriously addressed. Asad may have actually been hoping to become a bridge builder between Washington and Tehran, but if he did, he chose not to tell us about it.

With regard to Lebanon and Hizballah the response was, indeed, indirect. Lebanon, in the official Syrian version, is a sovereign country and Syria could not make commitments on its behalf. But if Asad made peace along one front, he would not allow anyone, Hizballah included, to disrupt or challenge the peace elsewhere.

On September 19 Ross and Indyk traveled to Damascus and on September 20 and 21 they conducted talks in Israel. Asad told them of his decision that when in the United States Shara' would grant an interview to Israeli television. Rabin, during his meeting with the two, was preoccupied with the Jordanian negotiations and with the prospect of bringing them to an early closure. For the first time he told his American interlocutors explicitly that it was important to ascertain that Syria would not obstruct Jordan's progress toward a peace treaty.

Rabin spoke in a similar vein to Secretary Christopher when the latter came to see him on October 9. He also spoke at length about the swelling opposition in Israel to any settlement with Syria that involved a massive withdrawal. It was not difficult for the secretary and his entourage to see the ubiquitous posters and placards announcing "The People with the Golan." But there was a less visible initiative in the political arena, supported by at least two Labor members of the Knesset, to tie Rabin's hands by requiring a special majority in the Knesset and in a prospective referendum to approve any agreement with Syria (see an elaboration of this issue in Chapter Six below). In the smaller meeting with Rabin, Christopher raised the idea of an American written summary of the negotiations thus far as a way of moving them forward. Rabin evaded. He was afraid of a premature bridging proposal, and he was not interested in a U.S. attempt at putting anything concerning withdrawal on paper.

The secretary met separately with Peres. Peres raised the Syrian issue and told Christopher that this had been coordinated with Rabin. The focus of Peres's presentation was economic cooperation between Israel and Syria in the Golan in the aftermath of a settlement.

A day later in Damascus, Asad, like Rabin, rejected the notion of a U.S. written summary. Asad, from his vantage point, saw the United States as too close to Israel and suspected that an American written summary would tilt toward the Israeli position. Asad agreed to a meeting between Israeli and Syrian high-ranking military officers, and did not respond when Christopher reported of the conversation with Peres. He then raised a new Syrian idea: how about implementing the agreement in one fell swoop? He was evidently worried by the passage of time.

Back in Israel the secretary tried to extract from Rabin a concession that would match Asad's goodwill with regard to the military talks and Shara''s interview. Rabin rejected offhand the idea of a one-phase settlement as well as the Syrian attempt to separate the establishment of diplomatic relations from the end of belligerency. These were the very foundations of his original package. But Christopher could tell Asad that "there will be some give" with regard to the time frame. Rabin promised that during his anticipated visit to Washington in November he would be more specific in this matter. But prior to that visit Christopher would come again to the region. He was definitely going to take part in the first Middle East regional economic conference in Casablanca on October 30, and should there be a Jordanian-Israeli signing ceremony he would participate, as well.

The accelerated activity on the Israeli-Syrian track produced in September 1994 an unusual spate of public diplomacy. Rabin set the stage on September 8 by making an authoritative statement in the cabinet meeting in response to media speculation on the issue of Israeli withdrawal from the Golan. The prime minister began by saying that "there was no agreement with or commitment to either the U.S. or Syria regarding the extent, depth and duration of withdrawal in the Golan Heights." But he continued with an explicit and affirmative presentation of his position: "Israel accepted the principle of withdrawal, linked to a process of normalization of her relations with Syria in the following fashion: During the first phase a very small withdrawal will take place . . . paralleled by a full normalization of relations. That normalization will be tested during three years without an additional withdrawal. . . . Only then and after a successful testing of a normalization will the next step be discussed . . . as has been mentioned in the past—withdrawal is conditional on a referendum."[4]

Rabin was walking a political tightrope. He was acutely aware of the mounting opposition in the Labor party's activist wing to an agreement with Syria that included a massive withdrawal. As he told Warren Christopher, a group of two to six Labor Knesset members could at any given moment join forces with the right-wing opposition and "handcuff" his Syrian policy through legislation. He knew that any affirmative statement of his on the negotiations with Syria could play into their hands. But he also realized that the negotiations with Syria had to be put in context, that without providing a context he would be exposed to the effects of unfettered speculation whenever a dramatic or significant development concerning the Syrian talks took place.

On October 3, speaking on the opening day of the Knesset's fall session, Rabin delivered a major address on the peace process. He devoted a significant portion of his speech to his most comprehensive public pronouncement ever on the negotiations with Syria and on the issue of the Golan. Rabin addressed the Golan settlers directly, and complimented them on the mission they performed and the accomplishments they had accumulated during the previous twenty-seven years. But, he argued, that mission was warranted as long as Syria refused to make peace with Israel. Syria had now accepted the principle of peace with Israel. Important gaps still separated Syria's position on the core issues of the negotiation from the Israeli position, but it was the government's duty to find out whether peace could be made. The "days of there's no one to talk to," and "we are waiting for a phone call from the Arabs," Rabin said, were over. He looked at the Golan Heights strictly through a security lens and any agreement with Syria would have to meet that test, but it was his aim to supplement security with peace, to avoid the next war and its price.[5]

Coincidentally, Hafiz al-Asad had spoken at some length about the peace process with Israel at the opening session of the Syrian parliament three weeks earlier. He criticized Jordan and the PLO, albeit mildly, for breaking ranks and making separate and unsatisfactory deals with Israel. Peace, he repeated, was Syria's strategic choice. Syria's concept of peace had been thoroughly thought through and was crystal clear. It had to be a just peace predicated on restoration of land and rights. An unbalanced peace could not be stable: peace had its "objective requirements," but it was dangerous to load onto them additional, extraneous issues. Asad expressed disappointment with Israel's failure to meet the requirements of "international legitimacy" in the Washington talks, and suggested that his real dialogue was being conducted with President Clinton and Secretary Christopher.[6]

It was, indeed, in response to the administration's pressure that Asad instructed his foreign minister to engage in public diplomacy. In early September, during a visit to London, he answered questions posed by Israeli journalists. Later that month, when he came to Washington, he met with a group of Jewish leaders, answered questions by Israeli journalists in a Middle Eastern forum, and culminated his efforts by granting a lengthy interview to Israeli television for its major weekend news program on October 7. This was the most ambitious attempt to have the Syrian leadership try to reach out to the Israeli public, and unfortunately it fell flat on its face. Shara' granted the interview grudgingly and spoke about peace and reconciliation without apparent conviction. The formal, cold spirit of Asad's speech set the tone for an interview that should have been characterized by warmth and charm. Israel's political establishment and population were not swept off their feet.

Three weeks later, on October 3, Syria's foreign minister presented his government's statement to the forty-ninth session of the UN General Assembly. The bulk of the statement dealt with Syria's position in the peace process and it contained no surprises; it echoed, often repeated, the formulations used by Asad in the speech he had delivered on September 9. But the interesting part of Shara'̔'s speech preceded the segment relating to the peace process, and was devoted to a criticism of Israel's refusal to sign the Non-Proliferation Treaty and to put her nuclear installations under the inspection of the Atomic Energy Agency. The issue of Israel's nuclear capabilities and policies was raised in the context of the debate on the indefinite extension of the Non-Proliferation Treaty that was to become a major bone of contention in Washington's relations with Cairo during the next few months.[7]

Syria allied herself with Egypt in this matter, but the issue went deeper than that. We had noticed earlier in our negotiations with Syria that our interlocutors had a fully thought-out position on this issue. Syria's position in 1992–1993 was not unlike that of Egypt in the 1970s: it was unhappy with Israel's nuclear potential but was not about to shoot itself in the foot and raise this as a major issue before regaining territory it was after. When the issue came up during one of our sessions with Allaf and his delegation, our impression was that the Syrians decided to define it as a "regional issue," tie it to the work of the multilateral "working group on arms control and regional security," and in this fashion establish a linkage between full normalization and Israel's nuclear capabilities. There were several allusions to this line of thinking in Shara'̔'s statement, and we registered the need to deal with it at the right time.

President Clinton's decision to take part in the Israeli-Jordanian signing ceremony sparked an interesting debate within the Clinton administration. One school of thought argued that in addition to the visit to Jordan and Israel the president should also travel to

Damascus. Asad, it was argued, was about to be humiliated twice, by Jordan signing peace with Israel and by the Casablanca conference, the highlight of the Israeli-Arab normalization process. The president, so the argument went, must not compound the injury by failing to visit Asad. And, in a more positive vein, the visit could be used in order to move Asad forward in the negotiations with Israel. The other school took a more skeptical view of the potential benefits of the visit to Damascus and was worried by the negative fallout from the visit to a state figuring so prominently on the State Department's terrorism and drug lists. Finally a compromise was struck. The president would travel to Damascus on the condition that Asad would publicly take exception to terrorism.

In the event, this formula failed to work. Clinton and Asad had agreed on the language to be used by the latter with regard to terrorism in their press conference. But when an American television reporter asked Asad about the State Department's list of states engaged in terrorism he reverted to the standard Syrian formula and failed to use the text that he and President Clinton had agreed upon. It may have been a deliberate snub or it may have been a genuine misunderstanding, but Clinton left Damascus angry. To me there was one clear lesson to be derived from the two presidential press conferences in Geneva and Damascus and from Shara‘'s interview to Israeli television: whatever we wanted to achieve by way of public diplomacy and confidence-building measures, the Western media were the wrong arena for Asad and his entourage.

In the substantive part of their meeting Asad made two concessions to the visitor: he agreed to a time frame of sixteen (rather than twelve) months, and to some kind of diplomatic representation three months before the completion of Israel's withdrawal. In their meeting in Jerusalem later that day, Rabin told the president privately that in his view Asad gave away too little. But out of deference to the president, Rabin stated in public that there was "a certain progress" in Damascus and announced that within the next month Secretary Christopher would be invited back to the region to help with the Israeli-Syrian negotiation.

The year 1996 was to be an election year both in the United States and Israel. This gave an additional urgency to the time dimension of the Israeli-Syrian negotiations. At some point in 1996 (some argued 1995) the issue would become too sensitive for a president and a prime minister seeking reelection. By all counts and accounts barely a year was left for effecting a deal between Rabin and Asad.

SIX

The Security Dialogue

ON MARCH 8, 1995, Secretary Christopher arrived in the Middle East after a comparatively long absence of four months in an effort to break the deadlock in the Israeli-Syrian security talks. His first host, Prime Minister Rabin, knew well that Christopher, like so many others, was doubtful whether Rabin, given the arduous negotiation over Oslo II and the mounting domestic opposition to his government's peace policies, was really interested in coming to an agreement with Syria. The prime minister decided to address the issue squarely and turn it into a challenge for the president of Syria. He began his meeting with Christopher by saying that he was aware of the fact that the question was being raised whether he wanted to or could conclude an agreement with Syria. "I want and I can," Rabin said, "and the time is now."

It was a low moment in the negotiations over Oslo II, and Rabin told Christopher that if Asad wanted to put new life into the Syrian-Israeli negotiation, to move it forward swiftly and place it at the cutting edge of the peace process, he would be willing to go along. There was no direct reaction to the challenge. Asad may have seen it as an attempt to play him off against Arafat (which he would resent) or simply as an unacceptable pressure tactic. For the next three months he continued to haggle over the notion of equality as "a principle of the security arrangements," and despite a second meeting between the chiefs of staff of the Israeli and Syrian armed forces in June a breakthrough failed to occur. The difficulties in the Israeli-Palestinian negotiation were overcome, the Oslo II agreement was signed on September 28, and the Israeli-Palestinian track remained the cornerstone of the peace process.

The March episode encapsulated the state of the Israeli-Syrian negotiation in 1995. More than once we felt that the security issue, the indispensable key to a breakthrough, was finally being addressed in a serious fashion, only to be frustrated by yet another Syrian decision to suspend the security negotiations. Some give-and-take had begun and areas of convergence had transpired, but the gaps remained very wide. Rabin and Asad remained suspicious of each other. Rabin saw Asad's negotiating style and the substance of his positions as further indication that the Syrian president was not interested in a genuine negotiation but rather in an American mediation or arbitration, and he was incensed by Asad's refusal to accept the very foundations of his own position. Asad in turn had become convinced that Rabin was not interested in finalizing an agreement before the 1996 elections, and suspected that his Israeli counterpart was stringing him along while he was negotiating with Jordanians and Palestinians and normalizing Israel's relations with all-too-eager Arab partners in North Africa and the Gulf.

The Clinton administration, for its part, grew increasingly conscious of the passage of time and the diminishing prospect of an Israeli-Syrian agreement as the crowning achievement of the first term's Middle Eastern policy. Given the American and Israeli elections in the fall of 1996, the White House and the State Department regarded late 1995 or early 1996 as the latest point for achieving the breakthrough. Without advertising the fact, they prepared time on President Clinton's schedule in November 1995 for a possible meeting with Rabin and Asad, but their efforts to build the critical mass that would warrant such a meeting were to no avail. And although all the parties to the negotiation were preoccupied with election dates as the terminal or interim point of this negotiation it was Rabin's assassination on November 4, 1995, that defined the transition to a new phase of the Israeli-Syrian peace process.

A year earlier, in early November 1994, the peace process had seemed to be in full swing. The Israeli-Jordanian peace treaty had just been signed, the first regional economic conference was held in Casablanca (October 31–November 1) with the Israeli political leadership and a large economic delegation in attendance, and on

November 2 a new phase was launched in the Israeli-Syrian security negotiation. Before we turn to that negotiation a particular byproduct of the Republican victory in the congressional elections of November 9, 1994, should be mentioned.

In May 1994 an organized campaign began in the United States against the idea of stationing U.S. troops on the Golan as "peacekeepers" (or peace monitors, to be more precise) in the event of an Israeli-Syrian agreement. The campaign was orchestrated and carried out by right-wing organizations and individual activists in the Jewish community with the occasional participation of visitors from Israel—the former director general of the prime minister's office (and my predecessor as chief negotiator with Syria), Yossi Ben-Aharon and the former minister for congressional affairs in our Washington embassy, Yoram Ettinger.

The organizers targeted Congress, the media, and the organized Jewish community. They sought to convey the message that sending U.S. troops as peacekeepers to the Golan was bad for America and bad for Israel. The Golan was a dangerous place, and the American soldiers stationed there would be exposed to terrorist attacks and other dangers. While the United States could lose the lives of its soldiers and become entangled in a dangerous foreign arena, Israel would lose her freedom of action and could jeopardize the whole fabric of the crucial relationship with the United States. This message was repeated in an organized letter-writing campaign, in briefings on Capitol Hill, and in a stream of memoranda by a former, non-Jewish Pentagon official, Frank Gafney, who ran a conservative think tank in Washington—the Center for Security Policy.

We saw the campaign as a shrewd effort to controversialize the Israeli-Arab peace process and to provide an American peg for opposing the notion of an Israeli-Syrian settlement. After all, why should an American senator or columnist take exception to the fact that Israel and Syria decided to end their conflict? He or she might think that Israel was foolish to give up land for a written agreement with Hafiz al-Asad's regime, but Israel was a grown-up country with a democratic government and was entitled to make its own decisions and its own mistakes. But once an American dimension was introduced into the equation—the stationing of U.S. peacekeepers—American decision makers and opinion makers and those concerned with the health of the U.S.-Israeli relationship were entitled to raise their voice and exercise their political weight. Whether in the more sophisticated style and tone of columnists and lobbyists or in the cruder style of the organized letter-writing campaign, the message was the same: "I as an American citizen believe that relinquishing the Golan Heights will necessitate the stationing of U.S. buffer troops who will be exposed to murderous attacks from Arab irregulars. The American people will not accept casualties among the U.S. peacekeeping forces and rightly so. Any such deployment of U.S. troops will begin with good intentions and end with American body bags and vehement American protest demonstrations. This will no doubt lead to a rise in anti-Semitism in the U.S."[1]

In May 1994 the organizers of the campaign took advantage of the "security package" discussed between the United States and Israel to demand discussion and clarification of the plan to place U.S. "peacekeepers" on the Golan. Senator D'Amato (R-N.Y.) wrote to President Clinton in this vein, and the president wrote back to explain that discussion of this issue was premature and to promise to advise Congress when it became more concrete.

On June 28 the *New York Times* columnist Abe Rosenthal published a column titled "Americans on the Golan: Will Congress Debate the Issue?" Three days later a conservative Republican senator from Wyoming, Malcolm Wallop, introduced an amendment to the defense appropriation bill stating that "none of the funds authorized to be appropriated for the Department of Defense by this or any other act may be expended for the support of any deployment of personnel of the armed forces of the United States to the Golan Heights as part of a multilateral peacekeeping force . . . or in conjunction with a peace agreement between Israel and Syria that results in the withdrawal of the Israeli Defence Force from the Golan Heights until the Secretary of Defense submits to Congress . . . a written report on a potential deployment."[2]

Senator Wallop was roundly defeated by a vote of 67 to 3, but the campaign continued. It acquired a new vitality and much greater significance after November 9, when the Republicans took charge of both houses of Congress and of all committee chairs. At issue were both the determination of the Republican Congressional leadership, headed by the speaker, Newt Gingrich, to demonstrate that the president was not free to run U.S. foreign policy by himself, and the specific objection of certain Republican senators and congressmen or of some of their supporters to the Clinton administration's and the Rabin government's policies in the peace process. Senator Jesse Helms, the new chairman of the Senate's Committee on Foreign Relations, and his staff were openly critical of Asad's regime, of Israel's willingness to make any territorial concessions as part of a settlement with Syria, and of any prospect of a U.S.-Syrian rapprochement. The chairman of the House Committee on International Relations, Benjamin Gilman, whatever his personal views, was under pressure from voters in his own constituency and other opponents of the peace process, with regard to both the Syrian and Palestinian tracks. Other senators and congressmen, whether in keeping with their conservative outlook on world affairs or because of a particular interest in things Israeli and Middle Eastern, formed a small but highly visible pressure group always skeptical of and often opposed to the notion of an Israeli-Syrian settlement (and for that matter to the Oslo accords, as well). In the absence of a breakthrough that focus of opposition did not impede any real progress, but it did cast a shadow over the prospect of a significant upgrading of the American-Syrian relationship in the event of an Israeli-Syrian agreement. Given Asad's expectation that peace with Israel would yield a significant financial and economic reward by the United States, comparable to the one offered to Sadat, this Congressional opposition had at least some negative impact on Asad's motivation to move forward in his peacemaking with Israel.

The actual negotiation between Israel and Syria during this period focused almost exclusively on the issue of security. It unfolded in three stages. First, during November and December 1994 the first meeting between the chiefs of staff of the Syrian and Israeli armed forces and the sequence leading to it took place. Second, from January to the end of May a non-paper on the aims and principles of the security arrangements was negotiated and finally agreed upon. Third, in late June the second chiefs of staff meeting was held, and shortly thereafter the negotiation was suspended until Rabin's assassination.

The security issue had been discussed, or rather debated, in earlier phases of the negotiations, and both parties had a fairly good sense of each other's outlook. The lengthy argument over the notion of "equal footing" reflected a wide gap between our positions as they were articulated in broad terms and through code words. In November a more detailed and concrete discussion began, and our positions transpired more clearly and more fully.

The Syrian position was predicated on a minimalist view of the security arrangements. Asad had accepted the notions of settlement and peace with Israel, but his concept of peace was consciously different from those of Sadat, Hussein, and Arafat. He saw the conflict with Israel in geopolitical terms and he saw its resolution through the same prism. Israel remained a rival, if not an enemy, and the terms of the peace settlement should not serve to enhance its advantage over the Arabs, Syria in particular, but rather to diminish it. In a similar vein the peace that Asad had in mind would be congruent with Syria's dignity and sense of dignity. From both perspectives modest and unobtrusive security arrangements were called for.

A whole line of argumentation was prepared in support of that position: security was not something that Israel alone needed. In fact, Syria, as its version of history clearly showed, had long been the victim of Israel's aggression and needed the protection afforded by sound security arrangements more than Israel did. Israel was not really in need of extensive security arrangements—it was militarily powerful and predominant, its air force could be over Damascus in two to three minutes, and it had a strategic relationship with the United States that guaranteed it a "qualitative edge." In addition, although it did not admit to this, Israel could also rely on its nuclear capability. In any event a state of peace was the best security arrangement. Excessive security arrangements would be counterproductive and would obstruct the evolution of a normal relationship between the two countries. The end of occupation would eliminate the motivation to wage wars, and Syria's record of keeping its commitments was excellent, as evidenced in the Golan since 1974.

A second Syrian tactic was to lay out a series of "general principles" from which the specific security arrangements should emanate, or on the basis of which they should be precluded— equality and equal footing, mutuality, reciprocity, protection of sovereignty, symmetry, and "on both sides."

When it came to a more concrete discussion, once the initial bargaining position was discarded, the following Syrian position transpired. The security arrangements should be limited to the Golan Heights, which would be divided into a demilitarized zone and a zone of limited deployment. An international force could be stationed in order to monitor and supervise the arrangements. Supervision by the parties should be done from the air without infringement of sovereignty. An early warning station on the Golan Heights manned by Israelis was out of the question; a station manned by a third party, say the United States, was not ruled out. The same elements should apply to the Israeli side of the line, perhaps not symmetrically but in a reasonably proportionate fashion.

The Israeli position with regard to the security arrangements lacked some of the cohesion and clarity of the Syrian position. The latter was evidently formulated by Asad, elaborated under his strict supervision, and applied in the regimented style of his regime. In Israel's case, although Rabin formulated the policy he allowed his generals and his foreign minister a degree of latitude that was unthinkable in Damascus. I am certain that in some cases our Syrian counterparts must have seen schemes and designs in an Israeli style of conduct that was actually a reflection of our loose notion of authority. This was compounded by Rabin's tactical decision not to announce his line of withdrawal and to keep a measure of openness and ambiguity in that matter. Consequently, whereas every

Syrian presentation began with an assertion that the security arrangements "must begin from the lines of June 4, 1967," our presentations were more ambiguous in this regard.

From Israel's perspective it would be more accurate to speak of a "security regime" than of "security arrangements." For Rabin the Golan presented first and foremost a security issue. He and the military leadership were primarily concerned with the prospect of several Syrian armored and mechanized divisions stationed in Syria's southwestern corner and in Lebanon launching a surprise attack against Israel. Israel maintains a comparatively small standing army, and her defense doctrine is predicated on the availability of adequate early warning that would provide the hours necessary for an effective mobilization of the reserve units. Despite the 1973 setback, they felt that Israel's military presence on the Golan Heights and the early-warning stations built on Mt. Hermon and elsewhere on the heights provided a satisfactory response to a potential Syrian attack. They recognized the fact that that very presence also provided the motivation for such a Syrian attack, but they could not envisage a significant withdrawal without extensive security measures that would make up for the loss of territorial assets. In the fullness of time, when peaceful coexistence had been a reality experienced and tested over a period of years, one could possibly dispense with such measures, but for the time being they were deemed necessary.

The security regime envisaged by Israel was designed to serve several purposes: reduce the danger of a surprise attack (by either party), minimize the risk of friction, and provide a mechanism for building up cooperation and confidence between the two defense establishments. With these aims in mind it was to consist of five integrated elements: one, the depth of the demilitarized area and area of limited deployment; two, the size and deployment of the Syrian armed forces; three, at least one Israeli early-warning station on the Golan; four, monitoring by a non-UN international force with U.S. participation; and five, a system of verification and transparency.

In October a sequence was put together by Christopher and his team for the first meeting between the Syrian and Israeli military. A senior Israeli military officer was to come to Washington for a preparatory meeting with Ambassador Walid Mu'allim. Next a Syrian counterpart would come for a similar meeting with me, to be followed by a meeting between the two military officers. Rabin insisted that the meetings not be publicized. For one thing, he was not interested in creating the (false) impression that a settlement with Syria was imminent when at least two members of his own party were threatening to cross the lines over the Golan issue. Also, since he had already decided to dispatch the chief of staff, he did not want to expose him to an interrogation by members of the Knesset's Foreign and Defense Affairs Committee. Rabin did not volunteer information on the state of the Syrian talks, but he and his generals when appearing before the committee would have to provide real answers.

On November 2 and 3 we went through the first leg of the sequence. Israel's chief of staff, General Ehud Baraq, accompanied by Rabin's military aide, General Danny Yatom, came for two days of meetings with Ambassador Mu'allim. Baraq's term as chief of staff was to end on January 1 but Rabin dispatched him all the same. It was generally assumed that following a brief transition Baraq would enter politics and eventually contend for the Labor party's leadership as Rabin's successor. By providing him with direct experience in the peace negotiations Rabin was helping him build up his political profile. Also by nominating his chief of staff he prompted Asad to do the same and designate his chief of staff, General Hikmat Shihabi, as his envoy. This meant that both countries would be represented by the most senior generals, who enjoyed a close rapport with the ultimate decision makers and moved comfortably across the military and political domains.

General Yatom (subsequently the head of the Mossad, Israel's foreign intelligence organization) was Rabin's chief aide in national security affairs and the liaison between him and the defense and intelligence communities. He was to provide continuity past the first of the year.

The meetings between Baraq, Yatom, and myself and Walid

Mu'allim were held on November 2 and 3 and were attended by Ross and Indyk. We were all animated by the potential significance of the sequence that was being launched. Mu'allim began with a brief introduction and Baraq responded with a long, comprehensive presentation of Israel's and his views. He responded to Mu'allim's customary insistence on the June 4 lines in two ways. He first said that there existed a "dialectical relationship" between the components of the settlement and that a deeper withdrawal would require more massive security arrangements. He then said, to Mu'allim's evident chagrin, that his professional view was that the border between Israel and Syria should be on the Golan Heights eight or ten miles east of the Jordan. He also recommended a time frame of more than five years for implementation but, he added, on both issues the final decision should be made by the political leadership. Baraq added in a similar vein that the demilitarized area should extend east of the present line of separation. He proceeded with a presentation of a full-fledged scheme of the security regime. It was very elaborate, but Baraq emphasized the mutual nature of the arrangements—Israel required a monitoring station on the Golan but was willing to have a Syrian station in the Galilee.

Mu'allim responded with apparent disappointment. Syria could not and would not give up one inch of land. He also emphasized that Syria would not accept any demands for changes in the order of battle of her armed forces or in their deployment. It might in the future decide voluntarily on some changes, but this could not be stipulated in the peace treaty.

Not much happened during the next few weeks, as Damascus reflected on Baraq's presentation and demanded that in any event the next phases of the sequence be publicized. Rabin's arguments were conveyed to Asad by the United States, but Asad was not impressed. He was vehemently opposed to secret (as well as, for other reasons, public) diplomacy and pointed to the fact that a vague reference to the military talks had already leaked to the Israeli media. On November 19, during Rabin's visit to the United States his hosts asked whether he could provide the secretary of state with "something for Asad" for his next trip to the region. Rabin agreed to a time frame of forty-two months (as compared to the forty-four months that separated the Camp David accords from the completion of the withdrawal process on April 1, 1982). Asad still argued that the relevant period began in March 1979 upon the signing of a formal peace treaty and not in September 1978, but he confirmed to Christopher in their December 6 meeting that General Shihabi would arrive in Washington later that month to meet first with me and then with Baraq and his military colleagues. Asad also insisted that as a reflection of the civilian political level's supremacy over the military the ambassadors should chair the sessions. It might have been yet another manifestation of Asad's special brand of humor, but there was nothing in the subsequent interaction of a Syrian chief of staff and a Syrian diplomat as we could observe it to suggest civilian supremacy.

My meeting with Shihabi took place on December 19. His meeting with Baraq and his two colleagues (General Yatom and General Uri Sagi, the director of military intelligence) was scheduled for December 21.

In nearly four years of negotiation with Syria, the first meeting with Hikmat Shihabi stands out as a special moment. The Syrian diplomats I had met and negotiated with were emissaries of Asad's regime about whom I knew little before we actually met. Shihabi came from the inner core of Asad's regime and was well known to every student of Syrian politics. He was a professional soldier, a Ba'th party man, and a confidant of the president. His direct participation in the negotiations was a sign of seriousness. The most vivid description of Shihabi that I had heard in the past was by a former student of mine, an Israeli pilot who was captured by the Syrians and was interrogated by Shihabi, who was then director of military intelligence. From that and other less personal and less dramatic descriptions, there emerged the figure of a tough and ardent foe of Israel, the embodiment of the Syrian military's and the Ba'th party's hostility to Israel. If he had undergone a genuine transformation and was now ready for reconciliation and if he represented and could carry with him a large part of Syria's military establishment, then the prospect of a settlement was brighter than we had come to assume.

Shihabi came to the meeting accompanied by Mu'allim and by Asad's interpreter, Buthena Sha'ban. Shihabi's English is adequate, but he preferred to speak through an interpreter. Buthena Sha'ban was known to our American colleagues as Asad's regular interpreter. More curiously, she was a Syrian feminist and the author of an interesting feminist book in Arabic.

Shihabi was dignified, polite, and reserved. He presented the Syrian view of the principles of the security arrangements with which I had by now become thoroughly familiar. He was not interested in entering into a discussion of his presentation but was willing to listen to comments.

Two days later, on December 21, the first meeting between Baraq and Shihabi took place. It was Baraq's turn to respond to Shihabi's presentation of the 19th. Whereas Shihabi had chosen to lay out general principles and draw the details from them, Baraq chose to build his case on a definition of the principal aims of the security arrangements. The presentation was not essentially different from the one made to Mu'allim on November 2. Both sides were clearly waiting for the give-and-take of the discussion in order to engage each other. A debate and a discussion ensued. The tone was matter of fact, and some potential avenues of progress were identified, but there was not enough time to explore them. Thus Ross proposed that we combine discussion of aims and principles. His proposal was accepted and it did introduce new life into the discussion, but the second and final day was coming to a close. We all went to a meeting with President Clinton in the Oval Office feeling that the two chiefs of staff needed a few more days. The president's personal participation was designed to underscore the importance that he and his administration attached to the prospect of a Syrian-Israeli breakthrough.

Rabin's efforts to keep the meeting secret unraveled in its immediate aftermath. As early as December 21 the Syrian News Agency (SANA) reported from Damascus that the Syrian and Israeli ambassadors to Washington met "with the participation of military experts." Two days later, Israel's second television channel, quoting "Egyptian sources," reported that a meeting between the two chiefs of staff had taken place. By the end of December SANA confirmed that the "military experts" were indeed the chiefs of staff. More significantly, the Syrian and Lebanese media began to publish more detailed reports about the meeting. According to these reports Syria rejected Israeli demands for "observation points" on the Golan and for "unequal demilitarization."

This was a bad omen. By publicizing his rejection of these Israeli demands Asad was deliberately tying his own hands. It also meant that by early January he had gone over the minutes of the meetings and disapproved of what he read. In Washington we all felt that the meeting had gone quite well and had prepared the ground for a continuation of the military dialogue at this senior level. Shihabi stayed on in the United States for a private visit, and Ross wanted to organize a follow-up meeting in early January. Rabin took exception. On January 1, General Amnon Shahak replaced Baraq as the IDF's chief of staff. Rabin thought that from that point on Shahak should represent the Israeli side, but both he and the new chief of staff did not think that he should travel to Washington to negotiate with his Syrian counterpart four days after taking office.

Later in January it transpired that in any event Asad was not about to dispatch his own chief of staff to a second round of negotiations any time soon. He objected to what he saw as far-reaching Israeli demands in the security area, and insisted that we reach an agreement on the underlying principles before resuming a detailed negotiation. To underline his unhappiness with the state of things, he kept Mu'allim in Damascus.

The negative symptoms multiplied. On January 23 two explosive charges killed twenty-one soldiers in a bus station near the Israeli town of Beit Lid. Responsibility for the attack was taken by the Shikaki wing of the Islamic Jihad in Damascus. Warren Christopher's efforts to persuade Asad to go through the sequence he had agreed to in the security talks, and at the same time to dissociate

Syria from terrorist attacks by radical opponents of the peace process, proved futile.

Asad's defiant mood was also reinforced by the success he registered in the Alexandria summit attended by Asad, Mubarak, and King Fahd. Mubarak was in the midst of his own confrontation with the United States over the indefinite extension of the Non-Proliferation Treaty. Egypt objected to the NPT's indefinite extension as long as Israel's nuclear potential was not addressed. It mobilized Arab and other countries against the U.S. nuclear policies, and obstructed the work of the multilateral Arab-Israeli peace talks on arms control and regional security as a means of pressure. Asad, on his part, was eager to slow down the normalization between Israel and the Arabs of the Gulf and North Africa. The separate agendas of Egypt and Syria thus converged, and together they prevailed upon the Saudis to join them and enhance the significance of their encounter. King Fahd's participation toned down the text of the final communique but the message was unmistakable—Syria's tactical needs in her negotiation with Israel and Egypt's deeper concerns with Israeli preeminence, nuclear and otherwise, required that other Arabs slow down their "race" (*taharwul* was the Arabic pejorative term used by the critics of swift normalization) toward Israel.

In early February Mu'allim returned to Washington, and the U.S. peace team set out to seek a way out of the stalemate. Ross went carefully over his own minutes and found three areas of potential flexibility in Shihabi's position: Shihabi spoke of potential voluntary redeployment, he agreed to transparency (mutual notification of large-scale exercises, etc.), and he alluded to a potential trade-off—Syria would agree to asymmetry in demilitarization if Israel agreed to a warning station manned by U.S. personnel. Mu'allim in turn insisted that since Syria had accepted our definition of the aims of the security arrangements we should now accept the principles that mattered so much to Syria, first and foremost that of "equality."

It was against that background that Christopher arrived in Israel on March 8 and conducted the discussion with Rabin that was described in the first paragraph of this chapter. Having stated his own intentions, Rabin asked the secretary for his estimate of Asad's intentions. Christopher's reply was that Syria was still interested in finalizing an agreement but had her own doubts regarding Rabin's intentions and timetable. In the course of discussion Rabin told Christopher that he could reassure Asad that Israel was not interested in extending the security arrangements deep into Syria. He accepted the concept of "relevant areas" for the security arrangements, and as far as he was concerned these areas stretched from Damascus to Safed (a town in the Galilee). Rabin envisaged an area of limited deployment on the Israeli side of the line in order to address Syria's concern with an Israeli surprise attack. Given the fact that the IDF's regular order of battle was comparatively small, and given its dependence on an elaborate reserve system, this was a gesture that Israel could offer with relative ease.

Christopher then shuttled back and forth to Damascus. Asad liked the notion of "relevant areas" but resented the inclusion of Damascus. He insisted that a "formula" be agreed upon with regard to equality before he would agree to send his chief of staff to a second session in Washington. We split many hairs in an effort to find that formula. The secretary of state was eager to be able to announce the resumption of the negotiations before he left the region on March 14, but more than one circle had to be squared. Asad was adamant in his insistence that the word "equality" or "equal" be included in the text without qualification, while Rabin was equally determined to insure that this was not the case —and in the event he was successful. A formula was finally worked out (Christopher and Rabin continued to argue over an open telephone line between Damascus and Jerusalem via Washington). On the basis of that formula Asad agreed that Mu'allim's meetings with me be resumed on March 20, but he would not authorize meetings between the military authorities.

On March 18 I was invited to see the secretary of state. His message was very clear: time and his own patience were running out. As he had indicated in the past, the Clinton administration's political schedule required that the negotiation end in 1995 (I naturally assumed that he was taking a safety margin of several months). He personally had no time for both parties' digging in on minor details. We should dispense quickly with general principles and formulations and focus on the actual negotiation. This was easier said than done; Asad continued to insist on his principles and terminology, and Rabin was equally determined not to buckle under his pressure. It took another ten weeks to finalize the brief "Non-Paper on the Aims and Principles of the Security Arrangements" that finally opened the way for the Shihabi-Baraq meeting.

It was during this period that former Secretary of State James Baker tried to help the negotiations in which he had invested so much in an earlier period. Accompanied by Ambassador Edward Djerejian, who had become the director of the James A. Baker III Institute for Public Policy at Rice University, Baker came on a private and confidential trip to Israel and Syria. Baker and Djerejian spent time with both Rabin and Asad, and apparently played a role in Asad's willingness to forgo his demand for "symmetry" but not for "equality." Upon his return, Baker updated President Clinton and Secretary Christopher on his mission. Surprisingly, the secret of the mission was kept for almost a year and a half until it was first reported in the Lebanese press.

During this period Ross and his team traveled to the region, and Mu'allim and I continued to meet with Ross and Parris in an effort to find the magic formulations that would break the deadlock. At the end of the first week in May, Rabin came to Washington for a policy conference of the American-Israel Public Affairs Committee. He met with the secretary of state on May 5 and the president on May 7. By that time Rabin had agreed to a compromise formula for the "non-paper" that Ross had prepared, and his discussion with Clinton and Christopher could be more relaxed and reflective. Rabin warned his hosts that Asad was in no hurry and felt under no pressure. He was relying on Iran and was not menaced by Iraq. Under these circumstances he was trying to obtain a better deal than those obtained by his Arab predecessors. Tactically he was trying to maneuver the United States into "delivering" Israel and to extract from either of us a written position on the issue of withdrawal. Rabin argued that against this background it was particularly important for the United States to be emphatic in explaining to Asad that he had nothing "in his pocket," that everything he had heard from the United States was hypothetical and conditional; we do not know what Christopher said to Asad in this regard when he went to Damascus during the second week of June, but on June 1, speaking at a news conference he held jointly with Mubarak, Asad said in response to a question on withdrawal: "regarding the withdrawal issue we have not reached an agreement so far. Of course, Syria's position is known and clear. Syria strongly adheres to and cannot give up the demand for the 4 June 1967 border. . . . The issue is settled at least as far as we are concerned."[3]

During the last week of May we finalized the "non-paper" and agreed on a sequence: Ross would arrive in Israel on June 4 (and proceed, of course, to Damascus), Christopher would follow suit on June 8, and Shahak and Shihabi would meet in Washington at the end of June. Rabin set the stage in Israel for the new intensification of the negotiations with Syria by speaking in a television interview about the prospect of dismantling one settlement as part of the first phase of implementation.

Ross arrived in the region accompanied by General Daniel Christman who, as the Pentagon's representative, was assigned the important task of seeking the professional middle ground. For the first few days on its own and then alongside the secretary, the American team shuttled between Syria and Israel. In Syria they met with Shihabi, who was joined by the two generals that would accompany him to Washington—General Ibrahim al-'Ammar (the director of military intelligence) and General Hasan Khalil of Military Security, an intelligence organization headed by General Ali Duba, a member of Asad's inner circle. In Israel, in addition to Rabin and Peres, they met Shahak and a group of intelligence and planning officers. The technique adopted by the U.S. peace team in order to close or at least narrow the gaps between the Israeli and Syrian positions was quite transparent. They asked both sides to arrange their objectives according to priority. By creating two hierarchies the ground would be prepared for trade-offs and compromises as the next step toward agreement. What we heard from Damascus indicated to us that in Washington Shihabi and his colleagues would seek to reduce the profile of the security arrangements as a whole, minimize the "relevant area," and object strenuously to our demand for keeping the early warning station on Mt. Hermon. Shahak, as instructed by Rabin, refused to link the security arrangements to one specific line.

Around June 20, about a week before Shahak and Shihabi were to begin their meeting, it transpired that the Israeli and Palestinian negotiations were coming within sight of an agreement on Oslo II. Both were eager to come to the United States for the final round of the negotiations. The Palestinians as a rule aspired to draw the United States into their track, and their Israeli counterparts were willing to oblige them if this would expedite the negotiation and bring it to conclusion. The administration was willing to help, but it was reluctant to encumber the Israeli-Syrian military talks. Asad, as everybody knew, was not enamored of Arafat or of the Oslo accords, and he would not want his chief of staff upstaged by a parallel negotiation on Oslo II. In the event, new difficulties slowed down the Israeli-Palestinian negotiations, and at least the first round of the Shihabi-Shahak talks could take place without a Palestinian backdrop.

Unlike the previous chiefs of staff meeting, this encounter was announced in advance. As expected, it generated a fresh wave of activity by the opponents of peace-with-concessions with Syria, including a demonstration in front of the chief of staff's private home. The opposition to the imminent Oslo II accord was becoming nastier and more violent, and the "pro-Golan" protest further electrified an overcharged political system.

The chiefs of staff meeting was held at Fort McNair in Washington and began on June 27. Shihabi and Mu'allim were accompanied by Generals 'Ammar and Khalil. Shahak came with his own retinue headed by General Zvi Shtauber of the IDF's Planning Division. We spent two days at Fort McNair, but our meetings were strictly limited to the conference room. General Shihabi was determined not to share a meal or even a cup of coffee with his Israeli interlocutors. Shihabi was more relaxed than he had been in our first meeting, but he was still quite tense and clearly conscious of the obligation of a senior Syrian officer to maintain his own sense of dignity and also a specific notion of decorum.

The meeting began inauspiciously. Shihabi was the first to speak. He warned that a failure of this second meeting could have dangerous repercussions, and proceeded to present a modest set of security arrangements that grew directly out of the agreed "principles." On both sides of the line demilitarized zones would be established in which international forces and local police could be deployed. Depth would be added to them by contiguous areas of limited deployment. Monitoring would be implemented by satellites, airborne radar, and other "nonintrusive" measures. Syria was also ready for mutual transparency afforded by prior notification of large-scale exercises and reserve call-ups.

Shahak responded by expressing disappointment. Israel could accept most of what Shihabi had just described, but this did not address her concerns. Demilitarized areas and areas of limited deployment were, indeed, an important component, provided they were established on the right scale. Transparency as such was a good thing, but the important thing was building trust and confidence and these must be built from a very low point of departure.

Following another brief exchange with Shihabi, Shahak asked General Shtauber to present the plan for a security regime that the IDF's planning staff had prepared. Shihabi reacted sharply and rejected the plan on grounds of principle without getting into detail. He objected to four aspects of the plan: first, it was not predicated on the assumption of Israeli withdrawal to the lines of June 4, 1967; second, it included an Israeli ground station on the Golan; third, it expanded the notion of "relevant areas"; and fourth, it interfered with the size and order of battle of Syria's armed forces.

At this point, General Christman went to work and presented "bridging questions" to both sides. Discussion of warning from the air followed. Part of the discussion was specific, professional, and at points impressive. Such issues as the distance of the armored formations of both sides from the future line were openly addressed.

At other moments the discussion was still plagued by slogans like "full peace will provide full security."

Back at Shahak's hotel we found out that in Israel the political system and public opinion were agitated by the publication of what became known as the "Shtauber document." The same General Shtauber who came with the chief of staff had been charged with the staff work that preceded the trip. The portfolio he prepared included an analysis of the "Non-Paper on the Aims and Principles of the Security Arrangements." The analysis was critical of the paper, but this was not the main issue at the moment. The important fact was that someone in the Israeli system who received a copy of Shtauber's analysis passed it on to the head of the opposition, Benjamin Netanyahu, who, shielded by his parliamentary immunity, quoted it in the Knesset. Netanyahu argued (incorrectly) that the paper proved the opposition's claim that Rabin had conceded the Golan and was negotiating on this basis. He further argued (incorrectly as well) that the paper also proved that Rabin did not live up to three principles he had been committed to in the past: inequality in the depth of demilitarization, an Israeli monitoring station on Mt. Hermon, and defense of Israel by Israeli forces alone.

The initial response by Rabin and Peres was to deny the authenticity of the document. Rabin had not issued written instructions to Shahak in anticipation of his trip, and was unaware of Shtauber's paperwork. The denial was then retracted and replaced by criticism of Netanyahu's willingness to expose an IDF classified working paper.

As we know, the claims made by the head of the opposition were unsubstantiated and the episode, awkward as it was, failed to obstruct the negotiation (or, to put it differently, it was not the publication of the Shtauber document that obstructed the military discussions between Israel and Syria). Its main significance lies in the light it sheds on two aspects of the negotiating process in Israel. One has to do with the relationship between the negotiator and the home gallery. The substance of our negotiation was known to very few individuals in Israel and comment on it, critical or laudatory, had to be speculative in nature. The "non-paper" was the first substantial text to become available to a larger group within Israel's national security establishment, and it naturally drew much comment, some of it critical. Of course, it was far from being perfect. It represented several compromises that Rabin agreed to when he overruled a professional recommendation and subordinated it to his broader view of the Syrian negotiation, the peace process, or Israel's relationship with the United States. On the Palestinian track it was usually Peres who drew the defense establishment's criticism for being willing to yield on specific points in order to reach an agreement, and Rabin who served as the arbiter. It is easy to draw a caricature of the two ends of the negotiating spectrum: those who would give away too much for the sake of obtaining an agreement and those who fight for every iota for the sake of perfection. The art of negotiation requires walking on the sensible middle ground where good and durable agreements are made.

The "Shtauber episode" also vindicated Rabin in his insistence that the details of the Syrian negotiation be kept within a very small and tight circle. As soon as the circle was expanded and orderly paperwork began, someone would be found who would see fit to leak a document publicly in an attempt to embarrass the prime minister. Of course the principal details of the negotiation could not be kept secret forever, but what Rabin wanted above all to avoid was a political furor over a hypothetical agreement.

The immediate fallout from the "Shtauber episode" did not interfere with the discussion on the 29th, the second day of the meeting. The discussion became more concrete. Shahak agreed with Shihabi that part of what both states required by way of early warning could be obtained from the air. In order to emphasize the limited value of coverage from the air, Shahak analyzed the sequence that produced a threat: first comes an idea, it is then converted into secret planning, which gives birth to commands, at which point activities begin to take place on the ground. Such activities, said Shahak, can be picked up from the air, but this represented an advanced stage of preparation and a warning obtained at that stage might be too late.

A discussion of territorial depth ensued. Shihabi argued that Damascus was much closer to the Golan than was Tel Aviv or Jerusalem. Shahak did not think that this was a valid comparison. Facing Syria was the narrow part of northern Israel known as "the finger of the Galilee." Shihabi retorted that this was an exception. Shahak argued back that beyond Damascus there were hundreds of kilometers of Syrian territory, whereas a force that cut through the "finger of the Galilee" would reach the sea. Shihabi's final argument was that Syria was indeed a large country, but the size of the inhabited part of Syria was similar to that of Israel. The exchanges became briefer and livelier. Shihabi argued that Israel's ability to mobilize reserves and rely on emergency storage was impressive. Shahak reacted by saying that in 1973 Syria tried to disrupt this very mobilization by firing Frug missiles, implying that the IDF's planners assumed that this was precisely what the Syrians would try to do, more effectively, in the event of another war with more sophisticated Scud missiles.

The discussion shifted to the issue of the "relevant areas." It was in this context that Shihabi made an interesting gambit when he pointed to the fact that according to the Syrian definition of "from Quneitra to Safed" (as against Rabin's original "from Damascus to Safed"), the proportion was 10:6. This was a clear departure from the mechanical approach to the notion of equality and an invitation to make a counter offer.

Shahak was in no hurry to make that counter offer, but he did present what became known in the parlance of the peace process as the "Shahak question." It came after yet another complaint by Shihabi that Israel's demands in the security area were excessive, that in any event peace was the best security arrangement. "If that is the case," Shahak asked, "why would you need to keep so many of your divisions so close to the Israeli border after we make peace? Syria has a territory nine times larger than that of Israel and it has common borders with five states; why should such a proportion of her military might be kept on one border?" Shihabi did not respond directly to the question, but he did say that in the event of an Israeli withdrawal Syria's "strike units" would not be moved forward from their present positions.

A final session was held on the morning of the 29th in the Oval Office. It was more ceremonial than substantive. We parted with a clear sense that a genuine negotiation between the Israeli and Syrian military establishments had begun.

During the next few days Ross and his team worked on a summary of the Shihabi-Shahak talks and prepared for their trip to the region on July 10. But the trip that was conceived as a follow-up to what was regarded by all of us as a successful meeting revealed instead a host of unanticipated difficulties. The first indication of an unexpected development was a peculiar commentary broadcast by Radio Damascus on July 10. According to that commentary:

> The military talks accomplished some progress on a number of points but failed to reach the phase of formulating even one paragraph in a practical and serious fashion so as to pave the way to security arrangements on both sides of the border in a manner that would guarantee the security and stability of both sides together in an equal and just way.
>
> When both parties reach a definitive formulation of the security arrangements there will be no need to build early warning stations that would keep part of the Syrian land under occupation. International gurantees and peace as such will be a safe substitute for any early warning. And even if there was a need to have early-warning stations on both sides of the border, this task could be given to international and friendly forces.[4]

We all assumed that a Syrian commentator on Radio Damascus would not let his imagination run wild on an issue of such great sensitivity. So what could we make of it? Was it a clumsy attempt to hint at a sensible compromise as a way out of an unfolding crisis? Or did something go wrong in Asad's system, and was the fallback position revealed much too early?

Rabin was not pleased with the summary prepared by Ross; it did not dovetail with what he had heard from Shahak. Nor was he pleased with the fact that Hizballah had fired Katyusha rockets across the length of the Lebanese-Israeli border. This was bad in itself as well as a negative message from Damascus.

Indeed, when Ross went to Damascus the next day he found Asad in a particularly foul mood. The Syrian president was unhappy with the second chiefs of staff meeting and unhappy with the general course of the peace process. He complained that at the end of every meeting that failed to produce results Israel proved to be a net winner and Syria the loser. So far, he continued, he had nothing to show for after nearly four years in the Madrid process, while the entire Arab world was opening up to Israel. He resented a mode of negotiation in which every difficult issue was pushed to the end of the process rather than being resolved on the spot. To be concrete, he would not agree to postpone the resolution of the ground station issue; it had to be resolved now (by which he meant that Syria's position had to be accepted). According to Asad the commentary on Radio Damascus was the commentator's own initiative. As long as the issue was not resolved to his satisfaction, Asad would not agree to a further round of military discussions.

Asad had obviously decided to bring matters to a head. His motivation and reasoning were manifold. For one thing, he was genuinely determined to do away with the notion of an Israeli warning station on Mt. Hermon and decided to turn it into a make-or-break issue. Asad knew that by agreeing to postpone the discussion of this question it would be added to the package of issues that would become the subject matter of compromises and trade-offs, and this was precisely what he decided to avoid.

Asad was also aware of the fact that every high-level meeting between Syria and Israel gave license to other Arabs to proceed with the normalization process with Israel. This was something he resented but could live with as long as Syria was also a beneficiary. As his complaints to Ross clearly indicated, he felt that both with regard to the peace process and in her bilateral relationship with the United States, Syria was not being sufficiently rewarded. Asad may have been particularly galled by the visit to Damascus of a member of Senator Helms's staff that had just taken place. To Minister

Shara῾ and to other Syrians the visiting staffer explained that Syria could not expect much from the U.S. government even if it made peace with Israel. Asad said nothing to this effect, but we assumed that he was also unhappy with the prospect of an Oslo II agreement, particularly one signed in Washington while his own negotiation with Israel was plodding along.

There were other difficulties, as well. Mu῾allim was unhappy with the summary that Ross had prepared. Shihabi's and Mu῾allim's reports to Asad may have contained some discrepancies. Asad's aides told the American visitors that on the basis of Shihabi's report the political leadership had been told that the early warning issue had been resolved. It would be awkward to reconvene the leadership and advise it of a different reality. Given the fact that this was the second time that a meeting between Shihabi and an Israeli counterpart gave rise to a misunderstanding in Damascus, we also wondered whether there was a personal domestic dimension to the travails of the Syrian-Israeli military talks.

Ross and his team traveled back to Damascus and returned to Israel on July 13. Late in the evening he went to see Rabin at the Ministry of Defense in Tel Aviv. Ross had not been received by Asad (the explanation given was that the president was suffering from back problems), and was told by Shara῾ that Syria was ready for further meetings between the ambassadors the following week but not for military meetings. The Syrians were adamant in their opposition to an Israeli ground station. With regard to the relevant areas, they repeated their willingness to keep their strike forces in place in the event of an Israeli withdrawal.

Rabin insisted that the procedure that had been agreed upon be kept. He had agreed to the compromise suggested by the United States on the "non-paper" as part of a package that included the procedure that Asad was now violating. Rabin reminded Ross that in May Secretary Christopher had specifically arranged to announce the agreement and the ensuing sequence in Damascus. At stake, he said, was the credibility of the whole process. He was not willing to pay with substance in order to keep the process going, and he expected the United States to make it amply clear who was to blame for the latest crisis. Rabin then added a point that did not please our American friends. Asad acted in this fashion, he said, because he felt free from pressure and it was a pity that one could not talk to Iraq.

Rabin was thus telling the United States that when perceived self-interest, goodwill, friendly persuasion, and gentlemanly mediation failed to produce results geopolitics and power politics were the only alternative. There was never a serious discussion of resorting to that alternative, and from all we knew of the Clinton administration it was not inclined toward choosing and exercising such an option. As for Iraq, ever since reports had circulated over a year earlier that a member of Rabin's cabinet had toyed with the idea of building a channel of communication with Baghdad, our American colleagues suspected that there was more than a kernel of truth to the story. The occasional willingness of other members of Rabin's cabinet to flirt with the idea of talking to Qadhdhafi's Libya reinforced that suspicion. There was no immediate response to Rabin's comment, but it registered.

The secretary of state instructed Ross to tell Foreign Minister Sharaʿ that Syria's position was unacceptable, but not to turn it into a public issue. The Clinton administration saw the July crisis in the Israeli-Syrian military talks as yet another temporary setback along the difficult road to an Israeli-Syrian agreement. It had no intention of publicly chiding Syria. Patient and creative as ever, Ross kept looking for the middle ground or the magic formula that would take these two reluctant protagonists across the new roadblock. His efforts continued during the next four months until Rabin's assassination transformed the landscape of the whole peace process.

We all returned to Washington around the middle of July and set to work. By the end of the month Muʿallim was given the green light from Damascus to offer some flexibility. This was conveyed to us as "personal ideas" that had yet to be endorsed by Damascus. In that framework Muʿallim offered five elements of flexibility: one, Syria's "strike forces" would not be moved forward in the event of an Israeli withdrawal; two, they would not be increased; three, they would not be given additional equipment; four, in some cases, a separation could be introduced between units and their ammunition; and five, over time, Syria could redeploy some of her forces on a voluntary basis and without any linkage to the phases of implementation.

Some of these ideas were not new and certainly not startling. They provided a point of departure for another lengthy negotiation. Having spent five months in negotiations over a "non-paper" that led to three days of security talks and to yet another crisis, we were not enticed by this prospect. Furthermore, the Syrians were raising these ideas in the expectation that Israel would match their flexibility, as it were, by removing her demand for an early-warning station. Our American partners never said a word in this regard but we could easily sense that in their minds they had already settled on the obvious compromise—early-warning stations operated by the United States.

Rabin's perspective was further compounded by other developments. On July 24 another terrorist act was perpetrated against civilians in Israel: a bus exploded in Ramat Gan, a city adjacent to Tel Aviv, killing six and wounding thirty-one Israelis. The attack was staged by Hamas in an effort to derail the negotiations on Oslo II. This it failed to accomplish, but its action did exacerbate the already charged atmosphere in Israel and contributed to further controversialize the Rabin government's peace policies.

In the summer of 1995 Rabin and the Labor party leadership were facing increasing difficulty in maintaining the cohesion of the Labor party caucus and the coalition's majority over issues concerned with both major tracks of the peace process. Two developments that had begun in 1994 confronted the government with major difficulties in 1995. In June 1994 an extraparliamentary movement was formed under the name "The Third Way." It consisted mostly of Labor party members and sympathizers, many of them with a military background, who felt uneasy with the government's peace policies. They argued that in the negotiations with the Palestinians and with the Syrians Rabin and his government had drifted to the left, and vowed to return Labor to its centrist tradition by exerting pressure from outside.

In the ranks of the new movement a special role was played by

the Golan settlers, many of whom had been traditional Labor supporters. These activists cultivated ties with several Labor members
of the Knesset, most notably a reserve brigadier, Avigdor Kahalani.
Kahalani was a decorated war hero who distinguished himself in
June 1967 in the tank battles of the northern Sinai, and even more
in October 1973 in the Golan. His political career drew on his war
record, and his statements on the Golan's indispensability to Israel's security had a special resonance. As a Labor member of the
Knesset he joined the parliamentary "Golan lobby" whose purpose
was to protect Israel's control of the Golan or at least part of it in
the event of a settlement with Syria. I remember a telephone call I
received from Kahalani in 1994, when he found out that we had
established a direct channel with Syria. He asked me to propose to
the Syrians that military officers who had fought on both sides of
the Golan War be brought together in a special encounter on the
cease-fire line. I actually raised the idea, and told Mu'allim and
Ross that this would be a very effective way of engaging a politician
like Kahalani in the Israeli-Syrian peace process rather than pitting
him against it. Needless to say, I was rebuffed.

In 1994 the Golan lobby raised for the first time the idea of a
"Golan entrenchment law"—a law to be passed in the Knesset that
would, according to various versions, require a special majority (of
70 or 80 members) in the Knesset in order to repeal the 1981 law
that had extended Israel's law to the Golan, and a special majority
of 65 percent in the referendum on a prospective Israeli-Syrian
agreement that Rabin had promised. This was part of an effective
political and public relations campaign that the Golan settlers,
their specific supporters, and other opponents and critics of
Rabin's policies put together. The inherent difficulties of a settlement with Syria, magnified by Asad's refusal to engage in significant public diplomacy, facilitated the campaign and cemented a
significant body of opinion against the prospect of a far-reaching
territorial concession in the Golan. In September 1994 a first serious effort was made to pass the "Golan entrenchment law" in the
Knesset, which Rabin was able to stem.

A second attempt was mounted in the summer of 1995. By that

time two members of the Golan lobby, Avigdor Kahalani and Immanuel Zissman, were on the verge of seceding from the Labor party and joining the Third Way and the opposition. Their shift was balanced by the disintegration of one of the right wing's caucuses (Tsomet) and the government's ability to win over two of its members. The vote was held on July 26, 1995, and ended in a draw 59:59, which meant that the motion failed to pass.

As the negotiations on Oslo II drew closer to agreement, the campaign against the government was stepped up. In retrospect, a direct line has been drawn from the violent demonstrations and ugly rhetoric in the summer of 1995 to Rabin's assassination in the fall of that year. But even without that specter it was obvious that the country and the government were going through an unusually difficult time. In more strictly political terms, the imminent conclusion of the negotiation of the Oslo II agreement brought to the fore practical questions that had to do with the need to marshal a majority for the vote in the Knesset.

The interim agreement was initialled on September 24 and the signing was set for September 28 in Washington. On October 6 it was voted on in the Knesset. Rabin and his aides were forced to invest considerable political capital in order to obtain a majority of sixty-one. Against this background the prime minister was not particularly eager to upset the two Labor members of the Knesset who were vehemently opposed to concessions in the Golan. He was ready for a domestic political crisis over a real issue, but he was not willing to risk his government over a negotiation that, he suspected, Asad was not really determined to bring to conclusion. In other words, although Rabin would not have precipitated a crisis in the security negotiations with Syria in order to facilitate the Knesset vote over Oslo II, he was not willing to go out of his way in order to overcome a crisis for which he held Asad solely responsible.

Asad, in turn, suspected that he was being subjected to a repetition of the summer of 1993, that Rabin was preoccupied with the conclusion of Oslo II, and that he was investing the bare minimum in order to keep Syria in the game. On August 8 a new element was added to the picture when Saddam Hussein's two sons-in-law fled across the border from Iraq to Jordan and were given political asylum in Amman. Thus began a Middle Eastern political drama that culminated in the deserters' silly return to Iraq in late February 1996, where they were killed by Saddam's men.

During the latter part of their stay in Jordan the deserters understood that they had reached a political dead end, which led them to the naive conclusion that they could negotiate their safe return with Saddam Hussein. But soon after their arrival in Jordan and during the late summer of 1995 their very escape and the activities it generated had created the impression that a serious effort could and would be launched to topple Saddam. This prospect presented Asad with a dual challenge. Every change in the status quo in Iraq would have enormous repercussions for his own regime. Saddam was a sworn enemy, but the sanctions regime kept him on his knees and neutralized him as an effective rival. Like so many others, Asad preferred a weak Saddam to the uncertainties of a fundamental change in Iraq. Any campaign to topple Saddam would have to be monitored closely by Syria. Asad was further concerned by the fact that the Clinton administration seemed to be consulting and coordinating its conduct toward Iraq with Israel and Jordan. Not much hard evidence was needed in order to feed Syrian paranoia and to conjure up images of an American-Israeli-Jordanian scheme to restore the Hashemites, or to prop up any other regime in Baghdad that would be totally undesirable from a Syrian point of view. In any event this was not the scheme of things Asad had in mind when he entered the Madrid process and began to build a dialogue with the United Sates. The whole purpose of that dialogue was to turn Syria into a country that the United States consulted and cooperated with in the formulation and execution of its Middle Eastern policies. Thus, throughout the month of August, while Rabin was preoccupied with the Oslo II negotiations and with their domestic Israeli dimension, Asad's attention was focused on the Iraqi crisis.

Rabin's visits to the United States for the signing of Oslo II at the end of September and for the fiftieth anniversary of the United Nations during the third week in October provided opportunities for consultation with the administration on the state of the Syrian talks. The Clinton administration's concern with the lingering crisis of the Israeli-Syrian track was intensified by the imminence of the second Middle Eastern Regional Economic Conference in Amman. At the end of October, Secretary Christopher would be traveling to what has become the most conspicuous symbol of Israeli-Arab normalization, an event boycotted by Syria.

As he had told Ross openly the previous July, Asad resented Israel's growing acceptance in the Arab world. He would certainly resent the political and economic benefits that would accrue to King Hussein during and in the aftermath of the Amman conference. A visit by Christopher to Amman without a stop in Damascus could be seen as a snub. Christopher and his aides had already decided that on his way out of Amman the secretary would make a brief stop in Damascus. Could it also be used as an opportunity to revive the negotiations?

Rabin agreed that at some point in November Ross would come to the region to launch an effort to break the deadlock. He also agreed that the United States would adopt a technique similar to the one used earlier in the year, when the "non-paper" was put together in order to try to settle the argument over the early-warning station and the depth of the relevant areas. He said to Christopher and to his team that from his point of view the efforts to bring about an Israeli-Syrian agreement could continue until April 1996. From that point on it would be too close to the Israeli elections scheduled for October 1996. Rabin's preference was that the American effort begin at Ross's level and that Christopher would not come to the region before January, when the Knesset was to vote on the budget. The budget vote was also a vote of confidence, and as such a vote that had to be won.

Asad's perspective on the negotiations with Israel during the same period was revealed in a lengthy, detailed, and fairly candid interview he granted to the editor-in-chief of Egypt's leading daily paper *al-Ahram*. The interview was published on October 11 and was probably conducted a few days earlier.

In typical fashion Asad began with a historical survey designed to show that Syria's policy had been and remained consistent. Waging war and pursuing a peaceful settlement were two different paths toward the same end; in Asad's own words: "We have always said—and recall this very well—especially after the October 1973 war that we want peace. . . . On October 6 [1973] I said in a speech to the nation in the first hour after the war started that we are advocates of peace . . . that position remained unchanged from 1973 until the 1990s." But peace had to be built on the right foundations and be congruent with Syria's principles and criteria. After arduous negotiations with the Bush administration, the Madrid framework was agreed upon. Nothing happened under the Shamir government because, as Asad argued, all he wanted was "to see time elapse; that is to gain time." Nor was Asad happy with the changes brought about by the advent of the Rabin government: "The atmosphere was quieter and the discussions were also held quietly. But there was no progress at all."[5]

As he had undertaken to do in the past, Asad avoided a frontal assault on the PLO and Jordan for breaking ranks and making separate deals with Israel, but he did not conceal his criticism and his determination to stand up to Rabin's pressure tactics: "A unilateral agreement was signed in Oslo and another agreement with Jordan followed. These matters, however, are sensitive. The Israelis want to exploit these processes by pressuring the other parties. Oslo put pressure on Jordan and Jordan and Palestine put pressure on others. In fact, while holding negotiations Syria does not take these matters into account at all. . . . We are with the peace process but we do not support efforts to scoff at us. It is out of the question . . . that we do not believe in or that we do anything contradicting pan-Arab interest, what we believe to be a pan-Arab interest."[6]

Asad then moved to a review of the chiefs-of-staff meetings and the collapse of the security negotiations. In his view a sequence had not been agreed to in advance, what had been agreed upon was a scenario in which every fresh step should grow out of the successful implementation of a previous step. As he did on other occasions when he felt pressured, Asad implied that the American messenger was to blame: "They left here and immediately communicated this to the coordinator of the peace process, who, in turn was supposed to present it to Christopher. I do not know whether the message was communicated to a higher level. This was the basis on which we agreed that the chiefs of staff [Shahak and Shihabi] would meet, and they really met. The fact is that our chief of staff returned with the impression that an agreement was reached on security arrangements [!]."[7]

Asad proceeded to describe the disagreement over early-warning and ground stations, and then repeated his opposition to meetings for meeting's sake. Such meetings were exploited by Israel in order to advance her policies: "Results must be reached. . . . Here no decisions were taken. Nothing was decided between the two parties. The matter was mere reports circulated by the media on the subject which had no shadow of the truth. This was also some sort of abuse. We know the objective of these steps. They want to create an Arab and a European and even a world climate to imply that the peace process is progressing . . . and that meetings are being convened."[8]

After speaking in general terms about the Israeli and U.S. elections of 1996, Asad released a tirade against the Middle East Economic conferences and against the Israeli vision of a "new Middle East":

I believe that they want a dark future for us. . . . I believe that the long-term goal of the others is to cancel what is called the Arabs, what is called Arabism. . . . I mean canceling Arab feelings, canceling pan-Arab identity. . . . I wonder about this notion in the far Arab future and what its values and role at present and in the future will be. . . .

This is the objective they are seeking. . . . Why is the Middle East being established? The Middle East does exist. The strange thing is that the Middle East is being presented as an alternative to Arabism. . . . We as Arabs certainly reject this because this is not the hands of individuals. Arabism is not a commodity to trade in.[9]

SEVEN

Bitter Harvest at the
Wye Plantation

THE LAST CHAPTER of the four-year effort to resolve the Syrian-Israeli conflict, Hafiz al-Asad's give-and-take with Shimon Peres, provided a complex, ambiguous, and ironic *dénouement* to a tale already rich in ambiguity and irony.

In the summer of 1995, Yitzhak Rabin and Shimon Peres made their final peace. Peres accepted Rabin's seniority, Rabin accepted Peres as his partner and second in command. A common agenda cemented the reconciliation that put an end to a long history of rivalry and grudging cooperation. Peres was clearly resigned to the notion that he would never again be prime minister of Israel, and yet in the aftermath of Rabin's assassination he found himself in the unexpected and unlikely position of Rabin's heir and successor, wrapped in his former rival's mantle.

During most of his tenure, Rabin had denied Peres real access to the Syrian track, and Peres in turn made no secret of his criticism of the conduct of the Israeli-Syrian negotiations and of his own desire to take charge of them. With Rabin's full knowledge, he often took exception to the prominence assigned by the prime minister to the security dimension of the talks with Syria and to the role he gave to the military. Peres was certain that financial aid, economic development, and economic cooperation provided better keys to a new relationship with Damascus. He felt keenly that he could break the rigid mold of this inexplicably tortuous negotiation. Having concluded the Oslo II agreement in September 1995, Peres and his inner circle indicated clearly that they were eager and ready to apply their negotiating skill and experience to the Syrian track. Rabin, in yet another manifestation of the new relationship with Peres, agreed to a somewhat greater involvement on their part in the Syrian talks.

It was against this backdrop that suddenly, in early November 1995, Peres, now holding the ultimate responsibility for Israeli policies, was free to deal with Asad according to his own preferences. What he encountered was not a Syrian president eager to conclude swift agreement with an Israeli prime minister unencumbered with most of Rabin's reservations but a conservative, suspicious counterpart, as uneasy with Peres's boldness and creativity as he had been with Rabin's trepidation.

The tug-of-war between Rabin and Asad, both authoritative, cautious, suspicious, and shrewd, and yet different in so many other ways, was the stuff of a great drama. The encounter between Peres and Asad became a tale of bitter disappointment. Asad was dogged in his insistence on an agreement that matched his terms and dogged in his determination to stand up to Peres and to the Clinton administration and then to punish them for what he regarded as undue application of pressure. What Peres applied was not pressure but creativity. For every obstacle put up by Asad there was an imaginative solution thought out by Peres. But the more innovative Peres proved to be, the more uncomfortable Asad grew as he had to contend with his new counterpart's restless and creative mind.

Many of Asad's decisions during this period have yet to be fully explained. His initial response to the new prime minister's gambit was disappointing. He conducted his side of the Wye Plantation talks with typical conservatism. His reaction to Peres's decision to move up the Israeli election and postpone the conclusion of negotiations with Syria was angry. His position during that time and subsequently on terrorism, the activities of Hamas and Islamic Jihad offices in Damascus, and Hizballah's attacks on Israel from south Lebanon defies the explanations that have been offered. By making these decisions Asad not only failed to advance his own cause but contributed directly to Peres's electoral defeat on May 29, 1996. It was only in the wake of that defeat that Asad grasped fully that he had missed not one but two opportunities to conclude

a deal with Israel and that a new reality was established by the
May 29 elections.

The Clinton administration, while it genuinely grieved and
mourned Yitzhak Rabin's assassination, immediately turned its attention and diplomatic efforts to the Israeli-Syrian track and to the
fresh prospect of a Syrian-Israeli agreement and a comprehensive
Arab-Israeli settlement before the end of 1996. But even the resources of the world's sole superpower and the priority assigned by
the president and the secretary of state to this issue failed to overcome the difficulties and peculiarities of the Syrian-Israeli track. As
time went by, the Clinton administration was forced to shift its
efforts from the quest for a spectacular breakthrough in the Arab-
Israeli peace process to a salvaging operation.

This period can be easily divided into three distinct phases: first,
the preparation for and the actual conduct of the new Israeli-
Syrian negotiation from Rabin's assassination in November 1995
to Peres's decision in January 1996 to move up the Israeli parliamentary elections; second, from that point to the actual suspension of the negotiations in early March; and third, the period leading up to the May 29 elections.

A New Quest for a Breakthrough, November 1995–January 1996

On November 5, President Clinton flew to Israel at the head of a
large, impressive American delegation to take part in Yitzhak
Rabin's funeral. It was a natural act of personal friendship, a trib-
ute to a brave statesman who paid with his life for the policies he
pursued, and a demonstration of solidarity with the people of Israel. But alongside the genuine anguish and emotion there was
sober attention to the policy agenda. A meeting was set between
President Clinton and Acting Prime Minister Peres for the early
evening on the day of the funeral. I was asked by Dennis Ross to
make sure that Peres would be fully briefed on the key details of
the Syrian negotiations, since the president was planning to ask
him whether he intended to continue Rabin's policy.

As a matter of fact, I did not know to what extent Rabin had briefed Peres on our negotiations with Syria and on his discussions with the president and the secretary of state in these matters. The arrangement the three of us had worked out in 1993 was that Rabin and Peres should update each other so that I would not have to brief either of them on the activities of the other. In this fashion I could manage in the often impossible situation in which I reported to Rabin as chief negotiator with Syria and to Peres as ambassador to the United States. Needless to say, the arrangement did not function in real life as well as it should have in theory. Peres would have had to be superhuman not to be irritated when he discovered every so often that he had not been briefed fully or in real time, while Rabin chose sometimes to overlook independent activities by Peres and his men. But as a rule I found out time and again that Peres was better briefed by Rabin than people assumed, and that even in time of manifest tension between the two men, the communication and ultimately the cooperation between them functioned at all times.

Whatever my assumptions, I gave Peres as full a briefing as I could prior to his meeting with Clinton in the evening. I spoke to him briefly at the cemetery and then arranged to see him alone for thirty minutes at the King David Hotel. We went through the essential record of the negotiation and of the American-Israeli exchanges in that regard. It was all done under immense time pressure, but I did make a point of warning Peres against the term "commitment" that, I suspected, might be used in the discussion with the president. It would be one thing for Rabin's successor to express a commitment to the late prime minister's policies and undertakings. But this would be different from implying, as the very term might, that an actual commitment had been made with regard to withdrawal.

During their brief meeting, President Clinton told Peres that he would be available until July 1996 to help with the Israeli-Syrian negotiation. Later, and certainly after Labor Day, he expected to be fully preoccupied with his own reelection campaign. As this discussion clearly indicated, the Clinton administration had resolved to seek a Syrian-Israeli agreement in 1996. If the Israeli elections were to be held on schedule in October (the U.S. presidential elections being held in November), then several months were available for completing the negotiations. But during the next few weeks it transpired that in the American-Israeli-Syrian triangle the Clinton administration was the only single-minded actor in this regard.

Israel's new prime minister grappled during nearly three months with the interrelated questions of his policy agenda, the optimal date for elections, and the prospect of a satisfactory agreement with Syria. Peres had three options with regard to the Israeli general elections: one, keep the scheduled date of October 29, 1996; two, call immediately for elections, which according to Israeli law would be held some three months later; or three, move up the elections but not immediately. His instinctive decision was not to call for an immediate election that would have been held in the context of the assassination. It would have been a very divisive election and Peres, who would probably have won it, would be perceived to have been elected in Rabin's shadow and not necessarily in his own right.

Peres could see the advantage of holding the elections on schedule, but he felt that in that case he would need an impressive achievement during the intervening period. His associate Yossi Beilin had just informed him of the draft agreement he had concluded with Abu Mazen, Arafat's second-in-command, regarding an Israeli-Palestinian final status agreement. Beilin was urging Peres to focus his agenda on the Palestinian issue, to turn the draft into an actual agreement by the spring of 1996, and conduct the election campaign on that basis. Beilin's argument was that the Israeli public, upon realizing the achievements inherent in such an agreement, would reelect the government. But Peres was not persuaded.

He was more attracted by the prospect of a breakthrough with Syria. If a satisfactory agreement could be made with Syria by the spring, and if that agreement could indeed provide the key to a comprehensive settlement of the Arab-Israeli conflict, it could become the substantive platform for the elections. But before he made a decision, let alone a commitment, in that direction Peres had to establish whether an agreement that met his terms was feasible within the relevant time frame. This was the focus of the exploratory efforts that were conducted through the U.S. peace team during the next few weeks.

The new prime minister's concept of an Israeli-Syrian settlement reflected his broader view of and experience in Israeli-Arab peacemaking, his perception of the distinctive characteristics of this particular track, and the constraints of the Israeli political system in the aftermath of Rabin's assassination and on the eve of a crucial electoral campaign.

Peres knew very well that Asad would not sign a peace treaty with Israel without a full withdrawal from the Golan Heights, but he believed that the actual line of withdrawal or, put differently, the border between the two countries, was yet to be negotiated. Unlike Rabin, Peres did not seek to extend the period of implementation. In fact, he saw potential advantages in swifter implementation and in having a stable peaceful relationship with Syria prior to the final phase of permanent-status negotiations with the Palestinians.

Peres also had a different view of the security dimension of the negotiation with Syria. Both formerly and currently minister of defense, he did not underestimate the importance of either the security arrangements in the event of withdrawal or the Israeli military establishment's prospective role in making any settlement with Syria acceptable to Israeli opinion. But although during the previous years the accent of the Israeli-Syrian talks had been on the security issues, and these issues were clearly depicted as the key to further progress, Peres sought a change of emphasis. He advocated a "simultaneous negotiation" over the principal issues on the agenda, thus taking away, at least implicitly, the primacy given previously to the security dimension.

More significant was the message that "real security" lay in economic development (for Syria) and in the development of economic interests along the border and of economic ties between the two countries. The Golan Heights should become a "free economic zone" or "a zone of economic development." For obvious reasons this was never stated explicitly or trumpeted in public, but Peres's own thinking in this matter was very clear. In part it was the notion written about in the foreign minister's 1994 book, *The New Middle East* and applied on the Palestinian track—economic development and increased prosperity on the Arab side would create greater political stability and a more significant stake in peace, and thus enhance security. When both sides were forced to engage one another they would have to create a new relationship, different and better than the unattractive "cold peace" between Israel and Egypt. The development of economic enterprises and interests in the area of the Syrian-Israeli border and of economic and trade relations between the two countries would be an important long-term incentive for keeping the peace and an important disincentive for contemplating war. There was an additional, more immediate, political calculus. Economic cooperation in the Golan would mitigate the immense difficulties and pain inherent in any withdrawal.

A meaningful economic relationship was but one aspect of what Peres viewed as "the quality of peace." He knew, based on the negotiations of 1994–1995, that Asad was ready for a formal contractual peace including full diplomatic relations and "movement of people and goods." But by all indications what Asad had in mind was the bare minimum that could be legitimately fitted into these categories. This had not been an issue that weighed heavily with Rabin. He did not believe that Syria would be willing to offer Israel more than Egypt did. Peres believed that for peace to be durable it had to be of a different quality. He also felt that, given the Israeli public's frustration with the "cold peace" with Egypt, it would not support concessions designed to produce yet another version of that peace.

The value of an Israeli-Syrian peace could, in Peres's view, be enhanced by its quality or depth, and by turning it into the stepping stone toward a comprehensive settlement of the Arab-Israeli conflict. The idea itself was not new. In 1994, when we had heard from our Syrian interlocutors that Asad had changed his view and definition of comprehensiveness we began to discuss the fashion in which recognition of Israel by the bulk of the Arab world would be tied to the conclusion of an Israeli-Syrian agreement and the signing ceremony in Washington. But Peres went further. He realized that comprehensiveness had become an issue that could benefit both Israel and Syria. Israel could conceivably obtain an agreement that covered a much broader scope than the conflict, or relations, with Syria. For Asad the concessions inherent in recognition of Israel and the establishment of a normal relationship would be mitigated by the seniority implied in his role as the provider of the Arab consensus.

Peres wanted a much deeper American involvement in the Israeli-Syrian negotiation. It had been a three-way negotiation since 1993, with the United States playing the multiple role of sponsor, facilitator, mediator, and participant. It was difficult to envision a more active and salient role in the negotiation itself that would not turn it into an outright mediation or arbitration. But what the new prime minister had in mind was not so much that as an integration of the Israeli-Syrian agreement into an all-embracing Clinton Plan for the region. If the Israeli-Syrian agreement would indeed lead to a comprehensive settlement of the Arab-Israeli conflict, one of the chief traditional impediments to the creation of a regional security organization would be removed. Peres was hoping to persuade Clinton to launch such a bold initiative under the title of the "Clinton Plan."

Finally, there was an issue that concerned the negotiation itself. Peres insisted on an early meeting with Asad as an essential component of a swift agreement. He preferred a meeting in Jerusalem or Damascus, and regarded a meeting in Washington as a third best. In his view only a drama of this magnitude would persuade the Israeli public that an extraordinary development was taking place. He never said so explicitly, but I felt that given the record of the previous three years he also needed to be persuaded that he had a genuine partner.

Uri Savir, the director general of the Foreign Ministry, the prime minister's confidant and his chief aide in the negotiations of Oslo I and II, emerged clearly as his point person for the Syrian track.

Savir had a comfortable relationship with Dennis Ross that went back to Peres's days as prime minister and foreign minister in the 1980s, and was cemented by common work on the Palestinian track. They now constituted the principal channel for exploring the prospect of an Israeli-Syrian agreement. During the first half of November, Ross conducted preparatory discussions with Mu'allim in Washington and (by telephone) with Savir in Jerusalem. On November 19 Ross and his team traveled to Israel for intensive discussions with Peres and his aides. By that time a sequence was constructed: Ross and his team would return to the region in early December, followed by Peres's visit to the United States and by Secretary Christopher's visit to Israel and Syria. At the end of that sequence the ground would have been prepared for the resumption of a direct Israeli-Syrian negotiation.

Ross was very clear in expressing the Clinton administration's conviction that an agreement could be reached in 1996. He also spent time conveying Asad's mood and perspective. Asad, according to that description, felt that he had been used and misled. In his own view, he who "had made Madrid possible" was the only participant who had so far failed to benefit from it. Asad believed that Rabin did not want to conclude an agreement before the elections, but felt that Peres did. He regarded the messages that had been transmitted to him in this matter in the past as too general and, in fact, misleading. Asad wanted to come to an agreement in 1996, but his agreement had to be different from everybody else's. In any event, said Ross, Asad was not interested in a change of format.

Peres, in his meeting with Ross and his team, explained his concept of the substance and process of a prospective agreement with Syria. He added a number of elements to the fundamental package: a definitive solution of the water problem, cessation of terrorism, and public diplomacy. More significantly, he said to Ross that he had yet to make a final decision. His decision would depend on Asad's response to Peres's ideas on both substance and process.

On November 22 Peres formed the new government. He chose Ehud Baraq, who had joined Rabin's government as minister of labor, as the new foreign minister, and kept the defense ministry to himself. Haim Ramon, Baraq's chief rival for future leadership, rejoined the government as minister of the interior. Yossi Beilin gave up the economic and planning portfolio in order to become a minister without portfolio in the prime minister's office. But Beilin was assigned to domestic issues and not to foreign policy. Foreign policy was to be divided between Baraq and Savir, who formally remained director general under Baraq but in practice operated out of the prime minister's office as his right-hand man. It was an awkward arrangement typical of the confusion and uncertainty of this transitional period.

Within this context I personally had to cope with Peres's decision to put Savir in charge of the Syrian negotiations. This did not come to me as a complete surprise, and I respected the prime minister's prerogative to entrust his closest aide with the most crucial issue on his agenda. I knew full well what kind of a relationship the prime minister and his negotiator should have. Peres and Savir had had that relationship for more than a decade, and Savir had negotiated the two Oslo agreements on Peres's behalf. I had greater difficulty in accepting the roundabout fashion in which the change was done and announced, and the negative background briefings offered to the media by some of Peres's aides and would-be aides. In any event I decided to stay on as ambassador, and in short order a satisfactory personal and working relationship with Peres was restored.

Dealing with my role in the Syrian negotiations was more complex. I could not dissociate myself from the principal issue in our relations with the Clinton administration at that time and remain an effective ambassador in Washington. All three parties to the negotiation wanted my participation in the negotiation as a representative of Rabin's legacy, as the "institutional memory" on the Israeli side and, I would like to hope, as someone who understood the nature of this negotiation. Finding the posture and profile that would enable me to function was not easy and became more difficult during the Wye Plantation negotiations, as will be described below.

Not much happened during the next two weeks. Israeli and Syrian delegations headed by the foreign ministers participated at the Barcelona conference, organized by the European Union, but nothing about the conduct of the Syrian delegation suggested that a dramatic change was around the corner.

On December 4, Ross arrived in the region and proceeded to Damascus. On the 5th, in the evening, he came to brief Peres on his four-hour meeting with Asad. Ross carried a letter from Peres. Asad responded positively but indicated that he would rather wait for his meeting with Secretary Christopher in order to elaborate on his position. But on one issue he was specific: he intended to keep Mu'allim as his negotiator; Peres could naturally appoint whomever he chose to.

In his two meetings with Ross, Peres spoke mostly about his idea of a "Clinton Plan." Peres sought to integrate Israel's prospective agreement with Syria into a larger scheme that would include a bilateral American-Israeli treaty and a regional security pact. Ross, while trying to understand what Peres had in mind, was noncommittal.

Peres came to Washington for a meeting with President Clinton on December 10. As usual it was preceded by a preparatory meeting with the secretary of state. Peres explained to Christopher that he was ready for any mode of negotiation and progress with Syria: "fast or slow, broad or narrow." It was up to Asad to decide what he wanted and to act accordingly. If Asad wanted an agreement before the elections he had to agree to a "dramatic step" (namely, a meeting). He presented the public line he was willing to adopt with regard to withdrawal. He was ready to state in the Knesset that the time had come to establish a permanent border between Israel and Syria based on Security Council Resolutions 242 and 338.

Christopher, in turn, told Peres that he was planning to travel to Syria on December 14, to proceed from there to Jerusalem, and to return to the region in early January after a round of direct Israeli-Syrian negotiations.

President Clinton's response to the idea of launching a major plan or initiative that bore his name was predictably cautious. He was clearly not eager to associate himself too closely with a project with such uncertain prospects. Nor was his administration interested at that stage in a formalization of the special and close relationship with Israel. It felt that the relationship as such had been accepted by the Arab world as a fact of life, albeit grudgingly, but that its formalization might provoke undesirable reactions and undermine Washington's ability to lead the peace process. There was much that could be said in response to this unspoken argument, but Peres chose to leave it at that.

On December 12 another meeting was held at Blair House, the president's guest house, between Peres and Christopher on the eve of the secretary's trip to Damascus. In retrospect one aspect of that meeting stands out: for the second time Peres asked Christopher to convey to Asad that the situation in south Lebanon and Syria's policies there were unacceptable to him and, his liberal position in the peace process notwithstanding, he would have to react forcefully if the violence continued.

On December 15 Christopher was in Israel after his visit to Damascus and his discussion with Asad. In a very informal setting at the prime minister's home he reported on Asad's response to the ideas that the secretary had presented to him under the heading of a "ten-point plan."

A version of Christopher's "ten points" became public a few days later when Peres briefed the Labor party's parliamentary caucus and dwelt on them at some length. Shortly thereafter they were leaked to the Israeli media. In any event, in the group that listened to Christopher's report on the 15th there were those who saw Asad's response as very positive and those who thought that it was long on atmospherics and short on substance. Thus with regard to keeping peace and quiet in south Lebanon, Asad expressed a preference for "a practical situation rather than a formal understanding." He favored, naturally, an active American role, but when told that Peres did not object to separate American-Syrian understandings, Asad reacted carefully and proposed that this be dealt with "at a suitable time." With regard to development projects he emphasized regional "development" rather than "cooperation," and expressed preference for development schemes in the Golan. He saw water as both a bilateral and multilateral issue, thus indicating that the water problems between Israel and Syria could not be resolved on a purely bilateral basis.[1]

The bottom line, in my opinion, was that Asad was ready for some upgrading of the negotiations. He must have heard from his American interlocutors that Peres was committed to the understandings with Rabin, that he was "softer" on the time frame and on security (if this particular message was conveyed in this fashion it would have been misleading), that he insisted on the depth and quality of peace and on some form of economic cooperation, and, finally, that he was willing "to fly high and fast or low and slow" depending on Asad's own decision.

Asad's response was cautiously positive but very guarded. This came as no surprise to those who had watched Asad's conduct of the negotiations since 1992 and Syria's behavior since November 4. Syria's direct response to Rabin's assassination was, at best, heartless. There was no fresh willingness to invest in public diplomacy or in curbing the violence in south Lebanon, so as to expand the base of public support in Israel for the policies of a new prime minister who was willing to transform the negotiation with Syria. Peres's gambit for a swift agreement predicated on an early meeting between the two leaders was rebuffed. Asad clearly wanted to find out more about what Peres expected and was willing to offer before he committed himself further.

On this basis the Wye Plantation negotiations were put together by Ross and his team. The Wye Plantation is a conference center on the Chesapeake about an hour and a half away from Washington. It belongs to the Aspen Institute but can be rented by other organizations. It is at its best in the spring and in the fall—it is too cold in winter and too hot in summer to enjoy the beautiful surroundings. But it offered a very comfortable and isolated setting perfectly located with regard to Washington that suited our needs and purposes at the time.

Asad did not want to send military officers to the first round of negotiations. Ambassador Mu'allim as head of the Syrian delegation was accompanied by Mikhail Wahba, his successor as head of Foreign Minister Faruq al-Shara⁰'s office and Riad Daudi, the international lawyer who had been a member of Muwaffaq Allaf's delegation in 1992.

The core of the Israeli delegation consisted of Uri Savir, Joel Singer, the Foreign Ministry's legal adviser, and myself. A much larger delegation came from Israel, comprising Foreign Ministry and the IDF's Planning Division experts who were in charge of staff work and paper work. They were reinforced by Yossi Vardi, an effervescent, bright businessman who for some time on a pro bono basis had prepared economic projects for the peace process with the Jordanians and the Palestinians. The experience that Savir had accumulated in his negotiations with the Palestinians and the staff and pool of experts he had developed were now mobilized for the Syrian talks.

Dennis Ross was accompanied by Mark Parris, the National Security Council's senior director for Middle Eastern affairs; Aron Miller, Ross's deputy; and Toni Verstandig, one of the senior persons in the Near Eastern Bureau at the State Department.

It was agreed that during the negotiations all delegations would sleep at the Wye Plantation and take their meals together. In Syrian terms this was a concession or a sign of progress and, in fact, an important one. The fact that a group of Syrians and a group of Israelis lived for several days under the same roof and met and communicated quite freely was one of the more attractive and significant aspects of the Wye talks.

The structured negotiation unfolded in three formats: plenary meetings, meetings of the heads of delegations, and meetings in which the legal advisers met separately while the other six continued the general negotiation. There may have been other meetings at Wye of which I was not aware. I certainly was aware of unadvertised meetings held by Ross, Mu'allim, and Savir at Ross's home prior to and in between rounds of negotiations. With my own experience in such meetings I could sense that they had taken place, that the actual dynamics of the negotiations were determined in the smaller meetings in Washington and at Wye, and that the plenary sessions—at least some of the time—were ritualistic rather than substantive.

It was agreed that the negotiations would begin on December 27 and would be held for six days in two sessions with a weekend break in between. At the round's end Secretary Christopher would travel to Israel and Syria to encourage and help the parties to make the new decisions that would surely be required.

In press briefings at the end of the first round at Wye a "senior American source" (later identified as Dennis Ross) stated enthusiastically that "more was accomplished during these six days than in the previous four years of negotiation."[2] I felt at the time that this was a gross overstatement, but I was in a bind. Any statement on my part to the contrary would be seen and depicted as part of a "sour grapes" syndrome. But now even the limited perspective afforded by the past eighteen months enables us to take a more balanced view of those proceedings.

The delegations that came to the Wye Plantation were clearly seeking an agreement in 1996. The basic strategy was quite simple and not very different from the strategy that had governed the negotiations earlier: suspend direct and explicit discussion of withdrawal and concentrate on the Syrian half of the peace equation. Once the contents of that half became mutually acceptable, withdrawal would be addressed specifically. At Syria's insistence discussion of the security issues was deferred. Mu'allim was quite open in expressing his expectation that these issues would be relegated to a later phase and to a secondary position, and fought to delay the arrival of military officers to the Wye talks. The Syrians were clearly acting on the assumption that Peres and his team would be "softer" on security, and regarded Israel's military establishment as "tough" on security and as a source of potential opposition to the model for an agreement they had in mind.

A significant "leg" among the four original "legs" of Rabin's conceptual table was "interface," his insistence on an unbalanced implementation of the agreement once it was achieved, with heavy doses of normalization preceding a meaningful withdrawal. Under Clinton's and Christopher's pressure Asad had accepted the principle of interface, and had agreed to apply it in a minor way, but he remained most uncomfortable with a notion that derived directly from the peace that Anwar al-Sadat had made with Menachem Begin.

At Wye, Mu'allim pressed consistently for a brief and simple application of the agreement once it was achieved. With that in mind he repeated an idea that had been tried in the past—let us dispense with the phases altogether and have the agreement implemented in one fell swoop, he said. Savir did not rule it out but offered a different approach—let us build a time line and place "stations of implementation" along that line. The concept as such was acceptable to Mu'allim, but discussion of the actual time frame and its relationship to the process of implementation never materialized.

Most of the discussion during this first round focused on the quality of peace, normalization, economic cooperation, and comprehensiveness. The discussion was governed by an urgent and practical question: Peres had to make a final decision with regard to the elections—keep the original date of October 29, or move them up to May 29. Establishing whether or not a swift agreement with Asad was feasible was a crucial element in his decision. Were the essential elements of Peres's concept of a satisfactory agreement with Syria acceptable to Asad? At this point the prime minister had one negative reply from Syria and one from the United States: Asad was not ready for an early meeting or for any other dramatic act of public diplomacy. President Clinton declined the invitation to launch a major plan carrying his name. So what about the other components of the prime minister's concept?

Asad had accepted the notion of "normal peaceful relations" in 1994, and Mu'allim was authorized to say it in a more forthcoming fashion at Wye. But in a situation in which the quality and depth of peace, normalization, and economic cooperation constituted the cutting edge of the prime minister's concept of peace, general statements did not suffice.

Savir pressed on, and Mu'allim responded by saying that economic cooperation presented a difficulty for him and that nor-

malization issues should be divided into those suitable for short-
term implementation and those that should be implemented "at a
more distant future." Savir pressed on again, and proposed that
Joel Singer, our legal expert and a veteran of the peace negotiations with Egypt, would share with us all his experience in establishing "a normal peaceful relationship" between two states that
had had no relationship in the past. Singer enumerated eighteen
areas that had to be covered by agreements in order to build an infrastructure for a normal relationship and to facilitate the transition from a state of war to a state of peace: diplomatic and consular
relations, abrogation of boycotts, the establishment of postal ties
and other forms of communication, economic and cultural cooperation, and so forth.

It was agreed that Singer and his Syrian counterpart, Daudi,
would meet separately to examine these issues, but when it came
to substance Mu'allim remained firm in his original position. As he
saw it, the natural progression for the two countries would begin
with termination of the state of war, which would be achieved first
and foremost by termination of occupation. Once this and security for both parties were achieved, normal peaceful relations
could be established. It was essential that a firm base be put in
place before Syria examined carefully her future relationship with
Israel and dealt with the issue of cooperation in a manner that
would best serve her national interests. Everything must be decided on that basis, and nothing must be construed or appear as a
condition. At this point he could not predict Syria's outlook on
Singer's eighteen points, as his feet were planted in the present,
the present being governed by the psychology of war and occupation. Syria's future outlook would be governed by interests and not
by commitments. For the sake of perspective it was important to remember that with the United States Syria had "normal peaceful relations" and did not have eighteen specific agreements. With Israel
nothing was excluded in the future but nothing could be promised
now. Mu'allim was more specific with regard to bilateral economic
relations with Israel; he could not say at present, when a state of

war obtained between the two countries, that Syria would establish bilateral economic relations with Israel.

During the weekend break Mu'allim softened his position on normalization somewhat. He still objected to the notion of eighteen different agreements and to a proactive approach to the issue of normalization. But he was willing to pursue a liberal interpretation of the three areas of "normal peaceful relations" that Asad had accepted in the past—diplomatic relations, termination of boycotts, and movement of people and goods. Such a liberal interpretation could cover most of Singer's points without being too much out of line. But Mu'allim remained adamant on the question of bilateral economic ties (and, by implication, of economic cooperation in the Golan Heights). He cited three reasons for Syrian trepidation: first, history and sensibilities ("we are still in a state of war"); second, the gap between the economic position of the two countries as reflected in the per capita income and other indices; and third, the Syrian—and broader Arab—fear of Israeli economic hegemony. The average Israeli citizen, said Mu'allim, would have a concrete sense of the new peaceful reality: embassies would be established, flags would be hoisted, the danger of war would be removed and new vistas would be opened; the Israelis would no longer be confined to the narrow boundaries of their country. They would be able, for instance, to get into their car and drive up to Istanbul. But for the time being at least intimate economic cooperation and other such ties could not be promised as part of the new reality.

Syria was, of course, interested in economic aid and development, and was hoping to see the United States lead such an international effort, but it wanted to shift the economic dimension of peacemaking from the uncomfortable context of the new bilateral relationship with Israel to the more comfortable rubric of comprehensiveness. In the vocabulary of the negotiations the term "comprehensiveness" acquired several layers: using an Israeli-Syrian agreement as the stepping stone toward a comprehensive settlement of the Arab-Israeli conflict, severing the linkage between the Syrian track and the Palestinian track, and instituting an international effort led by the United States for regional economic development. Comprehensiveness had been one of the least controversial issues in the Israeli-Syrian negotiation since 1994 and was certainly so at Wye, but a certain degree of ambiguity remained inherent in the Syrian position.

Shortly before the first meeting at Wye, on December 23, Asad, in response to a direct question at a press conference in Cairo, addressed the issue at length. He did say that "by a comprehensive solution we mean the people around Israel . . . who are directly concerned with the peace. Of course peace is a peace for all the Arabs . . . but things have always started from the surrounding, or cordon states. . . . Comprehensive peace will be achieved when Syria and Lebanon sign a peace agreement." And yet "the issues of the Arabs, no matter how they look and how some Arabs view them, will remain Arab issues. Assistance and feelings of pan-Arab responsibility will remain the basis."[3]

Asad also spoke specifically about the Israeli-Palestinian agreement. He did say that "they signed an agreement; it is a peace agreement." After all, what could he say in this regard if he wanted to sever the link between the Syrian and Lebanese tracks and the Palestinian track, on which he himself had insisted in the past? Asad also claimed credit (from the United States and Israel) for not obstructing an agreement he was not happy with, and yet he could not and maybe did not want to conceal his lingering opposition to the principle and details of the Oslo accords: "we clearly expressed our dissatisfaction for many reasons. I do not want to enumerate here. . . . We are clearly proceeding from the principles of the Madrid Process and what we had agreed upon before the peace process began in Madrid. . . . We agreed on certain principles. We are proceeding in accordance with these principles. We have not abandoned and will not abandon the principles that formed the basis of our endeavor. Some brethren, of course, placed themselves outside the scope of these principles."[4]

An Israeli prime minister who read these lines while grappling with the question of linkage between the Syrian and Palestinian tracks would have been wise to conclude that whatever formulae were to be agreed upon with regard to comprehensiveness, Asad's Syria could not be expected to dissociate itself fully from Palestinian politics.

The round was concluded with a view to the secretary of state's trip to the region. Ross prepared and read out a summary of the discussion emphasizing the points of agreement and convergence. This was another novelty. In three-way meetings in the past everybody took notes but a summary was not prepared. In the aftermath of the Shahak-Shihabi meeting in June 1995, Ross prepared a written summary that became a source of friction with the Syrians and was not acceptable to Rabin, either. At the Wye Plantation he read out a summary, which both sides endorsed. The summary dealt with four issues: the conceptual approach; the approach to the negotiations; comprehensiveness; and the international-economic dimension.

Ross presented his summary as the basis for the agenda of the secretary's trip, but two of the most crucial items of that agenda were not part of the summary. The administration knew very well that Peres was agonizing over the question of the election date or, in other words, whether the elections should be held in late October or moved up to late May. The prospect of a satisfactory agreement with Syria to be achieved by the summer was a crucial element in his decision. Syria's position on normalization and economic cooperation as presented by Mu'allim at the Wye Plantation was, from that point of view, discouraging. It was also necessary from Israel's perspective to begin a serious discussion of the security and water issues, and as Mu'allim had explained, given Asad's reluctance it was up to the secretary of state to persuade him to send military officers and water experts to the next round at the Wye Plantation.

The Israeli delegation traveled back home to brief the prime minister and the group of cabinet members he had designated as a steering committee of sorts for the Syrian negotiations. The circle around Peres was deeply divided in its assessment of the Wye talks and over the related question of the election date. These divisions were soon reflected in "pessimistic" and "optimistic" news and commentary in the Israeli media. Peres himself summed up the consultations that preceded Christopher's arrival in a sober fashion. In the next session at Wye, security and water should be discussed. The general statements regarding economic matters should be made concrete. And most important was the timetable: by the end of January, we must know what can be accomplished prior to October.

The secretary of state was at his realistic and dignified best. He defined the first round at Wye as "a new beginning." The tone and the atmosphere were positive. The underlying attitude was that of seeking solutions to problems rather than digging in behind barricades. But from a Syrian point of view Mu'allim had come to Wye on an essentially exploratory mission. From now on Asad would have to provide specific answers to the key questions. Christopher saw four achievements that had been accomplished at Wye: first, comprehensiveness was turned into a positive issue and a key to further progress; second, there was a sense that peace had an economic dimension and could build on the Syrian desire to have an American economic umbrella "as a bridge"; third, the concept of a time line was adopted and the need to build a critical mass on it was accepted; and fourth, the technique of working through an expanded core group was established. An honorable man, Christopher knew well that this list of achievements was padded, and in a less formal meeting he admitted to a certain disappointment with Asad's response as reflected in his envoy's conduct at Wye. For the venture to be successful much more would have to happen at the next session.

Peres, too, was very open with the secretary of state. Having heard from Christopher that Asad would not agree to a two-phased formula for dealing with the issue of withdrawal, he outlined his prerequisites for a swift negotiation: a genuine comprehensive settlement (with at least fifteen Arab states) and two or three working sessions with Asad. He told Christopher that given the practicalities of the Israeli electoral system he would have to make up his mind before February 5, and that he would need clear responses concerning substance and procedure by that date. He was quite open in sharing his calculus with the visitor. If he kept the October date for the election and continued with an accelerated negotiation with Syria, he could ill afford a crisis in that negotiation in the spring or summer. If that were to happen—and crises were part of any negotiation—he would be compromised by both failure and the concessions he would have made by that time with nothing to show for them. What Peres did not cite specifically but what we all understood was Asad's desire to have precisely that tactical advantage in the negotiations.

Christopher left for Damascus clearly troubled by the state of the negotiations and by the burden of responsibility for his share in the difficult decision Peres would have to make. He returned from Damascus with a new sense of optimism and confidence in the track's ability to yield an Israeli-Syrian agreement in good time. The secretary was impressed by both the atmospherics and substance of his visit to Damascus. He still could not give Peres a clear-cut recommendation, but he felt that Peres "had a real partner" in Damascus. Asad accepted the concept of comprehensiveness and the notion of "an economic bridge" as a way to overcome the gaps between Syria's and Israel's positions. He agreed to dispatch a military expert to the second round at Wye (set for the last week in January) but not a water expert. The water issue would be discussed by Mu'allim, who was also given a mandate to discuss the U.S. "economic leadership." Asad agreed that peace and quiet in Lebanon were essential, but soon after Christopher's departure from Damascus Hizballah's activity in south Lebanon escalated. (In this case it seems to have been initiated by Iran, contrary to Syria's own wishes.)

Careful as Christopher was, it was clear to us that he and the Clinton administration in general were hoping that Peres would decide to keep the original date of the elections and proceed with the accelerated Syrian negotiation. The same subliminal message was brought by Vice President Gore, who visited Israel on January 16. He emphasized to Peres that he was not carrying a message from the president and recommended that the prime minister "trust his own instincts" in this delicate matter, but he left little doubt as to the administration's real preference.

The second round of the Wye Plantation negotiations opened on January 24. Asad dispatched not one but two generals—General Ibrahim al-'Ammar and General Hasan Khalil, who had come with Shihabi for his meeting with Shahak in June 1995. The two legal experts, Joel Singer and Riad Daudi, continued their separate work on normalization, and the plenary sessions dealt almost exclusively with the security issue. In deference to the two generals, Mu'allim spoke in Arabic and the deliberations were translated back and forth by the State Department's Arabic interpreter, Gamal Talal.

In stark contrast to the chiefs of staff meetings, the Syrian delegation was dominated by Mu'allim. The Syrian generals spoke to their Israeli counterparts at the "military table" at dinner, but during the sessions Mu'allim was the only one to speak.

On the Israeli side, Peres decided to entrust the conduct of the security issues to General Uzi Dayan, head of the IDF's Planning Division, who had worked closely with him and with Savir in the Oslo II negotiations. But for the first three days he also dispatched General Danny Yatom, whom he inherited from Rabin as military secretary. Mu'allim did not quite try to conceal his different attitude toward the two Israeli generals. He clearly regarded Yatom as a representative of Rabin's legacy—someone who would insist on massive security arrangements as an essential component of any Israeli-Syrian agreement. Dayan, because of his role in the Oslo II negotiations or because the Syrians were led (or misled) to believe so, was seen by them as a "softer" Israeli general who would facilitate Israel's acceptance of a much more modest security regime. Their gradual discovery over the next few days that this was not the case, that General Dayan was a faithful representative of the positions worked out by the IDF's General Staff, was a source of disappointment and subsequently of manifest anger.

I did not know at the time, and I do not know now, to what extent the Syrians in general and Mu'allim specifically had been briefed by the U.S. peace team about the Israeli prime minister's intention to make a decision regarding the elections date on the basis of the second round's proceedings. The Israeli and U.S. delegations certainly acted with that imminent decision in mind. If Mu'allim was aware of such a consideration he seemed to be oblivious to it.

Daudi was quite forthcoming in his work with Singer, and they managed to fit twelve out of eighteen issues into the three categories that Asad had originally authorized. But six issues still remained outside the scope of the Syrian concept of "normal peaceful relations." Nor were the Syrians willing to envisage an elaborate section of the prospective peace treaty with Israel dealing with normalization. Our experience with Egypt had taught us that an impressive treaty and a panoply of annexes did not in themselves guarantee the degree of normalization desired by Israel. But the Syrian tendency to minimize normalization and treat it as a necessary evil did not augur well for the quest for an agreement predicated on the quality and depth of peace.

Mu'allim declined to discuss economic issues and economic cooperation. Instead, it was arranged that Toni Verstandig, the Bureau of Near Eastern Affairs expert on the economic dimension of the peace process, would remain in Damascus in the aftermath of Christopher's next trip to discuss these matters with the Syrian authorities. With regard to water, Mu'allim had a brief message—if the United States and Israel would help Syria resolve her water problems with Turkey, there would be no real water problem between Syria and Israel. In the event, there was no real opportunity to explore the potential inherent in this linkage, but the few discussions we and our American partners had with Turkish officials clearly indicated how difficult it would have been to find a formula acceptable to all three partners.

At the Wye Plantation these issues remained peripheral to the principal negotiation, which focused this time on the security issue. That negotiation was difficult and at times tense and strident. Mu'allim began with the familiar Syrian argument that a comprehensive and just agreement was the best way to prevent a future war. He then tried to find out whether the new prime minister's representatives would, indeed, be softer on security. With this in mind he proposed that security not be dealt with on its own but as part of an "integrated basket" comprising both military and political elements. If his approach were to be accepted, his next step would have probably been the argument that since Syria was providing Israel with a comprehensive settlement with the Arab world, Israel should moderate her demands in the security area. But Yatom and Dayan insisted on discussing the security arrangements first.

Dayan presented a concept for a security regime composed of six elements: a demilitarized buffer zone; a zone of limited deployment; early warning; control, inspection, and verification; dealing with terrorism and its infrastructure; and establishing a mechanism for communication, dialogue, and transparency. The ensuing discussion revealed that Mu'allim was willing to release one early concession—Syria would agree to the notion of confidence-building measures, which Americans and Israelis had been fond of and Syrians had not. But in return for this concession he wanted simplification and moderation of the security arrangements. In more concrete terms, Mu'allim proposed that relevant areas twenty-five kilometers wide be established on both sides of the border (which, he repeated, could only be on the lines of June 4, 1967). That area would be divided into demilitarized zones and zones of limited deployment. International forces and civilian police would be deployed in the demilitarized zones. Mu'allim thus chose to ignore Shihabi's gambit in June 1995, when he implied a 10:6 ratio in the relevant areas as his opening move. There was also a fresh emphasis on the notion of "on both sides," which in previous years had not been as prominent in Syrian presentations as the notion of "equality." Mu'allim was now insisting that there also be a demilitarized area on the Israeli side of the line, and that whatever international forces were deployed in the area be deployed on the Israeli side as well. Israel had accepted the notion of "equality in principle," but was categorically opposed to the notion of symmetry. We were willing to apply limited deployment on the Israeli side of the line. But the idea that Israel would go through a major withdrawal and then accept demilitarization and international presence on its side of the line had never been considered by us.

The heated discussion and the sharp arguments occurred when we reached the core of the IDF's position—dealing with the deployment of a sizable portion of Syria's strike forces near the Israeli border after peace was made. In the summer of 1995 Asad had agreed with Christopher and Ross that "Shahak's question" to Shihabi was legitimate. But when Dayan raised it at Wye, Mu'allim protested that Israel was meddling in Syria's domestic affairs. Syria might decide on redeployment at some future point, but only as her own free decision and not as an obligation or part of a treaty.

As Dayan became more specific, Mu'allim grew angrier. Dayan spoke of six Syrian divisions in the vicinity of the Golan Heights, of Syria's military presence in Lebanon, of Syria's Republican Guard (an elite fighting unit), and of Damascus. These were all relevant and legitimate issues for a genuine discussion of an Israeli-Syrian security regime, but when Dayan's hand touched Damascus on a map, Mu'allim burst out in an emotional and angry speech.

With a cooler head, Mu'allim later responded to the Israeli argument that there could be no security for us as long as Syria maintained a large standing army and kept a sizable part of it in her southwestern corner. He resorted to a line that had been used by him and his colleagues in previous exchanges: the military balance could not be measured locally but had to be seen within a larger frame. Overall, Israel had a clear advantage over Syria given the superiority of her air force, the strategic relationship with the United States, the U.S. commitment to Israel's qualitative edge and, of course, Israel's nuclear capabilities. Mu'allim proposed to avoid dealing with these issues since, clearly, any such discussion was bound to end in a stalemate.

This was a very curious and significant point. When Sadat had made his peace with Israel he chose to ignore these issues for the very same reason. But since Egypt agreed to a security regime that turned the Sinai Peninsula into an effective buffer zone, these issues could be finessed at the time. It was only much later, in the

1990s, that his successors chose to raise the issue and turn it into a major problem in the relationship between the two countries. With that experience in mind, Mu'allim's approach had no attraction for us. Was he proposing to ignore the issue for as long as Syria was seeking to regain the Golan Heights and keep the option of raising it at some future point at Syria's convenience?

A stalemate was clearly forming, and in order to preempt it a new idea was raised—a third category should be added (to the demilitarized zone and zone of limited deployment), so that the relevant area on the Syrian side could be expanded without inflicting a difficult concession on the Syrian side. The fresh idea was laid on the table, but Mu'allim did not respond. A novelty of this magnitude, we all knew by now, had to be taken up with Asad by the secretary of state during his next trip to the region.

By that time the agenda for the trip had been set. When Secretary Christopher came to the Wye Plantation on January 29 he had already been informed that Peres had finally made the decision to move up the elections. The Wye negotiation continued through January 30, but the American-Israeli dialogue shifted to the issue of damage control. The Clinton administration was not really surprised by the prime minister's decision, and if it was disappointed it managed to conceal its disappointment. In a typically pragmatic fashion it changed gears. An Israeli-Syrian agreement was not going to be achieved before May 29, 1996, but could it be achieved later in the year? Our American colleagues were preoccupied with Asad's reaction to Peres's decision. He was likely to respond with genuine anger, but also to use his anger to good advantage and to exact a price for a graceful acceptance of the Israeli decision. The truth of the matter was that Asad had no just cause for being angry. He had not met Peres's terms and had not provided him with real prospects of a good agreement in good time. But Asad must have felt that he had lost the tactical high ground, and according to his own lights he may also have felt betrayed.

Asad's anger was reflected initially in the Syrian media, where criticism of Peres and his policies began to appear. He must have been disappointed by more than just the change in the Israeli election date. As he saw it, he had made some significant concessions at Wye—he had agreed to a more specific discussion of normalization and to the notion of adding an economic dimension to his prospective accords with the United States and Israel. In Asad's book the change in Syria's position on water—linking it to Syria's water problems with Turkey rather than viewing it as both a bilateral and multilateral matter—was a show of flexibility. The Israeli concessions in the area of security that he had expected in return failed to be made, nor did he obtain an Israeli commitment to withdrawal. This certainly was not my view of the course and dynamic of the negotiation at Wye, but I was aware then as I am now of the Syrians' attachment to their own version of the same course of events.

Asad's apprehension was further fanned by the emergence during that very period of a close and formal relationship between Israel and Turkey. In February 1996 a defense cooperation agreement was signed between the two countries. Given the earlier history of Israeli-Turkish relations, this was a surprising and dramatic development. Israel and Turkey had established a close security cooperation in the late 1950s but it was kept secret at the time, due to the Turkish government's sensitivity to domestic Islamic opinion and Arab reaction. Later the relationship declined, and in the 1970s it was brought by the Turkish side to the verge of extinction. The rising power of Islamic forces, and, ironically, of the radical left, and hopes of access to Arab oil revenues were chiefly responsible for that negative Turkish attitude. The relationship improved gradually in the 1980s and dramatically in the 1990s. For one thing, the Arab-Israeli peace process facilitated and legitimized cooperation with Israel. Perhaps more important was the fact that the relationship with Israel became a litmus test in Turkish politics. If Necmettin Erbakan and the Islamists fought against it in the name of Islam, the military establishment as keeper of Ataturk's legacy pursued it with greater zeal and vigor. Furthermore, they chose to publicize a relationship that Israel was willing to keep discreet.

Israel had several good reasons for building a close relationship with Turkey—the natural affinity, its strategic importance, the significance of Turkey's civilian and economic markets, and the intrinsic importance of the security cooperation (to name one important element—the Israeli air force's ability to train in Turkey's open air space as against the limited possibilities afforded by Israel's own territory). The Turkish military's perception of an Iranian manifold threat reinforced the partnership and sense of partnership with Israel.

The notion of an Iranian threat did not apply to Syria. Turkey's rivalry with Syria is a well-known fact of life in the Middle East, and in an earlier decade Israel might well have seen a security pact with Turkey as having an anti-Syrian edge. This was not the case in 1996, but there was no persuading the Syrians that this was so. In retrospect it is significant to note that there was literally no persuading the Syrians; the issue was never brought up and addressed directly by the two delegations that negotiated so intimately during that very period. If the Syrians so deeply distrusted the Israeli-Turkish partnership being formed, why was Mu'allim not instructed to raise it with Savir or why did he not do it of his own initiative? The other side of the same coin is that we too did not initiate any discussion with the Syrians regarding this sensitive matter.

The public announcement concerning the new date for the Israeli elections was delayed by Peres until February 12 so as to enable Christopher to separate his trip to the region from this domestic political issue, at least as far as appearances were concerned. The secretary arrived in Israel on February 8 with a revised agenda. On the assumption that Peres was likely to win the elections, the United States wanted to keep Asad engaged in the negotiations and make whatever progress was possible in order to renew a full-steam negotiation soon after the formation of Israel's new government some time in June.

The secretary and his team were aware of Asad's foul mood. Christopher carried with him a reassuring letter from President Clinton, and was soon given a similar letter written by the prime minister of Israel. Christopher also tried to persuade Peres to offer Asad another sweetener—a willingness to accept the principle of demilitarization on the Israeli side. After some awkward give-and-take he left with an equivocal Israeli response.

On February 6, during the secretary of state's visit to Damascus, it was announced that the next round of talks at Wye would open on February 28. During the next few days we were briefed on the details of the Syrian position. Asad agreed to continue the negotiations and wanted to keep the emphasis on the security issues. He was interested in economic development and in the U.S. role in that regard, but the discussion that Toni Verstandig had in Damascus revealed the huge gap between the Ba'th regime's traditional approach to economic matters and the fundamental requirements of any international effort to boost the Syrian economy.

Asad remained firm in his position regarding the security arrangements. He rejected the notion of a third zone, and kept insisting on limited "relevant areas." The Syrians held on to a position which argued that deployment was a sovereign Syrian issue that could conceivably be pursued in the future on a purely voluntary basis. Given the preponderance of the security issue in the next round, the peace team, reinforced by General Christman, stayed in Israel to discuss it with our own team and the chief of staff. The discussion served to underline what we had all known—there was a very significant gap between the view of the IDF's leadership and the Syrian position as reflected this time in the presentation of the American team.

The third round of the Wye negotiations opened as scheduled on February 28 under the tragic and ominous shadow of the bus bombing that had occurred in Jerusalem on February 25 and of a second, less devastating attack in Ashkelon, in southern Israel.

This was the first in the series of three terrorist attacks (a second bus bombing in Jerusalem on March 3 and a suicide bombing in the heart of Tel Aviv on March 4) that shook the Peres government and had a major impact on the election results four months later. Peres had a comfortable lead over Netanyahu in the polls prior to the attacks, but his ratings and standing plummeted in their immediate aftermath. He regained some ground but never recovered fully. His defeat was the result of a cluster of factors and forces at work, but among these the decisive impact of this terrorist wave stands out clearly.

The waning of the Israeli-Syrian negotiation and the terrorist wave of February–March 1996 were related in more than one way. The Syrian refusal to denounce the terrorist attacks made our continued stay at Wye increasingly untenable, and finally led Peres to a virtual suspension of the negotiations on March 4. The political crisis in Israel and the threat to the very foundations of the peace process led the Clinton administration to organize an anti-terrorist campaign—the international summit in Sharm al-Shaykh on March 13–14 and the follow-up meeting in Washington at the end of March. Syria refused to come to the meetings and saw the campaign as directed not only against Iran but also against itself.

Asad found himself in a position he had known well in the past: seeking to spoil a Western effort to organize the region without and to some extent against Syria. It is difficult to understand Asad's conduct in Lebanon during the next few weeks except in this context. Lebanon had for more than twenty years been the arena in which he had defeated an array of regional and international challenges, and the escalation of Hizballah's attacks on Israel during this period cannot be explained except as a reflection of a Syrian decision to teach both the United States and Israel a lesson.

The clarity of Syrian policy with regard to Hizballah, Hamas, and Islamic Jihad once Asad decided to respond to what he regarded as bad faith and a challenge was not there in December and January. While Syria negotiated seriously at the Wye Plantation, Iran was trying to obstruct Arab-Israeli progress by escalating the activities of all three organizations. The Syrians were angered, and tension in their relationship with Iran ensued. The Syrian authorities restrained Hizballah's activities and imposed some limitations on the Hamas and Islamic Jihad offices in Damascus. But this was done quietly and with trepidation. There was not a clear and unambiguous message that Syria had made an irrevocable choice for peace with Israel, and that attacks against Israel, certainly attacks conducted from Lebanese soil or hatched in a Palestinian office in Damascus, had to be terminated.

All this was still not visible when the third round opened on February 28. We had a new face on our team—General Shaul Mufaz, about to replace General Dayan as head of the IDF's Planning Division and in the security talks with Syria (General Dayan was appointed general officer commanding Central Command).

In his opening statement, Dennis Ross acknowledged the impact of the terrorist attacks in Jerusalem and Ashkelon two days earlier by saying that the Israelis had arrived at the Wye Plantation "with a heavy heart." Ambassador Mu'allim found a way of being sympathetic without denouncing the attacks and drew our attention to the *Syria Times* editorial of that morning on the subject. The *Syria Times* editorial was the product of the pressure exerted by the Clinton administration on Asad's government to change its public line. The administration and, of course, our government and the Israeli media were exercised by Syria's original reaction to the attack in Jerusalem. Thus on February 25, on the Radio Damascus Hebrew service, a commentary was broadcast that justified the attack. It argued along lines familiar to us by now that this was the action of desperate people. The real terrorist, it argued, was the occupier and not the occupied. The choice of the *Syria Times* as the outlet for a softer response was interesting—it is a newspaper addressed to foreigners and hardly read by Syrians. The relevant passage read as follows:

> Incidentally, the Israeli negotiators will be coming to Maryland from the ordeal of two bombing operations that left a high toll among the Israelis. Although the incidents are condemned, these bombings and acts of violence and the ensuing closure of the occupied territories must be a lesson from which everybody should know that real peace is the only way to end tension and violence. Real peace means the return of land and rights to their indigenous owners.[5]

Mu'allim also spoke about the Israeli decision to move up the elections. Syria was unhappy with this development, but given her own "seriousness" and in appreciation of the "seriousness of President Clinton's and Prime Minister Peres's intention to reach an agreement by the end of the year" it had decided to proceed in the negotiations.

It soon transpired, though, that Mu'allim and his delegation came to Wye without new ideas and with no new instructions. The onus of moving the negotiations forward was on us. Indeed, General Dayan presented two new ideas. To begin with, he introduced the term "areas under consideration" as a substitute for "relevant areas." He was hoping that this change in terminology would facilitate Syria's acceptance of a larger area for the application of the security regime.

Dayan then expressed Israel's willingness to limit the IDF's deployment in its part of the "relevant areas" to a reinforced division. This was conceived as a trigger that would enable the Syrians to say explicitly that for their part they would be willing to pull back three of their divisions. This was something they had alluded to in their discussions with the American peace team. If they would be willing to spell it out during the formal session the security negotiations could be infused with new life at this delicate time.

But both gambits failed. Mu'allim rejected the term "areas under consideration" and pocketed the Israeli concession of voluntary limited deployment without offering a corresponding gesture. The discussion, while it lasted, consisted mostly of a familiar and sterile exchange between Mu'allim and the Israeli generals. Yet another effort by General Christman to revitalize the proceedings by addressing questions to both sides proved to be equally futile.

It is idle to speculate on our potential ability to keep the negotiation going for several more weeks. On March 3 the second terrorist act, which killed eighteen persons in Jerusalem, delivered the coup de grace to the Wye Plantation negotiations. Mu'allim's refusal to denounce the terrorist wave led us, under instructions from Jerusalem, to suspend the meeting. Israel's position during the next few days was that while it did not formally suspend the negotiations, our delegation would not participate in the negotiations as long as Syria could not bring itself to denounce terrorist attacks that were clearly designed to derail the peace process. Asad, in turn, did not even contemplate such a denunciation. The situation developed into a test of wills over this issue, and Asad was determined to win that test. The morning session of March 4 became the last act in the Israeli-Syrian negotiation of the years 1992–1996. Given the fact that no Israeli-Palestinian negotiations were scheduled after this period, and given the suspension of the multilateral peace talks, the peace process as it had been known for nearly four years came to a virtual end. Attention and activity shifted first to the campaign against terrorism and then to Operation Grapes of Wrath in Lebanon.

The campaign against terrorism was launched by the Clinton administration in order to save the peace process at the height of its most difficult crisis and to shore up the Israeli government, which was buffeted by yet another explosion in Tel Aviv and by the escalating violence in south Lebanon. The government was afflicted by loss of legitimacy, authority, and self-confidence, and the notion of an international campaign led personally by President Clinton had a reassuring impact. The original gathering in Sharm al-Shaykh in the Sinai on March 13 was an impressive affair. The follow-up meeting in Washington on March 28 was less so, and during the coming weeks the effort foundered altogether.

President Clinton's trip to Sharm al-Shaykh was followed by a visit to Israel. Most of his and his retinue's discussions with Prime Minister Peres and his team dealt directly with the terrorist challenge, but Asad, Syria, and Lebanon figured prominently as well. Americans and Israelis agreed that Asad felt cornered in the present situation and that it was important to extract him from that figurative corner. But how could it be done? How could the beleaguered Peres resume the negotiations as long as Syria adamantly refused to condemn the terrorist offensive, and in fact lauded it through the state-controlled media?

Peres was also worried by the rising tension in Lebanon as Hizballah stepped up its activities. Hizballah received its instructions from Iran, and Iran was clearly interested in fanning tension. The Labor government and the Israeli intelligence community shared the assessment that Iran was seeking at one and the same time to disrupt the peace process and to help bring down the Labor government that was committed to it.

With this Iranian policy in place, Syria did not have to encourage Hizballah to act, it only had to look the other way. This had been an important bone of contention between us during the past four years. We had not accepted the Syrians' contention that they only had "some influence" over Hizballah. We had felt all along that if Asad so wanted, he could have exercised a restraining influence over that organization. We had attributed his reluctance to a philosophy of negotiations that believed in using all means of pressure until the conclusion of negotiations, and did not believe in confidence building. (To my mind that interpretation was reinforced by the fact that in September–October 1996, when President Asad wanted to appear helpful to President Clinton's reelection, peace and quiet were kept in south Lebanon.)

In March 1996, in any event, Peres felt that Asad was actually stoking the fire and he asked his American visitors to convey a warning that at some point Israel would have to act. No one is fond of passing on such threats, and the visitors also saw fit to warn that a large-scale Israeli operation in Lebanon could very well play into Asad's hands.

But during the next four weeks Hizballah's activity continued to escalate, often in open defiance of the understandings that had governed, at least nominally, Israel's rivalry with Hizballah since August 1993. On April 2, the IDF launched Operation Grapes of Wrath. Like Operation Accountability of August 1993, its concept and course reflected Israel's limited ability to translate the IDF's overwhelming military superiority over Syria and the various actors in Lebanon into a swift and effective operation on the ground.

The constraints were familiar. Peres, like Rabin before him, believed that the only way to achieve a long-term solution to Israel's problem in Lebanon was through an agreement with Syria and subsequently with the government of Lebanon. Angry as he was with Syria's conduct, he still believed in a negotiated settlement with Damascus, and was determined to renew a full-fledged negotiation after the elections. An operation against the principal military force in Lebanon, the Syrian army, was not contemplated. An operation against Hizballah, a well-focused effort to destroy Katyusha rocket launchers and the teams that operated them, was part of the IDF's operational plan, but it was expected to have a limited value. At the core of the operation lay the notion that Israel could achieve at least some of its goals by exerting pressure on the government of Rafiq Hariri through destroying some economic targets and through causing the population in the south to flee to Beirut. Hariri would then be expected to use his influence with Damascus to change its own conduct. Hariri's influence in Damascus rested, so Israel believed, on Syria's awareness of the frailty of its own position in Lebanon. It had taken Syria a long time to put together a functioning government in Lebanon that would accept Syria's hegemony and yet enjoy a measure of legitimacy, and Damascus would have to take note of Hariri's pleas, the Israeli planners argued, if it wanted to protect its assets in Lebanon.

If the flaws inherent in this line of thinking were not self-evident, they should have been realized by any Israeli who studied the lessons of Operation Accountability. The prospects of actually achieving the operation's goals were limited, while Israel was bound to be cast in the role of a heartless, powerful state venting its rage and massive military power on innocent and helpless civilians. A large-scale military operation conducted among civilians carried the risk of unintended casualties, as happened, indeed, on April 19, when the IDF's artillery, seeking to hit back at a Hizballah post, shelled by mistake a group of civilian refugees in the village of Kafar Qana and killed more than a hundred. The ensuing wave of international and Arab indignation and condemnation made Israel's position practically untenable. All wars fought and military operations conducted in an Arab-Israeli context had a limited time frame, and the tragedy in Kafar Qana meant among other things that Israel had to bring its operation to a close swiftly. For a government facing elections in six weeks, the need to end the operation with a redeeming achievement was greater than ever. Operation Grapes of Wrath in general and the tragedy of Kafar Qana in particular demonstrated how difficult it was for Israel to conduct a punitive military operation in one part of the Arab world without affecting her new peaceful relations in other parts, such as Jordan. Furthermore, the events in Lebanon had negative repercussions among Israel's own Arab citizens, and ended up having a negative impact on Peres's would-be Israeli Arab supporters.

In the words of his biographer, "Asad saw Grapes of Wrath as directed primarily against him. He could not fail to see it as a replay, albeit on a more modest scale, of Operation Peace of Galilee, Menachem Begin's invasion of Lebanon in 1982." According to the same author, Peres's aim was to undermine Syria's position in Lebanon and to drive a wedge between her and Iran—"Robbed of his role of Arab champion, his regional pretensions exposed as hollow, Asad would have suffered a major political defeat and became less able to resist Israeli terms in future peace negotiations." The Clinton administration, according to the same line of argumentation, was a willing and a pliant partner in the Israeli effort to humiliate Asad and force him to make peace on terms that he found objectionable.[6]

Anyone familiar with the soul-searching that Peres went through before he finally authorized the operation in Lebanon or with the light touch that characterized the Clinton administration's give-and-take with Asad's regime may find this interpretation fantastic, and yet it is difficult to scrutinize Asad's conduct toward both Israel and the United States throughout the efforts to resolve the crisis without noticing a determination to punish both. It goes without saying that once the operation was launched and the challenge to him was presented, Asad felt that he was bound to win. As the operation unfolded and Israel's predicament transpired, he shrewdly realized that he was dealt a good hand and sought to maximize it. But when he chose to humiliate the secretary of state and let him complete a visit to Damascus without seeing him he overplayed his hand.

A cease-fire was finally arranged by the secretary of state on a basis that was not fundamentally different from the understandings that had been reached in the aftermath of Operation Accountability, except in two important points: the decision to establish a monitoring mechanism in order to help implement the new understandings, and the role assigned to France in that context.

A negotiation on the formation of the monitoring mechanism began in Washington on May 10. For several reasons it turned into an interesting and significant process. For one thing, it produced the only agreement we reached with Syria in nearly four years of negotiations other than the "non-paper" on the aims and principles of the security arrangements. The agreement was put together on the eve of the May 29 elections, but was finalized on July 3 after the formation of Netanhayu's government, the signing session providing the first opportunity for a direct encounter between representatives of Asad's regime and Netanyahu's government. The negotiation was conducted by five parties: the United States, France, Israel, Syria, and Lebanon.

France's inclusion was the second novelty. France, of course, had a long and cherished tradition of interest and influence in Lebanon, and had invested great effort in acquiring a new role and a new status in that country. French diplomacy had been encumbered by the need to reconcile France's championship of Lebanese statehood and sovereignty with its parallel effort to cultivate a close relationship with Syria. France's quest for a special role in the Israeli-Syrian track had been checked by the United States, Israel, and Syria. The United States saw France as a competitor, and Israel—Rabin in particular—regarded the United States as a much more effective and balanced facilitator. Syria tended occasionally to rely on European countries, France in particular, as a counterweight to Washington's special relationship with Israel. But Asad kept his relationship with France within well-defined lines, since he himself wanted to build a new relationship with the United States and realized that Washington alone had the capacity to serve as the honest broker of a Syrian-Israeli agreement and to underwrite it. And yet in April 1996, when he was angry at the United States, he resorted to the technique he had practiced in the days of the Cold War and played off Paris against Washington. It was Syrian insistence on a French role as a condition to cease-fire and agreement that brought France into the monitoring group.

On May 10 we began the negotiation on formation of the monitoring group. The meetings were held at the State Department building. The United States was represented by Dennis Ross and his team. France was represented first by Denis Bouchard, head of the Quai d'Orsay's Middle Eastern division. Israel, Syria, and Lebanon were represented by their ambassadors to Washington. Reconciling the diverse agendas of the five parties was an arduous task, but by the end of the third week in May an agreement was nearly ready. At that point Peres decided that it would not be wise to sign a potentially controversial agreement on the very eve of the elections.

The agreement as negotiated by us on behalf of the Peres government was concluded by his successor, Benjamin Netanyahu, on July 12, during his first visit to the United States as Israel's new prime minister. Netanyahu authorized me as Israel's ambassador (I stayed on after the May 29 elections for a transitional period of three months) and his foreign policy adviser Dore Gold to conclude the negotiation on the basis of the existing compromise. Netanyahu as leader of the opposition had been critical of some of the particulars of the new arrangement but he was in the process of moderating his views on Israel's relationship with Syria. Furthermore, he appreciated the impact of formal contact with Asad's Syria for a new Israeli leader who was being demonized by many in the Arab world.

The meeting in the State Department building provided an opportunity for one of Netanyahu's confidants, Dore Gold, to meet with Ambassador Mu'allim. At the same point Ross and I stepped aside so that messages could be exchanged freely. I do not know what was said by the two emissaries, but if the course of events during the next thirteen months is to serve as an index it did not amount to much. To the best of my knowledge this was the last direct contact between Israeli and Syrian representatives. The negotiation between the two countries may be renewed at some point, but the negotiation of the years 1992–1996 came to an end.

This account of nearly four years of serious negotiations between Israel and Syria raises several questions: why did the negotiations fail to produce an agreement? Was there a deal in the cards that was not turned from potential to reality? If so, why was a deal not made and what roles were played in this regard by the three participants in the negotiations, Israel, Syria, and the United States? Given the failure to reach an agreement, did the parties actually seek an agreement, or were they negotiating with other purposes in mind? What was the significance of the Israeli-Syrian negotiation within the larger scheme of the Israeli-Arab peace process and the regional politics of the Middle East? And finally, what has happened between Israel and Syria since the suspension of their negotiations, and what are the prospects of resuming a serious negotiation between the two countries in the foreseeable future?

At no time during this period (August 1992–March 1996) were Israel and Syria on the verge of a breakthrough. A breakthrough occurs when both sides realize that the main elements of the deal have been agreed upon; various details, some of them important, have yet to be finalized, a crisis may yet develop, but an invisible line has been crossed and both sides know that they have an agreement in hand.

The potential of getting to that point existed twice—in August 1993 and during the first few weeks of Shimon Peres's tenure as prime minister in November–December 1995. In early August 1993, Rabin sought to establish whether he had a viable option for a settlement with Syria as the cornerstone in his peacemaking strategy. Having failed in his persistent efforts to form a direct channel to Asad, he relied on the U.S. secretary of state and authorized him to use the "hypothetical question" technique in order to find out whether Asad was ready for the very specific package that Rabin regarded as acceptable to him and, ultimately, to the Israeli public. An element of flexibility was built into the package to be used in the inevitable process of bargaining, but a trained eye could easily identify the hard core of Rabin's position.

Asad's response was positive in principle, in that he told the secretary of state for the first time that, in return for the withdrawal he was asking for, he was willing to offer a full contractual peace. But his response to Rabin's specific peace package was disappointing. Two core elements were unacceptable to Asad: normalization and interface—Rabin's insistence on applying the Israeli-Egyptian model whereby a limited withdrawal would be matched by a comparatively long period of normalization so as to "test" the new relationship before a large-scale withdrawal was undertaken. Asad also rejected Rabin's demands in two procedural matters (which for the Israeli prime minister were most important)— engaging in public diplomacy and establishing a discreet, bilateral channel. On other issues—the security arrangements and the time frame—his response indicated that a long and arduous bargaining process lay ahead. Asad, in other words, had his own specific peace package and he was willing to come to an agreement only on the basis of that package or a close approximation of it.

Rabin's package reflected his principal considerations: peace with Syria was important in itself and as an indispensable component of an eventual comprehensive settlement. But Asad would not make peace unless offered a full withdrawal. This was a price Rabin was most reluctant to pay. Furthermore, even if he personally overcame his own feelings he would find it difficult to rally a majority of Israelis to endorse it unless Asad was willing to make an investment in converting the Israeli public. Rabin's package and his procedural concomitants were designed to guarantee that Israel ended up with a genuine peace, that the political and security risks were minimized, and that a political base of support for it could be built in Israel.

Rabin's reluctance was matched by Asad's ambiguity. He had made "a strategic decision for peace" in the sense that he was now willing to make a contractual peace with Israel. He wanted to regain the Golan and to build a new relationship with the United States, and he had come to the conclusion that the two could not be obtained unless he were willing to sign a peace treaty with Israel. Asad believed that he could cope with this radical emotional and ideological departure from his past record, and that his regime could absorb the shock waves and the impact of the changes entailed in this decision. But this could only be done within a very particular definition of peace and of the procedure that led to it. Dignity was an important consideration, as were the sense of lingering geopolitical rivalry with Israel and of Syrian society's and political system's vulnerability to the impact of opening up in general, and to Israel specifically. Hence the insistence on a modest set of political and security arrangements to be offered in return for a withdrawal that Asad regarded as his due. Here, too, was a curious symmetry between the Israeli and Syrian positions. Asad believed that Israel was bound to withdraw; in his terminology it was "an obligation" decreed by "international legitimacy." Israel did not deserve to be rewarded for fulfilling its obligation, and therefore everything that Syria might agree to that was not specified in Resolution 242 would be a concession. For Rabin, Israel's and his personal agreement to a massive withdrawal in the Golan would be a major concession, a radical departure from an entrenched policy, and a risky and costly step. For him what Syria was asked to give were not concessions but prerequisites for making his decisions justified and viable.

The gap between these two outlooks could conceivably be closed by the United States as the facilitator of the peace process and of the Israeli-Syrian track in particular. In Rabin's eyes this should have been done by pressuring Asad to accept the basic premises of his position. If the United States were to play the classic role of a mediator and come out with a compromise formula of sorts, his package would be eroded to the point of making the deal unacceptable. It is moot to speculate on the potential course of events had Asad accepted a greater part of Rabin's package or had the Clinton administration decided to tell Asad that it viewed Rabin's package as an integrated whole and expected him to accept it if he

wanted to move on in the peace process. Given the history of Washington's relations with Asad this could hardly be expected and, indeed, did not happen. During the previous two decades only one
administration, Reagan's, was willing to be tough with Asad to the
point of colliding with him in Lebanon, and it ended by withdrawing ignominiously. The Nixon, Ford, Carter, and Bush administrations all tried with varying degrees of success to engage
Asad. The Clinton administration adopted the same approach.
Nor did the administration expect Rabin to conclude the agreement with the PLO in Oslo within such a short time span. But
under the combined impact of Asad's response and the administration's attitude, Rabin chose to make his move on the Palestinian track.

Given this turn of events, the prospect of an agreement with
Syria before the end of Rabin's first term diminished progressively.
True, some very significant negotiations took place (the "ambassadors' channel" and the chiefs of staff's meetings in 1994 and
1995) and progress was made in the negotiations and in Asad's
give-and-take with President Clinton and Secretary Christopher,
but the passage of time had a negative effect on the Israeli-Syrian
track. The events of August 1993 predicated the peace process on
the Israeli-Palestinian track. The accent then shifted to the Israeli-
Jordanian track. As time went by, Asad's ability to obtain an agreement with Israel that would be implemented within Rabin's term
was lost. The passage of time also meant that opposition in Israel
to Rabin's policy in the peace process and specifically to a settlement with Syria was building up. Asad in turn felt more relaxed in
1995 than he had in 1991–1992, when the impact of the Soviet
Union's collapse and the Gulf crisis was fresh.

Asad and Rabin became increasingly skeptical of each other.
Rabin suspected that Asad was less interested in making peace than
in obtaining Israeli and American commitments for withdrawal,
that he was not interested in a genuine negotiation but in an American mediation that would meet him half-way without addressing
the fundamental elements of Rabin's package. Asad suspected that
Rabin had decided not to conclude an agreement with him dur-

ing his first term and that he was keeping him last in line, expecting to consolidate the peace process, negotiating with Asad from a position of strength, and seeking to force him to come to an agreement on Israel's terms.

Asad's suspicions were not totally unfounded, in that Rabin had indeed believed since August 1993 that an agreement with Syria during his first term was unlikely. The events of August 1993, Clinton's summit with Asad in January 1994, Asad's stiffer position in April of that year, and the two crises that followed the chiefs of staff's meetings in 1994–1995 all indicated to him that even if Asad had made a "strategic choice for peace" it was encumbered by so many conditions, reservations, and inhibitions as to make it impractical. Rabin did not expect the Clinton administration to deal with Asad more forcefully, and despite occasional references to the greater effectiveness of exerting geopolitical pressures on Asad he did not pursue this approach seriously.

Rabin knew that in the long term an agreement with Syria would have to be made for Israel's reconciliation with her Arab neighbors to be viable. But he was not in a hurry, and was certainly not willing to pay the price exacted in negotiations for being or appearing to be in a hurry. The Oslo agreements, peace with Jordan, and a degree of normalization with the Arab world were not a bad record for one term. If reelected, then from a stronger domestic base and with the achievements of the peace process under his belt he could continue the negotiations with Asad and seek closure with a surer hand. In the meantime he would respect his commitments to the American president and secretary of state, and keep Asad engaged in the negotiations even if that required occasional verbal concessions. Asad could, of course, upset this complex calculus by accepting the bulk of Rabin's package or by agreeing to a meeting, but this was not likely to happen.

Rabin was not alone in casting doubt on Asad's determination actually to conclude an agreement with Israel. Israeli politicians from both ends of the spectrum, policy analysts, and media commentators shared his skepticism. The fullest presentation of this interpretation was made by the American analyst Daniel Pipes. Writ-

ing in January 1996 at the high point of the Wye Plantation negotiations, Pipes argued that "the Syrian and Israeli governments—
despite their tense relations—have established the general contours of a peace agreement. In the four principal areas of
negotiations, the two sides have no profound differences." And yet,
Pipes continued, an agreement had not been made and was not
likely to be made because of President Asad's domestic political
constraints and considerations. As a member of the Alawi minority community, he wrote, Asad was primarily concerned with his
regime's survival and in a smooth succession, and he felt that by
making peace he would be undermining the position and loyalty
of the defense and security establishment, generate expectations
for greater freedom and democracy, and open Syria to Israeli
tourists and influence. Asad was, therefore, not interested in making peace but rather in participating in a peace process so as to
improve his standing in Washington and to distinguish himself
from countries like Iran and Libya. With more than a touch of
irony, Pipes added that this policy "worked best when Likud was in
power, for Asad could rely on Yitzhak Shamir's government to
maintain a hard line as well." But the advent of the Labor government, ready to make concessions for peace with Syria, undermined
the policy that Asad had pursued so successfully since the Madrid
conference.[1]

I do not share this interpretation. I believe that when he ago-
nized over George Bush's invitation to the Madrid conference,
Asad did think through the full ramifications of a positive answer
and made a decision to join a process that could very well lead him
to sign a peace treaty with Israel. I am also certain that there is a
Syrian narrative of this four-year saga that is very different from the
Israeli and American views of the same period and chain of events.
But when all is said and done it is difficult to understand why Asad,
despite his suspicions, reservations, and inhibitions, failed to take
the steps that would have produced an agreement on terms that
should have been quite acceptable to him.

These questions arise with greater poignancy with regard to
the second point in time at which a breakthrough was feasible,

November 1995 to January 1996. The Syrian negotiator, Walid Mu'allim, by way of expounding his government's line, argued that given the unprecedented pace of progress at Wye, "Uri Savir, Dennis Ross and I . . . decided that we would hold continuous talks to finalize the structure of an agreement on all issues. . . . We set a deadline for ourselves agreeing to close the remaining gaps and finalize all the elements of an agreement by June of 1996. . . . The expectation was that by September 1996 the final document would be ready. . . . So we were very surprised when soon afterward Mr. Peres called early elections."[2] The Israeli negotiator Uri Savir has not complained of missed opportunities and has not allocated blame or responsibility, but he has argued in a television interview that much had been accomplished at the Wye negotiations and that Israel and Syria were on the verge of coming to an agreement.

But in December 1997 the Israeli newspaper *Ma'ariv* published a story under the headline "This Is How We Missed the Peace with Syria." Savir was not quoted directly in the story, which revolved mostly around him, but what the Israeli press likes to call "sources close to him" argued, in line with Mu'allim's claim, that Savir, Mu'allim, and Ross brought the negotiations to the verge of agreement—"all disputes between the two states could be bridged with relative ease. All that had to be done was to make a decision, but Peres could not make that difficult decision, not he, not in the position he was in." And in case this was not clear enough, and as if the unwarranted insinuation concerning Shimon Peres did not suffice, the correspondent summed up: "The bottom line is that at the end of the first round at the Wye Plantation Uri Savir presented Shimon Peres with the general contours of the peace agreement he could bring to Jerusalem before November 1996. . . . Peres equivocated . . . he knew that he would have to make difficult decisions; to moderate the army's demands, to give up the Golan Heights. He knew that Rabin could have done it; he was not certain that he could. Peres decided to move up the elections. . . . This is how the opportunity was missed for a peace agreement between Israel, Syria, and the rest of the Arab world."[3]

Secretary of State Christopher, during an interview granted to the diplomatic correspondent of *Ha'aretz* in late October 1997 when he came to Israel to take part in the inauguration of the Peres Peace Center, spoke at some length and quite freely about these issues. When asked whether Asad miscalculated and missed an opportunity, or whether he saw peace as a long-term threat to his regime, the former secretary argued, "My own view is that he missed an opportunity, an historic opportunity to achieve the return of the Golan, or return of territory. I account for it not by his fear, but his mistrust and suspicion of what was being offered. He examined it so extensively and exhaustively that he missed the opportunity. If he had been responsive and done the public things that we urged and also responded substantively I think much more progress would have been done. Rabin had the strength and the conviction that Syria was and is a threat and it would be a great service to Israel if that threat were removed. One of Asad's miscalculations was that time is and was on his side." From a perspective of nearly two years Secretary Christopher argued that, in fact, there was no real possibility of concluding an agreement during Peres's brief tenure: "I really respected that when Prime Minister Peres felt that he needed a mandate for himself . . . and I think that pushed him to the early election decision. The time was very late then, even if the elections had been held in November [October 1996]. They were supposed to conclude a deal in the midst of an election campaign when there had been kind of a historic event like an assassination and then a change of government. That would have been very, very short, very tight."[4]

Asad's biographer, Patrick Seale, in addressing the same issues took an entirely different line. Under the subtitle of "missed opportunities," he begins by referring to the argument "that Asad missed the chance of peace with Israel—and of a return of the Golan—when Rabin was alive and then when Peres inherited the prime minister's mantle. . . . Peace was there for the taking, it is said, if only Asad had made some gesture such as agreeing to meet Peres, or allowing Israeli journalists to visit Syria." Seale opens his response to this argument by admitting that "Asad had always been extremely cautious in negotiation, insisting on proceeding step by careful step, seeing a trap in Israel's repeated probing for "back channels. . . . Asad seems unable to set aside his deep conviction that Israel is not ready for an honorable peace, not ready to be simply one player among others in the Middle East system . . . but conspires instead to hold sway over the whole region . . . with the aim of reducing the Arabs to a subject people." Seale quotes in this context Asad's interview to *al-Ahram* in December 1995 (see Chapter Six) and his scathing attack on Peres's vision of a "New Middle East."[5]

With regard to the Wye Plantation negotiations, Seale maintains that "while Syria offered total peace for total withdrawal" Israel never responded in a clear-cut fashion. The withdrawal "was always hedged around by numerous preconditions. First it was to be subject to an Israeli national referendum then it was to be accompanied by such draconian conditions as the thinning out and restructuring of the Syrian armed forces, the placement inside Syrian territory of an Israeli warning station, only token Israeli withdrawal pending proof of Syrian good behavior and full normalization: in the sense not just of diplomatic relations but of the free movement of goods and people, joint projects, integration of utilities and the like." Seale then complains that at one of the last sessions at Wye Plantation the Israelis apparently submitted more than a score of projects for integrating the two economies. "Most Syrians," he says, "would have seen any such settlement as exposing their society, nascent industries, cultural traditions and national security to hostile Israeli penetration. For Asad it would have made a mockery of his entire career."[6]

Seale ends with two very different conclusions. One is that an agreement between Israel and Syria during these years was not in fact feasible. For one thing, on the key issues—withdrawal, security, the timetable, and normalization—"no agreement was reached." But beyond this lay the more fundamental incompatibility between two very different visions of peace. For Asad, he says, the essence of any settlement is not the recovery of this or that piece of occupied territory but the "containment" of Israel, just as his notion of a "comprehensive peace is not about normalization but . . . about holding the line against Israel . . . to shrink its influence to more modest and less aggressive proportions, which the Arab players in the Middle East could accept and live with." This vision could not coexist with Israel's view, which sees peace as a means to extend its influence to every corner of the Arab world. But while Seale writes that "it was these conflicting visions of peace which very probably doomed the talks to failure," the blame for missing the opportunity to make peace was Israel's rather than Syria's. "Israel wanted too much and overreached. It could have peace but she wanted peace *and* hegemony, and that was not and is not realistic."[7]

Seale is not a Syrian spokesman, but he is Asad's semiofficial biographer, and he has access to and he understands Asad and his policies. When Ambassador Mu'allim argues that peace at the Wye talks was within reach, he has an axe to grind. His government's line is that much was accomplished at the Wye Plantation, that it was formalized, that it is binding, and that the negotiations should be resumed at the point at which they were interrupted. Seale's version, while not free from partisan baggage, is less self-serving and offers a valuable insight into Asad's view of the negotiations with Israel and of the contours of an acceptable settlement.

Asad was probably genuine when he spoke of concluding a settlement in 1996, but his definition of an acceptable settlement was far apart from that of Shimon Peres. It might have been possible to bridge that gap, but certainly not within the time frame dictated by the Israeli prime minister's domestic political calculus. This was an issue that Asad failed or refused to understand. He did not want to make the investment that Peres viewed as indispensable if he were to commit himself right away, and he responded angrily when Peres decided a few weeks later to move up the elections. By venting his anger in Lebanon, where he gave Hizballah a free hand and possibly a green light to ignore the "understanding," he drew Peres into launching Operation Grapes of Wrath, which contributed to his electoral defeat and to the rise of an Israeli government that he found far more difficult to comprehend and contend with.

Asad's failure to empathize with his Israeli counterpart's domestic political constraints and calculus reflected the deliberate and limited fashion in which he and his subordinates came to accept the complexities of and rules of the game in the Israeli political system. It was a slow, manifold process. It began with a stereotypical view of Israeli society and politics, colored by hostility and lack of interest, a tendency to view all Zionist parties as being essentially the same, and a suspicion that what we viewed and presented as complexities and difficulties were in fact finely orchestrated negotiating tactics. Over time a more credulous and nuanced view was adopted in Damascus, but the extent and pace of this development were too limited to have a real impact at the crucial moment. The election results of May 29, 1996, and their subsequent impact on the Syrian-Israeli track provided a rude awakening and led Asad in the summer of 1997 to start addressing the Israeli political system as such, but for the 1995–1996 window of opportunity it was too late.

Asad's Israeli counterparts had an easier task in dealing with a centralized, stable system dominated by one person. They realized, of course, that authoritarian leaders are not free from opposition, that they have to contend with their brand of public opinion and prepare it for changes of line and policy, but they believed all along that they had to focus their efforts on one person, who had the power to make the decisions and carry his country with him. The Israelis assumed that the Syrian public was ahead of its government in being willing to settle with Israel, that opposition to a decision by Asad within the regime could transpire but would remain marginal, and that the real impediments were to be found within Asad's own mind. Asad had been a significant figure in Syrian politics since the mid-1960s, and Rabin and Peres in the course of their public and political careers had each formed a view of the Syrian ruler. These personal views were supplemented by the contribution of Israel's national security bureaucracy, whose analysts had scrutinized Asad's actions and statements over the years. The missing element was personal acquaintance. It is difficult to envisage the Egyptian-Israeli peace treaty of 1979 without the meetings between Sadat and Begin (not to speak of the personal relationships between several other Egyptians and Israelis), or Oslo II without the personal give-and-take that Rabin and Peres had with Arafat and his group during the previous two years. Except for two formal meetings with General Shihabi, personal contact with Asad and his team was denied to the two Israeli prime ministers who dealt with him. For them he remained an abstract enigma, his aims and motives undeciphered.

It is this view of the discrepancy between the influence of the domestic dimension on the respective positions and conducts of Israel and Syria in their negotiation which accounts for the meager space devoted in this book to the political and socioeconomic aspects of Asad's policies.[8] During the past three decades Syria has undergone profound demographic and socioeconomic changes that will probably be translated to political changes at some future points. But thus far Syria is governed by a stable, powerful, and monolithic regime that is totally dominated by one person. This person has undoubtedly thought through the potential repercussions of a prospective settlement with Israel on the nature and stability of his regime, and he has defined his concept of an acceptable peace arrangement in this context, as well. A close scrutiny could possibly identify nuances regarding the issue of a settlement with Israel within the Asad regime's political spectrum, but Asad's unquestioned dominance has denied such nuances any practical significance. From Henry Kissinger's memoirs we know that during the negotiations he conducted in 1974 before signing a disengagement agreement, Asad invested a visible effort to insure the support of the senior military echelon for his policies and arranged for frequent meetings between these officers and the secretary of state. The year 1974 was Asad's fourth in power, and he had yet to consolidate his position fully. Twenty years later Asad was firmly entrenched, and if he had to invest efforts in keeping the defense establishment's support, he certainly did not have to involve the secretary of state in them.

An entirely different set of domestic issues came to the surface in late 1995 and early 1996, due to the special emphasis on the economic dimension of peace and the issue of Israeli-Syrian economic cooperation in Shimon Peres's concept of peace. The Israeli prime minister's approach was unacceptable to Asad for a number of reasons: he opposed any component in the peace settlement that could be perceived as an Israeli *diktat* and therefore humiliating; he was opposed to any expansion of the notions of peace and normalization; and he rejected anything that he perceived as an attempt to interfere in his regime's internal affairs, be they political or economic. Seale's description of Asad's response to Peres's new ideas seems authentic.

In the absence of an agreement, what did the Israeli-Syrian negotiations produce? In fact, quite a lot. Both sides became thoroughly familiar with each other's positions. The general contours of a prospective settlement were sketched and several important barriers were crossed. Two Israeli prime ministers have indicated to the Israeli public their willingness to make massive concessions in order to achieve peace with Syria, and Hafiz al-Asad has publicly agreed to make full peace and to offer normalization with Israel. But the negotiation has created a negative legacy, as well. A powerful opposition was built in Israel to the notion of a settlement based on withdrawal from the Golan. Asad, on the other hand, by claiming publicly to have obtained an American and Israeli commitment to such withdrawal will be hard put to settle for less, and so will his successors. The present Israeli government was elected on a platform rejecting the model of an Israeli-Syrian agreement that was adumbrated in its predecessors' negotiations with Syria. It is now trying to construct an alternative model, one that Asad is vowing to reject. It will be difficult, though perhaps not impossible, to obtain an agreement under these circumstances.

The Syrian-Israeli negotiation of the years 1992–1996 had a significance that exceeded the bilateral relationship between the two countries. Hafiz al-Asad and Syria had a special role and a special status in the Madrid process. President Bush and Secretary Baker invested a special effort in bringing Asad to Madrid. They wanted his prestige and his resources harnessed to the peace process rather than mobilized against it. His resources included Syria's innate power, its influence over the Palestinians, and its position in

Lebanon. Asad's prestige rested on his record and on his claim to pan-Arabism's residual mantle. President Clinton and Secretary Christopher inherited this view of the peace process, and viewed a Syrian-Israeli agreement as the key to a durable comprehensive settlement.

This view was shared some of the time by Rabin and Peres. But Rabin also drew on his experience as a peace negotiator in 1949 and as the prime minister who cooperated closely with Henry Kissinger in making the interim agreement of 1975. If Syria was not a genuine partner to a comprehensive settlement that Israel could live with, he would rather proceed gradually and incrementally, and deal with individual Arab partners and not with the Arab collective. Ironically Asad found himself hemmed in by his participation in the peace process and by the prospects opened to him in the negotiations with Israel, and was unable to put up serious opposition to Israel's agreements with the PLO and Jordan and the normalization process with the larger Arab world.

The chapters of this book are rich in raw material that would interest students of the arts of negotiation and bargaining. No attempt will be made here to fit this raw material into a general theory of negotiations. But it is important to make some comments with regard to academic literature on negotiations, as well as draw some lessons in the specific context of Israeli-Arab peacemaking.

The failure to come to an Israeli-Syrian agreement should naturally be measured against the three achievements of the peace process—the much earlier Egyptian-Israeli peace, and the contemporaneous negotiations and agreements with the PLO and Jordan.

The Camp David accords of September 1978 and the Israeli-Egyptian peace treaty of March 1979 were the culmination of a diplomatic process that began in the immediate aftermath of the October 1973 war. The October War ended the stalemate that followed the 1967 Six Days War, and enabled two of the parties to the conflict to end their bilateral dispute by trading the Egyptian territory that Israel captured in 1967 for peace and acceptance. There was much more to Israeli-Egyptian peacemaking than this simple formula, of course. Egypt made peace with Israel as part of a comprehensive reorientation of her domestic and foreign policies. Egypt was led by a bold visionary leader who made big decisions and refused to be bogged down by details. In his different style, his Israeli counterpart, Menachem Begin, was capable of breaking the mold and taking a decision that ran against the grain of his public image. Sadat did not act in a vacuum. He spoke and acted with the confidence of a leader who came from the heartland of a country with a long tradition of raison d'etat. Begin had the advantage of being a right-wing leader who could afford to antagonize some of his own supporters, knowing that he could count on the center and left-wing's support when making peace. Sadat and Begin had the support—and prodding—of an American president who, having overcome his initial reluctance, devoted himself to seeing the negotiation through. And they had the Sinai Peninsula as a natural buffer zone between the two countries. Both leaders understood the value of an early secret "walk in the woods," and both allowed their military establishment to build channels of communication and a relationship of trust that facilitated the agreement.

The dramatic impact of Israel's agreement with the PLO was at least equal to that of Sadat's journey to Jerusalem. It is easier to explain the PLO's or Arafat's decision to make the agreement. They were at a low ebb and they could see the value of making the concessions that were required on their part in order to reach a compromise that brought Yasser Arafat from Tunis to Gaza. These were decisions he could have made in the past, probably on better terms, but in 1993 he finally chose to act rather than let another opportunity slip by. The Israeli government's calculus was more complex. Israel was clearly the stronger party in the conflict, and the temptation to hold on to Israel's traditional position vis-à-vis the PLO or to try to dictate terms to a weakened PLO was there. But Rabin and Peres decided as a lesson of the intifada that Israel had to seek a political settlement with the Palestinians, and were persuaded by the course of the Washington talks that the PLO was indeed the *interlocuteur valable*. Constructing the agreement as a phased agreement with the more painful final-status issues left to the end made the pill easier to swallow, at least at the outset. The availability of the Oslo channel was of immense value in making these decisions. For several months authorized representatives could meet and negotiate secretly, away from public scrutiny and political interference. An effective private channel and the direct contact between authorized representatives were indispensable for effecting the Israeli-Palestinian breakthrough.

When it came to peacemaking between Israel and Jordan, the difficult decision was King Hussein's. Compared to the concessions it had to make in other tracks, Israel's concessions to Jordan were not particularly painful. It was the king who had to overcome his reluctance to antagonize Asad and a significant segment of his own constituency by making full peace with Israel. His decision was facilitated by the resolution of disputed land and water issues, by the Clinton administration's encouragement, and by the new realities of Palestinian politics in the aftermath of the Oslo accords. Between Jordan and Israel there existed a long tradition of contact and cooperation that was one of the best-advertised secrets of Middle Eastern politics. This enabled the two governments to negotiate at the highest level. It was at that level that the special personal relationship between King Hussein and Prime Minister Rabin was formed.

Against the backdrop of these three breakthroughs, both the missing elements and the principal impediments in the Israeli-Syrian negotiation become more clearly apparent. Hafiz al-Asad is not Anwar Sadat. He is not a bold and visionary decision maker but a meticulous tactician. Yitzhak Rabin was ready to make a bold decision, but he ended up making it in the Palestinian and not in the Syrian context. Bill Clinton is a different president from Jimmy Carter and George Bush, and during his first term he found out that even if his priorities lay in the Israeli-Syrian track he could with less pain and cost push the Israeli-Arab peace process on other tracks. Moreover, the Golan Heights are different from the Sinai. It is a comparatively small area, bordered by four states, close to Damascus as well as to Israeli-populated areas, militarily crucial, and commanding Israel's water resources. Another factor was that Yitzhak Rabin and Shimon Peres realized, as they had suspected, that it was indeed more difficult for leaders relying on a center-left coalition to make peace than it would have been for a right-wing leader. Their efforts to come to terms with Syria generated opposition from the right as well as from segments of the center. In the absence of Syrian cooperation in addressing Israel's public opinion, the domestic political price seemed prohibitive.

Asad's refusal to meet personally with his Israeli counterparts and the restrictions he imposed on his negotiators were another major obstacle. At any given point during the four-year negotiation a decision by Asad to come to a meeting with President Clinton and the prime minister of Israel would have produced an agreement based on a compromise. But Asad was hoping to do better than the projected compromise, and was not willing to take the small risk that the meeting would not produce an agreement.

For adversaries like Israel and Syria to make the difficult decisions that produce an agreement, a combination of pain and hope is required. The pain makes the status quo unbearable, the hope and vision of a better future facilitate the decision. That combination was glaringly absent during four years of negotiation.

The academic literature dealing with conflict resolution refers to such a combination of actual pain and anticipated gain as "ripeness" (and more recently "readiness"). Those writers who advocate the usefulness of this concept have argued that as long as a conflict has not reached a point of ripeness, be it "positive" (when expectations of relief or gain provide the momentum that is indispensable for overcoming the forces acting to perpetuate the conflict) or negative (when the pain or cost exacted by the status quo become the primary motive for accepting a compromise), all efforts to resolve it are bound to fail. Conversely, they maintain that the availability of such ripeness will account for the success of negotiations or other efforts at reconciliation and settlement.[9] The concept of ripeness can be a very useful analytical tool in understanding the course of a successful or abortive negotiation; but it is less valuable as an operational tool to serve policy makers in making the decision to launch an effort to resolve a particular conflict or in formulating their strategy.

The same academic literature that has provided us with the concept of ripeness has also offered us important distinctions between a very basic and broad term—negotiations—and the more specific terminology of prenegotiations, bargaining, and mediation. The distinctions are not merely semantic.

The term "bargaining" refers to the give-and-take between two parties, each seeking to make the best deal from its point of view. The process of bargaining is obviously a very significant part of the larger negotiations in the context of which it is being conducted. Without a successful conduct and conclusion of the bargaining process a negotiation will not be brought to a successful end. But this does not quite sum up the complex interplay between the bargaining dimension and the broader negotiation.

In a successful negotiation, the process of mutual discovery and confidence building should facilitate the bargaining, while the emerging shape of a mutually acceptable deal would reinforce an unfolding reconciliation. Together they create a new and shared calculus that replaces the erstwhile zero-sum game, a distinctive component of conflict situations. Thus on the way to the Oslo accords the Israeli side chose to moderate its bargaining position, having recognized its greater power and having decided that by dictating terms to the weaker Palestinian party Israel might end up undermining her future partner in the implementation of the agreement. No such dynamics developed in the Israeli-Syrian dialogue, when the deal defined by Asad as the essential minimum was well above the line drawn by Israel. The tough bargaining combined with Syria's reluctance to accept reconciliation and normalization as legitimate elements of the negotiation to produce a negative dynamic much of the time.

The mediation between Israel and Syria was, as we know, conducted by the United States. Other actors, governments, and individuals tried their hand at mediating but ended up adding curious episodes to the saga of the negotiations rather than affecting their course. Of the two protagonists it was Syria that was more interested in Washington's mediation. For both Washington and Damascus this was also a mechanism for building an American-

Syrian dialogue, so much so that in short order the negotiation turned into a three-way negotiation. Within this triangle it was often clear that Damascus was more interested in its dialogue with Washington than in its bargaining with Jerusalem.

In fact, Israel also wanted the United States to play a role, but from her perspective a successful negotiation with an Arab party should rest on the right mixture of direct negotiations and American involvement (as was the case between Israel, Egypt, Jordan, and the Palestinians). The Clinton administration was willing, indeed eager, to play the roles of sponsor, mediator, and arbitrator in a negotiation it regarded as the cutting edge of the peace process. But at the end of the day Washington lacked the will and the power to force on the parties a formula and was unable to bridge the gap that separated them.[10]

An important recent trend in academic writing on conflict resolution and negotiations emphasizes the distinction between the actual negotiation and an earlier phase—"prenegotiations." The earlier phase is defined as the time span during which the parties make the transition from a unilateral search for conflicting solutions to a shared problem, to a joint search for a common solution. The passage from one phase to the next is marked by the inauguration of a formal negotiation. In operational terms the prenegotiating phase is to be used in order to maximize the prospects of success once a full-fledged negotiation is launched. The underlying assumptions are that the opportunity for a formal negotiation must not be squandered—it would be dangerous and wasteful— and that a correct construction of the prenegotiating phase by narrowing differences and reducing skepticism and hostility is essential for a subsequent success.[11] Unfortunately, in reality it is quite difficult to construct the process of reconciliation according to the optimal model proposed by the experts. At the end of the war, in the shadow of a crisis, given the fear that the window may close, the parties will begin to talk or be summoned to the table according to the circumstances of the moment.

In the history of Israel's peace making with Egypt, the years 1973 to 1977 can be seen as a phase of prenegotiations, which effectively set the stage for a successful negotiation that was concluded less than a year after its formal inauguration. But this course of events was not foreseen when both a direct dialogue and an American mediation between the two countries began in the murky aftermath of the October War. By the same token, the architects of the Madrid process did not know at the time that from the perspective of August 1993 the formal talks between Israeli and Palestinian delegations would appear as part of a preparatory phase for the informal and semiformal give-and-take that led to the Oslo breakthrough.

The course and outcome of Israel's negotiation with Syria contain many lessons for those interested in conflict resolution and negotiations either in general or in their Middle Eastern context, but the principal lessons concern the Israeli-Syrian relationship itself. The conflict between the two countries is open and it needs to be managed, settled, and resolved. Some would argue that given the failure of the major effort invested in the early and mid-1990s one should wait for a profound change in the Israeli-Syrian equation— a geopolitical change in the region, a political change in Syria, the introduction of novel and hitherto unfamiliar elements into the proposed formula—that would provide for an entirely different negotiation. But such changes may never happen or may happen at such a late point as to make them irrelevant.

Discussion of the prospect of renewing the negotiations should focus on Israel and Syria as we know them. Hafiz al-Asad has no intention of lowering his demands. He has also managed to tie the hands of his successors by publicly claiming that he had obtained an Israeli commitment to and an American endorsement of an agreement predicated on full withdrawal. But if Asad wants to reach an agreement with Israel, he will have to offer more for what he demands. The United States will remain a crucial intermediary between Israel and Syria, but without a direct, discreet dialogue between the two countries it will be very difficult to reach an agreement. The hard core of bargaining and deal-making will have to be wrapped with a thick and effective crust of public diplomacy, without which the Israeli public will not endorse an agreement with Syria predicated on a territorial concession. Only if Israel, Syria, and the United States draw the lessons offered by three and a half years of negotiation and a year and a half of breakdown in communication will Israel and Syria be able to cross at the decade's end the brink they failed to cross in the early and mid-1990s.

Benjamin Netanyahu's victory in the Israeli elections of May 1996 and the formation of his government were the dominant elements in a cluster of developments that transformed the Israeli-Syrian relationship over the past two years. For nearly four years, from the summer of 1992 to the late spring of 1996, the two countries were seriously groping for an accommodation. That process was accompanied by much suspicion, frustration, and anger, but it was gradually changing the relationship of two countries that had fought several times in the past decades and had been on the verge of a collision on several other occasions. This has not been the case since June 1996. The negotiations have not been resumed; there was one brief direct contact between the two governments followed by the exchange of several messages by proxy, but they have all failed to clarify the positions, build trust, or restart a dialogue. In the absence of a dialogue and of the prospect for a renewal of the negotiation, bellicose rhetoric and fear of war reentered the picture.

The period from June to September 1996 can be described as a transitional phase in Israeli-Syrian relations, as it was in the larger Israeli-Arab relationship. The general Arab reaction to Netanyahu's victory was marked by a mixture of dismay and relief. Israel's new prime minister had won his victory by vilifying Rabin's and Peres's peace policies, and many Arabs suspected that despite his promise to respect the agreements signed by his predecessors, he and even more so some of his ministers and coalition partners would in effect seek to undermine the accomplishments of the peace process, particularly on the Palestinian track. But those in the Arab world who had felt uneasy about the extent and pace of the Arab-Israeli normalization process felt also a certain sense of relief. Whatever was to happen on the various tracks of the peace process, Arab-Israeli normalization would be limited and slowed down. Anyone who attended the third Middle Eastern economic conference in Cairo in November 1996 could not fail to notice the Egyptian leadership's satisfaction with that aspect of the new situation. An Israeli delegation did attend the conference and some Egyptian businessmen were allowed to meet with Israeli colleagues, but as a whole Israel had been relegated to the margins. The contrast with the centrality of Israel's role in Casablanca and Amman was stark. Egypt remained committed to its own peace treaty with Israel, and had a distinct interest in the continuation of the peace process, particularly on the Palestinian track. But just as Egypt was worried by the fear of a total collapse of the peace process, it was relieved by the waning of what had been seen just a year earlier as the quest for an Israeli regional hegemony.

Indeed, each Arab state and actor had a particular perspective on these developments. Jordan was initially quite pleased with the prospect of slower movement on the Palestinian and Syrian tracks. The Palestinians, who were most intimately affected by the changes in Israel, were most alarmed. The Syrians were worried by a whole set of developments that could not augur well for their track: Netanyahu personally had criticized Rabin's and Peres's policies in the negotiations with Syria. He had accused them of agreeing to withdraw from the Golan Heights, and personally publicized the "Shtauber document" in June 1995 in order to alert the Israeli public to what he saw as a willingness to withdraw and to settle on inferior security arrangements. The Golan lobby and settlers were represented in his government, and his cabinet included two of the principal authors of the 1982 war in Lebanon—Ariel Sharon and Raphael Eytan.

Furthermore, Netanyahu's public statements with regard to Syria during his first weeks in office were ominous. In a press conference during Warren Christopher's visit to Israel on June 25, 1996, and in various press interviews Netanyahu criticized Syria as a promoter of terrorism. He spoke specifically about terrorist organizations hosted in Damascus and about Syria's relationship with Hizballah. Netanyahu announced that he would not negotiate with Syria under the shadow of Hizballah's activities, and threat-

ened to launch a campaign to "contain" Syria alongside Iran and
Iraq. All this was, of course, not lost on Asad, who was hard put to
assess the implications of the change in Israel for his country.
Should he be worried by the prospect of an anti-Syrian diplomatic
offensive? Could this new Israeli government escalate the level
of military action in the event of another incident or clash in
Lebanon? And what about the legacy of four years of negotiations—was it about to be written off?

In the aftermath of the Israeli elections of May 1996, Asad and
his government have indeed invested considerable efforts in formulating and protecting their version of that legacy. This effort has
had several purposes. One is to defend the achievements that Syria
had registered in the negotiations against the new Israeli government's quest to redefine the paradigms of the negotiations. Another is to set the stage for a prospective resumption of the negotiations under the most advantageous circumstances. But the
decision in September 1996 to go public with this effort suggested
that Asad may also have been responding to criticism inside Syria.
Was it not possible that people were asking what had the regime
accomplished in four years of negotiations? The leadership and
the rank and file of the Ba'th party and the Syrian public had been
hearing for years about the follies of Sadat and about King Hussein's and Yasser Arafat's deviation from the right path. But all
three had produced results and regained land from Israel, and
what did Asad have to show for his efforts? If Asad could not produce recovered territory, could he at least produce a claim to have
won an Israeli "commitment" to return that territory and an
American endorsement of that commitment?

The initial and all subsequent efforts to resume the Israeli-
Syrian negotiations collapsed against two sets of obstacles. The first
is of an apparently procedural nature—Asad's demand that the negotiations be resumed "at the point at which they had been interrupted" (and thereby subsume the legacy of the previous four
years), and Netanyahu's rejection of that position and his counter
demand "to resume the negotiation without prior conditions." But
at a deeper level lies a more fundamental obstacle—Asad continues to insist that the negotiation be predicated on an acceptance

of his demand for full withdrawal, while Netanyahu refuses to accept this premise even when couched in hypothetical or conditional terms. The farthest that the Israeli prime minister has been willing to go is to offer through a third party a formula according to which the depth of withdrawal would reflect the depth of the security arrangements. According to an Israeli news report that the government did not quite deny, this offer was made in July 1997, and was rejected by Asad as inadequate.

The impact of this stalemate was magnified by the change in Washington's perspective on the Israeli-Arab peace process and particularly the Syrian track. The change became apparent in the summer of 1996, and was quite stark after the formation of the second Clinton administration in January 1997. The Middle East peace process had been one of the most important areas of the administration's foreign policy during Bill Clinton's first term, where considerable success was achieved in return for a comparatively small investment and limited risks. True, the administration and the secretary of state personally were criticized in the media and during the 1996 presidential elections campaign for making more than twenty trips to the Middle East and to Damascus specifically, but this was a small price compared to the agony and the acrimony that were entailed in the Bosnian, Somali, or Cuban issues.

By January 1997 that perspective had changed radically. The Arab-Israeli conflict required costly investment in order to be salvaged rather than yield the spectacular exploits of the years 1993–1994. The intimate relationship of the American president with the prime minister of Israel had been replaced by an awkward relationship with an Israeli leader who was determined to change the rules of the game, who had a different vision of peace and the peace process, and was quite willing to engage the administration in the U.S. domestic arena. Asad and Arafat had never been easy partners to work with, but with a sure footing in its relationship with Israel the United States was better equipped to deal with them. During President Clinton's second term his personal and domestic calculus was different, as was the perspective of a new secretary of state, Madeleine Albright, determined to shape her own different agenda and profile.

The Arab-Israeli peace process remained a significant foreign policy issue, but in this context the Israeli-Palestinian relationship had clear precedence. At issue now was not a comprehensive Arab-Israeli settlement but the prevention of a total collapse of the peace process that events like the "tunnel incident" and the Palestinian-Israeli violence of September 1996 seemed to presage. This called for a focusing of the U.S. efforts on the Israeli-Palestinian track. Here the danger was imminent, it threatened to affect other countries such as Jordan, and it was an issue about which the rest of the Arab world cared. Asad may have been held in high regard in the Arab world, but most other Arabs were not necessarily keen to extend to him active support. And the same lack of a sense of urgency that had militated against the completion of the Israeli-Syrian negotiations in previous years was now reinforcing the sense that whatever efforts the United States was willing to invest should be channelled to the Israeli-Palestinian front.

In the absence of a negotiation, the Israeli-Syrian agenda has been defined by other issues. One is the ongoing indirect confrontation in Lebanon. The "understandings" of May 1996 and the comparatively effective functioning of the monitoring committee mitigate but do not quite cushion the effect on Israel of the fighting and casualties inside the "security zone" in south Lebanon and of the occasional Katyusha rocket attacks on northern Israel. Early in his tenure Netanyahu raised the idea of "Lebanon first," based on a unilateral Israeli withdrawal from south Lebanon, preferably in concert with Syria but possibly without it. Syria responded negatively. The notion of any partial arrangement remained an anathema. But even an uncoordinated Israeli withdrawal struck Damascus as a bad idea. If Israel was bleeding and hurting, let the pressure continue and serve as a means of pressure on Netanyahu to return to the negotiating table on Asad's terms. Damascus was also worried by the prospect of an uncontrolled deterioration if Israel withdrew. The conflict in south Lebanon had been unfolding along patterns that had become familiar, almost predictable, for well over a decade. An Israeli return to the international border without a resolution of the underlying dispute would be construed as an Israeli defeat and as a Syrian achievement, but the conflict could soon get out of hand and expose Syria to the risk of entanglement with an Israeli government it could not fathom.

The fear and threat of a Syrian-Israeli military confrontation came to the fore in the summer of 1996. It seems to have been a classic case of an unintended escalation. Following Netanyahu's harsh anti-Syrian rhetoric in June, the Syrian chief of staff Hikmat Shihabi resorted to threatening language by alluding to the possibility that Syria would choose a "military option" if the diplomatic stalemate continued endlessly. Shihabi's statement generated a wave of speculations and counter statements in Israel. Next came a redeployment of some Syrian units from the Beirut area to the Bekaa Valley. As far as can be ascertained, this was a move conducted in a Syrian-Lebanese context, the implementation of a long-standing scheme to move some Syrian units away from urban areas in the aftermath of the Lebanese elections. Against the background of the mounting Syrian-Israeli tension, there were those in Israel who saw the move as preparation for a limited military operation. Israel responded with public statements of her own, and apparently with some changes in deployment. Since Syria had not contemplated any operation at that time it responded nervously to what some Syrians, at least, interpreted as preparations for an Israeli operation. This particular tension dissipated quite soon, but its impact registered. Both sides were evidently suspicious of each other and the possibility of a military confrontation, whether unintended or deliberately planned, became a significant component of their relationship.

In the broader context of the Israeli-Arab peace process, Syria has taken advantage of the stalemates and crises of the past two years in order to return the peace process to the original course envisaged at the time of the Madrid conference—unified and coordinated Arab position, no separate agreements, no early normalization. Rabin had made no secret of his quest to change the Madrid rules and had registered several successes in that regard, and Asad was clearly seeking to take advantage of the changes in Israel's policies in June 1996 to undo those successes. This was apparent during the Arab summit that met in Cairo in June 1996, and remained so through the next two years.

During the same period Prime Minister Netanyahu and his government sent Syria a very mixed message. In various private meetings Netanyahu left his interlocutors with a distinct impression that somewhere down the road he was planning to seek a settlement with Syria, even though he knew very well "what it would take." The messages he sent through a variety of third parties were on the whole conciliatory. As we saw above, Asad rejected the formula linking the depth of withdrawal to the depth of the security arrangements. But Asad must have realized the implications of a formula that was quite similar to Rabin's original formulation that had linked the depth of withdrawal to the depth of peace.

But Asad could not ignore other acts and statements by Netanyahu and his government that indicated a very different attitude to Syria and to the issue of an Israeli-Syrian settlement. The most significant development in this regard was the Knesset's vote on July 23, 1997, on the third attempt to entrench the Golan law. As will be recalled, the "Golan lobby" in the Knesset had tried twice during Rabin's tenure to entrench the 1981 Golan law by initiating a law requiring a special majority (of 70 or 80 members) to repeal it. Rabin fought hard and defeated both initiatives. On July 23, a right-wing member of Netanyahu's coalition made yet another bid to entrench the Golan law. The cabinet discussed the new initiative and decided to vote against it, but when it came to the vote the cabinet members, including the prime minister, voted for the proposal, which passed by a majority of 43 to 40. It was subsequently explained that this was the first of three readings, and the vote as such had no operative significance. This may have been true, but to Asad it must have reinforced the message that Netanyahu did not want or was unable to come to an agreement on terms acceptable to the Syrian president.

Netanyahu then articulated his concept of peace and settlement in terms reminiscent of his book and of the first statements he had made in the aftermath of the 1996 elections.[1] He did so in a speech he delivered to the graduating class at the Israeli National War College on August 14, 1997. The accent of the speech was on Israel's current dispute with the Palestinian Authority, but the prime minister's comments were placed within a broader outlook on peacemaking with Israel's Arab neighbors. Israel, he said, could not hope for some time to come for a peaceful coexistence with her Arab neighbors along lines familiar to West Europeans or North Americans. That kind of coexistence could only prevail between democracies, and Israel's neighbors were not likely to become democratic in the near future. By the same token, normalization of relations, a positive development in its own right, could not replace balance of power and deterrence as guarantees for peace. This was true not only of Arab-Israeli relations but also of inter-Arab relations. "Our region," Netanyahu said,

> is rich in inter-Arab peace agreements and declarations of friendship and brotherhood that could unfold over many years and disappear overnight. There is no reason, therefore, to expect that the quality of Arab-Israeli peace will be better than that of inter-Arab peace. It follows, then, that normalization of relations, dialogue, commercial relations and cultural exchange are very important, but they are not the primary principle and cannot serve as a substitute to a clear superiority of Israeli power over Israel's Arab neighbors as a guarantee for obtaining peace and preserving it. . . . As long as the regimes around us are not democratic and peace-seeking by nature we will not be able to afford settlements in which the security component is not dominant. No settlement will endure unless we keep security and defense areas. . . . As long as our area is characterized by nondemocratic regimes, we will have to pursue a policy that will preserve our ability to deter, and will not give up strategic assets that are vital for our security. I believe that these principles can guide us also in obtaining a peace settlement with Syria . . . principles that place security as the first and most important tier in obtaining and maintaining peace.[2]

Without stating so explicitly, Netanyahu was criticizing his predecessors' peace policy and presenting an alternative vision. When applied to the Israeli-Syrian context, for instance, the alternative vision meant that Israel should hold on to territory rather than pay with territorial assets for a normalization that, according to Netanyahu, "is always conditional, always partial, always vulnerable, and always reversible." The Israeli prime minister did not specify whether what he had in mind was simply a perpetuation of the status quo or a formalized security regime that he would seek to negotiate with Hafiz al-Asad.

Asad is evidently perplexed by his inability to decipher Netanyahu's intentions. On August 12, 1997, he addressed a visiting group of Israeli Arabs and told them among other things that "Netanyahu has thus far made strange statements. He proposed exchanging peace for peace and later he proposed exchanging peace for security. Afterward he announced that he is with Resolutions 242 and 338, but according to his own interpretation."[3]

The invitation of the Israeli-Arab delegation to Syria in August 1997 was itself indicative of a Syrian willingness in view of the confounding new realities to change some of the rigid assumptions and criteria that had guided Syrian policy toward Israel in previous years. As will be recalled, there was an earlier visit by an Arab-Israeli delegation to Syria in March 1994. The delegation headed by Knesset member 'Abd al-Wahhab Darawsha came to console Asad over the death of his son Basel. It was an American initiative to which Syria responded with evident ill will, so that the original purpose of building goodwill was totally missed. In 1997 it was the Ba'th regime that initiated the visit. It was clearly trying to make a goodwill gesture and to start building its own constituency inside the Israeli political system. There was also a related effort to differentiate the Labor party from the Likud and the present government, and to present the former in a more favorable light. It was all done in a clumsy and awkward fashion. Damascus still refused to understand that by inviting a group of Israeli Arab citizens and by referring to them as "the Palestinians of 1948," it was sending a negative message to Israel's Jewish majority. But Damascus did understand that it had missed the opportunity to come to an agreement with two Israeli governments that were willing to make it on terms that should have been acceptable to Syria. It understood also that all Israeli parties are not the same, and that from then on it had to address the Israeli political system and its complexities if it wanted to resolve the conflict with Israel through politics and diplomacy rather than through confrontation.

NOTES

PREFACE

1. J. Burton and F. Dukes, eds., *Conflict: Reading in Management and Resolution* (New York, 1990); J. Bercovitch and J. Rubin, *Mediation in International Relations* (New York, 1992); G. Alexander and J. Holl, *The Warning Problem and Missed Opportunities in Preventive Diplomacy* (New York, 1997).
2. For criticism on the "new historians" see Efraim Karsh, *Fabricating History: The New Historians* (London, 1997). Karsh addresses in his book, among others: Avi Shlaim, *The Politics of Partition: King Abdallah, The Zionists and Palestine, 1951–1971* (Oxford, 1990); Ilan Pappe, *The Making of the Arab-Israeli Conflict 1947–1951* (New York, 1988); Benny Morris, *1948 and After* (Oxford, 1994).
3. Neil Caplan, *Futile Diplomacy*, Vol. 3 (London, 1997), pp. 276–77.

CHAPTER ONE
TRYING TO RECAPTURE
YESTERDAY'S SHADOW

1. See Ambassador Mu'allim's interview in the *Journal of Palestine Studies* 26.2 (Winter 1997): 404.
2. Ibid., p. 403. Emphasis added.
3. See Orly Azulay-Katz, *Ha'ish shelo yada lenazeakh* (The Man Who Could Not Win) (Tel Aviv, 1996).
4. Ibid., pp. 15–27.
5. *Ha'aretz*, November 17, 1995: "40 Dakot historiot 'im Clinton" (40 Historical Minutes with Clinton), p. B2.
6. *Qol Israel*, July 14, 1996.
7. Ibid., September 14, 1996.
8. In September 1996 the Netanyahu government decided to open the Hasmonean Tunnel in Jerusalem. It thereby played into the hands of Yasser Arafat and the Palestinian Authority, which responded with a wave of violence and forced the new Israeli government to renew the dialogue with them.
9. See *Foreign Broadcast Information Service* (FBIS), October 1, 1996: "Syria's Al Asad Discusses Resumption of Peace Talks."
10. Yukihiko Ikeda in conversation with an American diplomat, September 1996.

11. See Mu'allim's interview, p. 405.
12. Oslo I is the Israeli-Palestinian agreement concluded in Oslo in August 1993 and signed in Washington in September 1993. It was followed by the Cairo agreement signed on May 4, 1994, which dealt with its implementation, and by the Oslo II agreement signed in Washington on September 28, 1995, which provided for the extension of Palestinian self-rule in the West Bank.
13. *Ha'aretz*, January 19, 1997: "Artzot Habrit le Netanyahu" (The United States to Netanyahu), p. A1.
14. *FBIS*, November 6, 1996: "Syria's Al Asad, Egypt's Mubarak Hold News Conference."
15. *Al-Ahram* (Cairo), December 28, 1996, "Interview with President Asad," p. 1.
16. *Ha'aretz*, August 13, 1997: "Asad le mishlakhat Arvit me Israel" (Asad to an Arabic Delegation from Israel), p. A1.
17. *Ha'aretz*, August 28, 1997: "Tik Pocket" (Pocket Case), p. B2.
18. *Ma'ariv*, August 30, 1997: "Hak Barak" (MK Barak), p. 1.

CHAPTER TWO
ISRAEL AND SYRIA, RABIN AND ASAD

1. The best and most comprehensive book on Israel's conflict and relations with Syria in those years is Moshe Ma'oz, *From War to Peace Making* (Brighton, 1994). For illuminating insights into the Syrian point of view and Asad's perspective on the conflict and on the early peace process with Israel, see Patrick Seale, *Asad of Syria* (London, 1988).
2. For Egypt's position see Itamar Rabinovich, "Egypt and the Palestine Question before and after the Revolution," in Shimon Shamir, ed., *Egypt from Monarchy to Republic* (Oxford, 1995), pp. 325–39.
3. For a thorough study of the armistice regime between Syria and Israel, see Nisim Bar Ya'acov, *The Israel-Syrian Armistice* (Jerusalem, 1967). Among the several general studies of the first two decades of the Arab-Israeli conflict, see especially Nadav Safran, *From War to War* (New York, 1969).
4. These differences are described in Itamar Rabinovich, *The Road Not Taken* (New York, 1991), pp. 65–82.
5. Ibid., pp. 99–110.
6. This process is analyzed by Safran, *From War to War*, who describes it as "the festering of the conflict." A different version, more sympathetic to the Arab view of the process, is Fred Khouri, *The Arab-Israeli Dilemma* (New York, 1968).
7. Bar Ya'acov, *Israeli-Syrian Armistice*, pp. 77–79.
8. For an analysis of the interplay between Syria's domestic politics and its conduct on the issue of the Israeli overland water carrier, see Itamar Rabinovich, *Syria under the Ba'th* (Jerusalem, 1972), pp. 94–95.
9. A particularly useful analysis of the process of deterioration leading to the Six

Days War is Shimon Shamir, "The Middle East Crisis: On the Brink of War," in Daniel Dishon, ed., *Middle East Record 1967* (Tel Aviv, 1971), pp. 183–204.

10. Moshe Dayan, *Moshe Dayan: The Story of My Life* (New York, 1976) p. 475.

11. Itamar Rabinovich, "Continuity and Change in the Ba'th Regime in Syria 1967–1973," in Itamar Rabinovich and Haim Shaked, eds., *From June to October* (New Brunswick, N. J., 1978), pp. 219–28.

12. Dayan, *Story of My Life*, p. 491.

13. The best account of the Arab regimes' success in coping with the impact of the 1967 defeat is Fouad Ajami, *The Arab Predicament* (Cambridge, Engl., 1982).

14. See the complementary versions by Henry Kissinger, *White House Years* (Boston, 1979), pp. 597–617, and Yitzhak Rabin, *The Rabin Memoirs* (Boston, 1979) pp. 178–79.

15. The best account of the internal conflict within the Ba'th regime in the late 1960s is Nikolaos Van Dam, *The Struggle for Power in Syria* (London, 1981).

16. *FBIS*, March 9, 1972: "Al Asad Notes Progress on Revolution Anniversary," pp. 1–15.

17. Itamar Rabinovich, "Hashpa'at Milkhemet Yom Kipur al emdata vemedinyuta shel surya basikhsukh im Ysrael" (The October War's Impact on Syrian Position and Policy in the Conflict with Israel), in Adir Cohen and Efrat Karmon, eds., *Betzel milkhemet Yom Hakipurim* (In the Shadow of the October War) (Haifa, 1976), pp. 211–22.

18. See Kissinger's classic account of his negotiations with Asad in Henry Kissinger, *Years of Upheaval* (Boston, 1982), pp. 777–87.

19. Ma'oz, *From War to Peace Making*, pp. 144–52.

20. Rabin, *The Rabin Memoirs*, pp. 242–45.

21. Itamar Rabinovich, *The War for Lebanon 1970–1983* (Ithaca and London, 1984).

22. Steven L. Spiegel, "The Carter Approach to the Arab-Israeli Dispute," in Itamar Rabinovich and Haim Shaked, eds., *The Middle East and the United States* (New Brunswick and London, 1986), pp. 93–117.

23. Jimmy Carter, *The Blood of Abraham* (Boston, 1985), p. 73.

24. Jimmy Carter, *Keeping Faith* (Toronto, 1982), pp. 285–86.

25. See the text of the Camp David accords in Appendix E to William B. Quandt, *The Peace Process* (Washington, D. C., and Berkeley, 1993), pp. 445–56. The book itself contains the most complete study and analysis of the accords.

26. Asad's response to the Camp David accord is vividly described by Seale, *Asad of Syria*, pp. 304–10.

27. For the origins of the 1982 war in Lebanon, consult Ze'ev Schiff and Ehud Ya'ari, *Israel's Lebanon War* (New York, 1984).

28. David Kimche, *The Last Option* (London, 1991), passim.

29. Itamar Rabinovich, "Syria's Quest for a Regional Role," Woodrow Wilson Center, Working Paper 79 (Washington, D. C., December 1986).

30. For three Israeli versions of Shamir's path to Madrid, see Yitzhak Shamir, *Be-*

sikumu shel Davar (In Conclusion) (Tel Aviv, 1995), pp. 263–91; Moshe Arens, *Broken Covenant* (New York, 1995); and Eithan Ben Tzur, *Haderekh lashalom overet be Madrid* (The Road to Peace Goes through Madrid) (Tel Aviv, 1997).

31. Eyal Zisser, "Syria," in Ami Ayalon, ed., *Middle East Contemporary Survey 1990* and *1991* (Boulder, San Francisco, and Oxford, 1992 and 1993), pp. 649–68 and 664–89, respectively. The Taif accords were signed in Taif in Saudi Arabia in 1989 with a view to normalizing the political conditions in Lebanon. They also provided rather vaguely for the future departure of Syria's troops.

32. The efforts invested in and negotiations conducted before the Madrid conference are described in detail by the architect of the conference James A. Baker, *The Politics of Diplomacy* (New York, 1995), pp. 417–20, 425–28, 447–49, 454–57, 459–63, 468–69, 487–89, 500–07.

33. Lea Rabin, *Our Life—His Legacy* (New York, 1997).

34. Karim Pakardouni, *Stillborn Peace* (Beirut, 1985), pp. 71–74.

CHAPTER THREE
FIRST CRACKS IN THE ICE

1. No text is available. I have been able to consult notes taken by one of the participants.

2. *Al Manar,* September 21, 1992, p. 7.

3. The crisis of the Hamas deportees erupted after the expulsion from Israel to Lebanon of some 400 Hamas activists in December 1992. The Palestinians, and in solidarity with them Syria, Jordan, and Lebanon, suspended their participation in the peace process. See also p. 84 in this chapter.

4. *FBIS,* September 9, 1992: "Al Asad Meets with Golan Heights Delegation," p. 41.

5. *FBIS,* November 31, 1992: "Hafez Al Asad Interviewed by Time Magazine," pp. 39–44.

6. *FBIS,* December 16, 1992: "Al Asad Inaugurates Trade Union Congress," pp. 41–47.

7. *Qol Israel,* September 9, 1992.

8. *FBIS,* September 10, 1992: "Rabin Denies Map Drawn," pp. 18–20.

9. *FBIS,* October 27, 1992: "Rabin Delivers Political Address to Knesset," pp. 30–33.

CHAPTER FOUR
THE WING BEATS OF HISTORY

1. Martin Indyk, *Dual Containment,* Washington Institute lecture, May 18, 1993.

2. Ibid.

3. Transcript of the president's script, March 1995, courtesy of AIPAC.

4. *New York Times,* May 11, 1993: "Full Peace for Full Withdrawal," p. A21.

5. *Al-Wasat*, May 10, 1993: "Interview with President Asad," pp. 12–20.
6. *FBIS*, August 16, 1993: "Al Safir Interviews President Asad," pp. 53–58.
7. *New York Times*, September 11, 1993: "Clinton Says Support of Israel Will Not Waver," p. 1.

CHAPTER FIVE
BETWEEN AMMAN AND DAMASCUS

1. *Ha'aretz*, April 22, 1994: "Rabin: Lema'an Shalom mutar lehorid yishuvim bagolan" (For the Sake of Peace It Is Permissible to Dismantle Settlements in the Golan), p. A1.
2. *Ha'aretz*, April 18, 1994: "Mosad mamlakhti . . ." (Government Agency . . .), p. A1; ibid., April 11, 1994: "Misrad Hakhutz hekhin . . ." (The Foreign Ministry Prepared . . .), p. A1.
3. Anthony Lake, "Conceptualizing U.S. Strategy in the Middle East," Washington Institute lecture, May 17, 1994.
4. *FBIS*, September 9, 1994: "Rabin Comments on Golan at Cabinet Meeting," pp. 36–37.
5. *FBIS*, October 4, 1994: "Rabin Speaks at Opening of Winter Knesset Session," pp. 41–45.
6. *FBIS*, September 12, 1994: "Al Asad Addresses People's Assembly," pp. 41–48.
7. *FBIS*, October 4, 1994: "Al Shar' Addresses UN General Assembly," pp. 59–60.

CHAPTER SIX
THE SECURITY DIALOGUE

1. Part of a letter addressed to me in my capacity as Israeli ambassador to Washington.
2. *Congressional Record*, Senate, July 1994.
3. *FBIS*, June 2, 1995: "Al Asad, Mubarak Hold News Conference," pp. 50–52.
4. *Radio Damascus*, July 10, 1995.
5. *Al-Ahram*, October 11, 1995: "Interview with President Asad," p. 1.
6. Ibid.
7. Ibid.
8. Ibid.
9. Ibid.

CHAPTER SEVEN
BITTER HARVEST AT THE WYE PLANTATION

1. *Jerusalem Post*, December 19, 1995: "Peres: No Precondition for Renewing Negotiation with Syria," p. 1.
2. *Ha'aretz*, January 7, 1996: "Ross: 'Be shisha Yamim . . .'" (Ross: In Six Days . . .), p. A6.

3. *FBIS*, December 26, 1995: "Mubarak, Al Asad Hold News Conference," pp. 21–24.
4. Ibid.
5. *FBIS*, February 29, 1996: "Syria: Bombings in Israel 'Condemned'. Seen as Lesson for Peace," p. 46.
6. Patrick Seale, "Asad's Regional Strategy and the Challenge from Netanyahu," *Journal of Palestine Studies* 26.1 (Fall 1997), pp. 27–42.

CONCLUSION

1. Daniel Pipes, "Just Kidding," *New Republic,* January 8 and 15, 1996, pp. 18–19.
2. See Mu'allim's interview in *Journal of Palestine Studies* 26.2 (Winter 1997): 401.
3. *Ma'ariv,* December 12, 1997: "Kakh Fisfasnu et hashalom im Surya" (This Is How We Missed the Peace with Syria), section 2, pp. 1–3.
4. *Ha'aretz* (English edition) October 24, 1997: "A Believer in the Road already Traveled," section 2, p. 5.
5. Patrick Seale, "Asad's Regional Strategy and the Challenge from Netanyahu," *Journal of Palestine Studies* 26.1 (Fall 1997), p. 36.
6. Ibid., p. 36.
7. Ibid., pp. 36–37.
8. For a detailed account of these issues see Volker Perthes, *The Political Economy of Syria under Asad* (London and New York, 1997). For a comprehensive and updated review of the relationship between political and economic issues in Asad's Syria and their relationship to his policies in the peace process, see Glenn E. Robinson, "Elite Cohesion, Regime, Succession and Political Instability in Syria," *Middle East Policy* 4, no. 4 (January 4, 1998), pp. 159–79.
9. The concept of ripeness is treated by a rich body of literature. Some of the important original contributions to that literature were made by Richard Hass, who left Harvard University to serve in the Bush administration's National Security Council. In the Middle Eastern context, William Zartmann of Johns Hopkins University's School of Advanced International Studies has devoted a particular effort to the development and application of this term; see William Zartman, "Explaining Oslo," *International Negotiation* 2.2 (1997), pp. 195–215; and also Dean Pruitt, "Ripeness Theory and the Oslo Talks," *International Negotiation* 2.2 (1997), pp. 237–50.
10. For intervening mediation by a superpower, see Saadia Touval, "The Superpowers as Mediators," in J. Bercovitch and J. Rubin, eds., *Mediation in International Relations* (New York, 1992), pp. 232–48.
11. On prenegotiation, see William Zartman "Prenegotiation: Phases and Functions" in J. Gross-Stein, ed., *Getting to the Table* (Baltimore, 1989), pp. 1–17. Alongside the academic literature in this field, mention should be made of the book written by the American diplomat Harold Saunders, published under the

title *The Other Walls* in the mid-1980s and in revised form in the early 1990s. Saunders, who played a senior role in the formation of Middle Eastern policy under Nixon, Ford, and Carter, devoted the core of this book to a discussion of the construction of the correct process of dialogue between Israel and the Palestinians. See Harold Saunders, *The Other Walls* (Princeton, 1991). Saunders draws a clear distinction between the early phase of prenegotiation and the negotiation itself. For another study by a former diplomat in collaboration with an academic student, see Samuel Lewis and Kenneth Stein, *Making Peace among Arabs and Israelis* (Washington, D. C., 1991).

POSTSCRIPT

1. Benjamin Netanyahu, *A Place among the Nations* (New York, 1993).
2. *IDF Radio,* August 14, 1997.
3. *FBIS,* August 12, 1997: "Syria: Al Asad Discussed Peace with Israeli Arabs."